NATIONS OF THE MODERN WORLD

ARGENTINA
    H. S. Ferns
    Professor of Political Science,
    University of Birmingham

AUSTRALIA
    O. H. K. Spate
    Director, Research School of Pacific Studies,
    Australian National University, Canberra

CEYLON
    S. A. Pakeman
    Formerly Professor of Modern History, Ceylon
    University College; Appointed Member, House of
    Representatives, Ceylon, 1947–52

CYPRUS
    H. D. Purcell
    Lecturer in English Literature,
    Queen's University, Belfast

EAST GERMANY
    David Childs
    Lecturer in Politics, University of Nottingham

MODERN EGYPT
    Tom Little
    Managing Director and General Manager of
    Regional News Services (Middle East), Ltd, London

ENGLAND
    John Bowle
    Professor of Political Theory, Collège d'Europe,
    Bruges

FINLAND
    W. R. Mead
    Professor of Geography, University College, London;
    Formerly Chairman, Anglo-Finnish Society

MODERN GREECE
    John Campbell
    Fellow of St Antony's College, Oxford
    Philip Sherrard
    Assistant Director, British School of Archaeology,
    Athens, 1958–62

MODERN INDIA   Sir Percival Griffiths
President of the India, Pakistan and Burma
Associations

MODERN IRAN   Peter Avery
Lecturer in Persian and Fellow of King's College,
Cambridge

ITALY   Muriel Grindrod
Formerly Editor of International Affairs *and*
The World Today
Assistant Editor of The Annual Register

JAPAN   Sir Esler Dening
H.M. Ambassador to Japan, 1952–57

KENYA   A. Marshall MacPhee
Formerly Managing Editor of The East African
Standard Group; *producer with British Broadcasting*
Corporation

LIBYA   John Wright
Formerly of the Sunday Ghibli, *Tripoli*

MALAYSIA   J. M. Gullick
Formerly of the Malayan Civil Service

MOROCCO   Mark I. Cohen
Director of Taxation, American Express
Lorna Hahn
Professor of African Studies, American University

NEW ZEALAND   James W. Rowe
Director of New Zealand Institute of Economic
Research, Inc.
Margaret A. Rowe
Tutor in English, Victoria University, Wellington

NIGERIA   Sir Rex Niven
Colonial Service, Nigeria, 1921–59; Member of
Northern House of Assembly, 1947–59

PAKISTAN	Ian Stephens *Formerly Editor of* The Statesman *Calcutta and Delhi, 1942–51; Fellow of King's College, Cambridge, 1952–58*
PERU	Sir Robert Marett *H.M. Ambassador in Lima, 1963–67*
SOUTH AFRICA	John Cope *Formerly Editor-in-Chief of* The Forum; *South African Correspondent of* The Guardian
SUDAN REPUBLIC	K. D. D. Henderson *Formerly of the Sudan Political Service; Governor of Darfur Province, 1949–53*
TURKEY	Geoffrey Lewis *Senior Lecturer on Islamic Studies, Oxford*
THE UNITED STATES OF AMERICA	H. C. Allen *Commonwealth Fund Professor of American History, University College, London*
WEST GERMANY	Michael Balfour *Reader in European History, University of East Anglia*
YUGOSLAVIA	Muriel Heppell and F. B. Singleton

NATIONS OF THE MODERN WORLD

PERU

PERU

By

Hugh Kirk

SIR ROBERT MARETT

PRAEGER PUBLISHERS
New York · Washington

BOOKS THAT MATTER

Published in the United States of America in 1969
by Praeger Publishers, Inc.
111 Fourth Avenue, New York, N.Y. 10003

Library of Congress Catalog Card Number: 71-85541

Printed in Great Britain

FOR

Suzanne and Hamish

Preface

I SHALL ALWAYS BE GRATEFUL to a kind fate which sent me on two separate occasions to Peru: in 1948 as First Secretary in the British Embassy for three years; from 1963 to 1967 as British Ambassador. In these diplomatic capacities I was able to travel widely in the country and meet a great number of Peruvians in all stations of life. Everywhere we went, whether moving in the high society of the capital or visiting the most humble Indian villages, my wife and I were treated kindly. We have left Peru with nothing but affectionate memories. It is my hope that this book will be of service to others in opening the door to this most fascinating of lands.

I owe a very special debt of gratitude to Mr Stephen Clissold for his help, advice, and encouragement in writing this book. I am also greatly indebted to Mr David Huelin of the Bank of London and South America who vetted the economic chapter; Mr Jack Harriman for help in selecting the illustrations; Miss Valerie Jefferey, Mrs Warren-Knott, and Mrs Hollman who at different stages assisted me on the secretarial side.

Jersey
May 1969
R.M.

Contents

4 CONTENTS

PART FOUR

PROBLEMS AND PROSPECTS

List of Illustrations

Part One
THE ANCESTRAL ROOTS

Chapter 1

The Setting

A SPACE TRAVELLER in search of a pleasant place to land on earth might be excused if he turned away hastily at his first sight of Peru. For, if viewed from the stratosphere, the country would appear to consist of nothing but three equally uninviting kinds of wilderness – a pitiless desert running down the whole length of the Pacific coast; a few miles inland, one of the most formidable mountain systems in the world; and to the east of the Andes, perhaps the most forbidding wilderness of all, a green carpet of Amazonian jungle extending without a break to the horizon. Our spaceman would need a powerful telescope to discover any redeeming features in this grim landscape – to observe, for example, that the yellow strip of the coastal desert was not continuous but was cut through at intervals by thin green lines indicating the presence of irrigated valleys; or to pick out from among the folds of the high mountains an occasional basin, valley, or plateau wide and fertile enough and at a low enough altitude to support civilized life. Even in the 'Green Hell' of the Amazonian rain-forest, as a British explorer once described it, occasional signs of human life would be discovered along the banks of the meandering rivers. But however closely the ground might be examined, such oases would be found to be few and far between compared with the immensity of the surrounding wilderness.[1]

During his election campaigns in 1962 and 1963, President Belaúnde (1963–68) used as his slogan the title of a book he had written called *The Conquest of Peru by the Peruvians*.[2] The history of Peru according to Belaúnde's version, has consisted of an unremitting struggle against a hostile environment. Peru is blessed with many potential riches – an abundance of minerals hidden away in the Andes; oil and gas waiting to be tapped under desert and forest; coastal waters teeming with fish; wide variations in altitude and climate making it possible to grow almost any kind of crop; and in the highlands ample pasturage for domestic animals. But in a land consisting almost entirely of desert, mountain, and tropical forest,

---

[1] Of Peru's total land area only about 2 per cent was cultivated in 1961.
[2] Fernando Belaúnde Terry, *La Conquista del Perú por los peruanos* (Lima, 1959).

the exploitation of many of these assets requires an extraordinary amount of work performed in conditions of extreme hardship. For example, many of the mines are situated at altitudes above 15,000 feet. The roads, so urgently needed to open up the country, have to be built on the sides of tremendous precipices in the mountains, or driven through virgin forest in tropical country which as soon as it has been cleared becomes a sea of mud. Vast engineering works, involving the driving of tunnels through the solid rock of the Andes, are needed in order to bring more water to the parched desert on the coast.

While, then, it is no doubt proper for Peruvians, looking back over their history, to take pride in the organizing genius of the Inca, the courage and determination of the Spanish conquistadores, the vision of the founding fathers of the republic, and the good works of some of their successors in high office, the real hero in the Peruvian saga, according to Belaúnde's philosophy, is the common man, which in Peruvian terms means, in effect, the poor, humble, and illiterate Indian. Without the toil of generations of nameless Indians it would have been impossible for such an inhospitable land to have become the cradle of civilization in South America, the seat of the proud Inca empire, one of the two great bastions of Spanish colonial power in the New World, and the homeland of the 12 million people – Indian, Spanish, and of mixed blood – who comprise the modern republic of Peru. But, Belaúnde's doctrine continues, there can be no relaxation for the Peruvians in their struggle against a harsh environment so long as the majority of the inhabitants continue to live miserably at no more than a bare level of subsistence.

Of the three principal geographical zones, arranged in parallel strips, into which Peru is divided, the Amazonian rain-forest, known in Spanish as the *selva*, presents the greatest difficulties to man; and indeed in most of its extension it has defeated altogether his efforts to exploit it. The extent of his failure is revealed by the following simple statistics: while 63 per cent of the land area of Peru lies east of the Andes in the *selva*, only 14 per cent of the population manages to make a living in this region.[1]

Before the coming of the Spaniards, the Indian inhabitants of the Amazonian rain-forest were never able to do more than establish primitive settlements along the banks of the rivers. Many of the tribes have remained completely savage to this day. The forest in this zone was too thick and the ground mostly too waterlogged to permit the development of any large-scale agriculture, such as was so successfully undertaken by the Maya Indians in the tropical regions of Mexico and Central America. Colonel Fawcett died in

[1] David A. Robinson, *Peru in Four Dimensions* (Lima, 1964), p. 80.

vain in his search for El Dorado in the South American jungle. No great ruined cities, like Palenque in Mexico, have been uncovered to indicate that there was ever any similar flowering of an ancient Indian civilization in this tropical region.[1]

Nor have the subsequent European immigrants, despite their superior technical resources, been much more successful in exploiting the potential riches of the Amazonian rain-forest, let alone in turning it into a habitat suitable for large-scale settlement by man. At the beginning of the twentieth century this region was important for a time as a source of natural rubber, and the Peruvian city of Iquitos on the upper Amazon became a boom town. But it is a forlorn-looking place now, with its old wooden houses on stilts beginning to come to pieces, and in constant danger of being washed away by the muddy stream of the Amazon. In more recent times oil has been discovered in the region, but there is as yet no important centre of production in this part of Peru. Such commercial activity as exists is centred upon the great rivers, along the banks of which there are occasional lumber camps or plantations, but nothing more. There used to be in Iquitos an enterprising Chinaman, called Mr Wong, who would take tourists in his launch a few miles down river to show them a 'genuine' savage tribe, the women with their breasts bare, the men in their war paint. But even if it was possible to suspect that Mr Wong's Indians had dressed up, or undressed, for the occasion, he was giving the visitor an essentially correct impression of the realities of life in the Peruvian *selva*. Even today Iquitos, with its 50,000 inhabitants, is no more than a lonely outpost of civilization in the midst of an almost entirely savage wilderness.

The prospects for successful exploitation are, however, a good deal more encouraging on the western edge of the *selva*, in the zone more usually known as the *montaña*, where the valleys descend from the eastern slopes of the Andes. In these rich, tropical valleys, or at any rate in their upper reaches, the Indians in prehistoric times did manage to clear the bush for agriculture, for it is known from the accounts of the sixteenth-century chroniclers that the Inca imported tropical products from this region. However, in spite of their genius for organization the Inca do not seem to have penetrated very far down these valleys. The rain-forest successfully barred the expansion of the empire eastwards.

As we shall see later on, it was one of President Belaúnde's most cherished dreams to convert the potentially rich region of the *montaña* into a garden, capable of supporting a large population and producing every kind of tropical product – bananas, sugar, cocoa,

[1] Colonel Fawcett explored the jungles of Brazil; the conditions are similar in the Amazonian jungle of Peru.

tea, coffee, etc. – which at different levels of altitude can successfully be cultivated in these valleys. The land is there in abundance. The problem is mainly one of communications and settlement. It was accordingly a major plank of Belaúnde's programme to build roads connecting these remote valleys with the rest of Peru.[1] Some of the more important centres of population in the region can also now be reached by air from Lima.

Such few roads as already exist connecting the *selva* with the *sierra*, as the central mountainous zone of Peru is called, follow the courses of the river valleys up the eastern slopes of the Andes, climbing from almost sea-level on the Amazonian plain to passes which may be as high as 15,000 feet. At the entrance to these valleys there is dense tropical forest; but from between 3 to 5,000 feet the jungle begins to thin out, and this is the ideal part of the valley for settlement and agricultural development. Above 6,500 feet the *sierra* begins. The valley will become narrower; the steep hillsides on this favoured side of the Andes where there is plenty of rain will be covered by a patchwork of little fields, green, brown, or yellow, devoted to the cultivation by Indian communities of crops such as maize or barley which flourish in a temperate climate. Above 11 or 12,000 feet the mountainsides will become increasingly rugged and bare, at best with only a covering of coarse grass or scrub to hide their nakedness.

The Andes have to be experienced to be believed. The sheer size of the landscape – beetling cliffs and yawning chasms in the upper part of the valleys; on what feels like the top of the world the cold, empty, grass-covered *puna*; and finally the great ramparts of rock, ice, and snow of the high mountains – so overwhelms the visitor that any attempt at description is likely to get bogged down in superlatives. It is important to get the scale of these mountains into perspective. The highest peaks rise to over 20,000 feet above sea-level (Mont Blanc is 15,782 feet), these heights being matched by a rift in the bottom of the Pacific ocean, just off the Peruvian coast, of approximately the same depth. In other words, such was the violence of the crumpling of the earth's surface when the Andes were created that within a distance of only about 200 miles there is a difference of altitude of 40,000 feet between mountain peak and sea-bottom. The highest peak in Peru, Huascarán, reaches a height of 22,180 feet; the snow-line in the latitude of Lima (the whole of Peru lies within the southern tropics) is at about 16,500 feet; the average altitude of the *sierra* is about 13,000 feet. This is quite high enough, however, to make many people suffer the agonizing headache and nausea of *soroche*, which results from lack of oxygen. Fortunately it

[1] See below, pp. 231–2.

does not usually last very long. If it does, it is always possible, in most parts of the Andes, quickly to seek relief at a lower level; for by no means all of the *sierra* consists of such high country. In the deep gorges cut by the rivers the altitude may quickly descend to only a few thousand feet. Thus, depending on altitude, there can be experienced within a very small compass of time and distance amazing changes of climate – a tropical hot-house atmosphere in the depths of the gorges; some perfect, well-watered, almost English-looking country in those rare and precious valleys and basins which lie in the temperate zone between 8 and 11,000 feet; higher up the cold, lonely, wind-swept, but unbelievably beautiful, *punas*; and, above 16,500 feet, the eternal snows and glaciers of the mountain peaks.

It is customary to describe the Peruvian Andes as consisting of three principal ranges or *cordillera*, running approximately from north-west to south-east in parallel with the coast, and separated one from the other by high plateaux and river valleys. But this, like all attempts to describe the Andes, is an over-simplification. Only the western range, overlooking the Pacific coast and forming the continental divide, runs in a continuous chain down the whole length of Peru from Ecuador to Chile. The so-called central and eastern *cordillera*, while well defined in the north and reappearing in a more or less recognizable form in some parts of the south, become merged and lost in the great knots of transverse mountain ranges which at intervals block north–south communications. These knots have the effect of dividing the *sierra* into a number of separate basins, each of which is almost entirely hemmed in by mountains except where the rivers escape through deep gorges, either to the Pacific or to the Amazon.

These fertile basins contain the principal towns of the *sierra*. Indeed, apart from some of the valleys of the *montaña*, they are the only parts of the Andes capable of supporting a dense population. In prehistoric times they were sufficiently isolated from one another to become local centres of cultural development, each inhabited by its own tribe or group of tribes. Even today in an age of railways (but not many of them), motor-roads, and aeroplanes, they have retained a good deal of their local character. From north to south the six most important centres of population in the Peruvian Andes – there are many lesser centres, of course – may be listed as follows.

Cajamarca, in the northern Andes, has been thickly settled since prehistoric times. It was the meeting place of Pizarro and the ill-fated Inca, Atahualpa. Today it is an important centre for cattle-breeding. The Andes in the north of Peru are lower and less rugged than in the south. Now that a road across them has been built they provide relatively easy communications between the Pacific coast and the tributaries and main valley of the Marañón on the Atlantic watershed – a potentially rich semi-tropical region which is now being opened up to commercial exploitation by the new highways.

The Callejón de Huaylas is a long, narrow corridor, through which the river Santa flows northwards before turning left and plunging down through a gorge to the Pacific ocean. The valley is flanked by two tremendous mountain ranges, known as the *Cordillera Negra* and the *Cordillera Blanca,* the former so-called because it is almost always without snow, in contrast with the white *cordillera* which contains some of the finest snow-clad peaks in the Andes, including the mighty Huascarán. This rich but narrow valley has been cultivated intensively by the Hayla Indians since time immemorial. It is one of the beauty spots of Peru.[1]

The Central Andes contain a number of fertile valleys which today can be reached fairly easily by road from the capital, Lima. The central highway (or the British-owned Central Railway if one prefers it) climbs from sea-level at Lima 15,000 feet up the barren slopes of the western *cordillera,* passes through an awesome canyon, appropriately named *infernillo* (little Hell), near the top, and emerges finally through a pass guarded by snow-capped mountains into the bleak, lunar landscape of the mining region of Cerro de Pasco. From here there is a choice of three routes. One road descends by easy stages – and what a pleasant contrast it is – into the green fields which surround Huancayo, famous for its Indian market and in the midst of a very rich agricultural area. Another road turns north, crosses some very high and bleak country known as the Pampa de Junín, and then descends from Huánuco through a series of valleys and gorges down into the *selva,* ending up at Pucallpa, a river port on the banks of a tributary of the Amazon. But perhaps the most dramatic of the three routes is one which goes through Tarma, and from here plunges down the eastern slopes of the Andes in a series of terrifying hair-pin bends to San Ramón. This little town is situated in an extensive area of tropical plantations producing anything from bananas or *papaya* to coffee in the higher ground of the neighbouring hills. The region is a splendid example of what can be achieved when roads are built to open up the *montaña* to commercial exploitation. But as soon as the roads peter out, the bush immediately takes over. Only by taking a canoe and risking the rapids of the fast-flowing river Perené is it possible to proceed from this region further into the *selva.* San Ramón itself can be reached by motor-car in a single day of hard driving from

[1] It can be reached in a day by car from Lima. There is a tourist hotel at Juaraz.

Lima. But in the riverside villages of the Perené, although so close
to the capital, the Indian chiefs still wear the headdress and carry
the staffs of their pagan ancestors; doctors and priests are practically
unknown; and life goes on very much in the same way as it did
before the coming of the Spaniards.

Arequipa is today the most important city in the southern Andes.
It is situated at the relatively low altitude, by Peruvian standards,
of 8,000 feet in a beautiful setting dominated by three snow-capped
volcanoes. It enjoys sunshine all the year round. The surrounding
countryside is arid and agriculture is only possible where the neighbouring valleys have been irrigated. However, commercially and in-
dustrially Arequipa is important as a half-way house between the
sierra and the coast. The British-owned Southern Railway, with its
headquarters in Arequipa, connects the ports of Mollendo and
Matarani on the Pacific coast with Puno on Lake Titicaca; a branch
line continues to Cuzco in the heart of the *sierra*. The railway company's steamers run across the lake at night to Bolivia. Thus Arequipa, with its railway and ports, is a focal commercial centre providing an outlet for the minerals, alpaca wool, and other products
of the southern *sierra*. In atmosphere it is European, and gives little
impression of belonging to the *sierra* – Cuzco, for example, is like a
different world. But the *Arequipeños* regard themselves as high-
landers, and indeed have acquired some of the characteristics of the
Scots. The home of many revolutions, a surprising number of Arequipa's sons have occupied high office in the republic.

Cuzco, situated inland from Arequipa in a high basin at about
11,000 feet, is, of course, the most famous city of the *sierra*. In the
Quechua language the word Cuzco means navel. It was chosen by
the Inca as the name of their capital to mark its position as the
centre of the known civilized world. In the city as it is today the
towers and domes of fine Baroque churches dominate the skyline,
but most of them are built upon solid foundations of Inca masonry.
In this superimposition of two architectural styles is symbolized the
history of Peru – the rise and fall of the Inca, the shift of power
from an Indian to a Spanish élite, and the triumph of Christianity
over the cult of the sun. Even so, the spirit of the Inca still lingers in
Cuzco. The descendants of their Indian subjects throng the narrow
streets in their colourful costumes, and in the outskirts of the city
there can be seen some fine examples of the megalithic architecture
of these master-builders. Cuzco today is no more than a provincial
capital, depending for its existence on tourists and the produce of
three rich agricultural valleys in the neighbourhood. In one of these
valleys, that of the Urubamba, there can be seen fine examples of
Inca terracing, showing how, at a tremendous cost in human labour,

every inch of cultivable land even on the steepest slopes was put to use.[1]

Lake Titicaca, lying half-way between Peru and Bolivia, 3,500 square miles in area and situated at 12,500 feet above sea-level, is one of the most remarkable stretches of water in the world. Its banks lined by giant reeds and with the clouds reflected in the water, the lake has a haunting beauty in its setting of bleak moorland. In this part of southern Peru the dominating geographical feature is a cold, treeless, high plateau which separates the western and eastern *cordillera,* the latter just visible from the lake as a line of jagged white teeth on the far-away Bolivian horizon. But cold and forbidding though it is, this southern Peruvian *altiplano* has always, rather surprisingly, managed to support a large Indian population. Wherever possible in the vicinity of the lake, patches of potatoes, and even sometimes maize, are grown. Herds of llama and alpaca (and, since the time of the Spaniards, sheep as well) are grazed in the surrounding grasslands. On this double economic foundation of agriculture and animal husbandry life has gone on with virtually no change for thousands of years. A few miles inland on the Bolivian side of the lake there stand the ruins of an ancient Indian city, with its great stone ceremonial gateway still intact. Tiahuanaco flourished between the second and sixth centuries A.D. It was a religious and possibly also a political centre of importance in its time, for pottery and other cultural manifestations in the Tiahuanaco style have been found widely spread in Peru at an archaeological level preceding that of the Inca, suggesting the diffusion of a religious creed from this centre and possibly also a period of military conquest.[2] The glory of Tiahuanaco has long since disappeared, but the descendants of the Indians who created this civilization survive. Most of them live today in dire poverty, tilling the poor soil and grazing their animals around the shores of this sad, cold lake on the roof of the world.

Some 53 per cent of the population of Peru (mostly Indians or *mestizos*)[3] live in the *sierra*. The basic industries which sustain this population are mining (of great importance to the economy of Peru), agriculture, and the grazing of animals. The majority of the inhabitants of the *sierra* live in one or other of the densely populated areas, the most important of which have been briefly described. It is in these fertile basins that the large agricultural estates are to be found, most of them devoted to dairy-farming. In the market-towns

[1] There is a daily air service from Lima to Cuzco.
[2] See below, p. 38.
[3] People of mixed Indian and Spanish blood.

of the *sierra* the small middle class is reasonably prosperous; but the standard of life of the peasants, whether working on the large estates or on their own land, is generally extremely low. An important minority of the Indians live in their own isolated communities, far from the cities, cultivating small patches of land on the steep hillsides and in the narrow valley-bottoms, and grazing their small flocks of animals in the higher ground of the *puna*. Like the *selva* a large part of the *sierra* is useless to man, and consists of nothing but high mountains or expanses of *puna*. It is possible to travel for days through the *puna* without the sight of a man or a tree to break the solitude. In those relatively rare parts of the *sierra* which can be made habitable for man the Malthusian principle would seem to apply. The size of the population is always nicely adjusted to the amount of available land capable of supporting a family at a level of bare subsistence.

It now remains to describe the third and, economically, the most important geographical zone of Peru – the *costa*. It comprises the coastal strip and the lower part of the western slopes of the Andes which face the Pacific. The problems of this region can be summed up in one word – water. It never rains – or, to be accurate, it hardly ever rains – on the Pacific coast of Peru. Both the mountainsides and the coastal plain are therefore completely desert except along the bottom of the river valleys which bring down water from the Andes.

The cause of this lack of rain is the intensely cold Humboldt current which sweeps northward from Cape Horn up the Chilean and Peruvian coasts, and finally turns out to sea at almost exactly the latitude of the boundary between Ecuador and Peru. The sudden alteration in course of the current at this point is matched by a dramatic change of climate on the coast; north of the border in Ecuador the vegetation consists of tropical forest or mangrove swamp; on the Peruvian side the country is a desert – it is as though the map had been cut with a knife. Along the whole length of the Peruvian Pacific coast the effect of the cold Humboldt current is to cool the air above the sea and reduce its capacity to retain the moisture which in normal circumstances would have fallen on the land as rain. Moreover, once the air passes over the land it is warmed up again, which increases its capacity to retain moisture and makes precipitation impossible. One beneficial result of this peculiar condition is a temperature on the Peruvian coast on average some 7 degrees F. cooler than is normal in these tropical latitudes. Another result – a mixed blessing – is a climate sunny and pleasant enough in the summer months (December to May), but plagued by fog and cloud in the winter. In Lima for weeks on end in the winter there is never a sight of the sun, and the only way to escape is to climb a

few thousand feet (it can be done in less than an hour by car) into
the Andes to one of the resorts situated above the clouds. Quite
often in Lima, especially in the evenings, it drizzles, but there is
never what in England or the U.S.A. would be called good, honest
rain. Only on the coast of northern Peru are there occasional down-
pours when – at intervals of between five and ten years – a rogue
current of warm water from the Equator temporarily displaces the
Humboldt current. When this happens the *adobe* huts of the poor
people dissolve into mud, normally dry river-beds become raging
torrents, and the desert suddenly blossoms miraculously and is
covered by a carpet of flowers.

But for most of the time along the 1,400 miles of Peru's Pacific
coast it is, strangely enough, water from the far distant Atlantic
ocean which makes life possible in this otherwise desert wilderness.
The south-east trade winds, blowing from the southern Atlantic
across the Amazonian jungle, cause a heavy rainfall on the eastern
slopes of the Andes, especially between October and May. Most of
the water flows uselessly back into the Amazon; but, fortunately for
Peru, some of the clouds manage to get through to the heights of
the western *cordillera*. From the snow and ice of the peaks in this
range, more than forty normally completely rainless valleys on the
western slope obtain enough water not merely to give life to the
coast but to allow it to become the most prosperous region in Peru.

Thus the Pacific coastal strip consists of an alternation of fertile
irrigated valleys, some more important than others, depending upon
the volume and regularity of the supply of water, and separated
from each other by stretches of anything from a few to 50 miles of
the most arid desert imaginable. It can readily be understood that
to drive along the coastal Pan-American highway from Tumbes on
the northern frontier to Tacna in the south is not a very exhilarating
experience. Each new desert or irrigated valley looks very much
like the last. Even so, the coast has a certain beauty – one which is
perhaps more suitable for water-colours than oils on those frequent
occasions when the hills are shrouded by mist; in the haze the reds,
browns, and yellows of the desert blend gently into the green of the
irrigated fields. Seawards, great Pacific rollers rear themselves up
from a glassy and colourless ocean and beat monotonously upon the
lonely shore.

The coastal valleys of Peru have been intensely cultivated by the
Indians for thousands of years. The more important valleys, or
clusters of adjacent valleys, became the centres of independent
Indian kingdoms, until they were conquered and absorbed by the
Inca in the fifteenth century. The Spaniards, in their turn, upon
their arrival in Peru, established a number of important cities, such

as Piura and Trujillo in the north, and the capital, Lima, in the centre, in the mouths of the coastal valleys close to the sea. They chose these sites in order to safeguard their communications with Spain, which could so easily have been cut by rebellious Indians if the capital had been established in Cuzco or some other city in the *sierra*. And so the *sierra*, which had been the backbone of the Inca empire, with the coastal valleys attached to it like so many ribs and forming an integral part of the body politic, became under the Spaniards a neglected hinterland. The Spaniards were mainly interested in the *sierra* because of its mineral wealth. Otherwise most of their energies were devoted to developing the resources and enjoying the amenities of the coast. Until very recently most of the leaders of the Peruvian republic have been content to follow in this tradition.

Although occupying only 11 per cent of the area of the country, some 33 per cent of the inhabitants of modern Peru, and most of the wealth of the republic, are concentrated in the Pacific coastal strip. In the rich, irrigated valleys large well-run estates produce the sugar and cotton and other cash crops which figure as important export items in Peru's balance of trade with the outside world. On the coast in the north, near Talara, are to be found the most extensive oilfields in Peru; in the south, at Marcona, there are large deposits of iron-ore. Even the Humboldt current has made its contribution towards the industrial revolution on the coast by filling the sea with anchovy. These little fish provide the raw material for the fish-meal industry which in the last few years has suddenly blossomed forth in Peru in a most spectacular manner. Thus, while the *sierra* sleeps and dreams of past glories, the coast is forging ahead. Lima, once a quiet and dignified colonial capital, is now a booming city ringed by factories and the shanty towns of the new industrial working class. In short, it is a completely different world on the coast compared with the rest of Peru.

Chapter 2

The Indian Heritage

WHEN CHRISTOPHER COLUMBUS LANDED in Hispaniola he made the mistake of thinking that he had reached the East Indies by the westerly route. Ever since this time the original inhabitants of the New World have been called 'Indians', although the name does not properly fit them at all. The ancestors of the Indians of America did, however, come from Asia, although not from the East Indies. Short of stature, stocky, solidly built, with an olive brown complexion, high cheekbones, straight black hair, sparse beard – these and other physical characteristics indicate beyond any reasonable doubt that the Peruvian Indians, like all their cousins in the New World, are an offshoot of the Asiatic Mongoloid branch of the human family.

The generally accepted theory is that the remote ancestors of the American Indians emigrated from Asia by way of the Bering Straits in late glacial times. This may not by itself be a complete explanation of the presence of man in America in prehistoric times; there may possibly have been earlier waves of migration from the Old World. But it is certain that men of roughly the same physical type as the present-day Indians have been established in the New World for a very long time, probably for at least 10,000 years, and possibly a good deal more. Their ancestors must anyhow have been in Peru long enough for environment to have had time, through natural selection, to do its work. For the Quechua Indians of the Peruvian highlands have developed some very distinctive physical characteristics. In order to equip them to live and thrive in the high altitudes of the Andes nature has given them a torso, lung capacity, and blood volume much greater than those of other American Indians. Such a radical adjustment to the environment could only have taken place as the result of thousands of years of undisturbed residence in this mountainous habitat – a conclusion of physical anthropology which is supported by the archaeological evidence so far as it goes.

Enough in the way of hard fact is now established by archaeology to make it possible to trace, at least in outline, the evolution of civilization in Peru from its earliest beginnings up to the time when, in the sixteenth century, history takes over the story. Evolution seems to be the right word to describe what happened. No professional archaeologist today takes seriously the more exotic diffusionist theories which had a popular following in the past, such as that the Indians of America are one of the lost tribes of Israel, or that Peruvian civilization was imported into South America more or less ready-made from ancient Egypt. This is not to deny the possibility that at different periods of their history the Peruvians may have had some contact with Mexico and Central America – the other important centre in America where Indian civilizations of a high order were developed – and perhaps also with some other places further afield such as the Pacific islands, Malaya, China, or even Japan. But the intensive digging which has been done in some of the coastal valleys of Peru makes it clear that it was essentially the Peruvians themselves who conquered Peru, with only possibly some very occasional inspiration or interference from outside. The following is a summary of the successive phases of the social and economic development of the Peruvian Indians insofar as archaeology has managed to piece their story together.[1]

THE EARLY HUNTERS (BEFORE 7500–2500 B.C.)

The first chapter in the story of the Peruvian Indians is still very largely hypothetical. Mongoloid immigrants from Asia, wandering in small primitive hunting-groups, are presumed to have drifted southward into America in search of game and food, gradually occupying those parts of the continent which were habitable. It has been established by excavation that human beings were hunting sloth, horse, and guanaco in southern Patagonia at a date estimated to be shortly after 9000 B.C. Their ancestors presumably passed through Peru at some earlier date. However, the earliest trace of man so far discovered in Peru, in caves at Lauricocha in the highlands, has a radio carbon date of about 7500 B.C.

On the coast the earliest remains of man which have been subjected to a radio carbon test give a date of only about 3000 B.C. This discovery was made by Frederic Engel in an ancient cemetery which he excavated near the seaside resort of Paracas, south of Pisco. It has provided a good picture of what life was like 5,000 years ago in Peru. There is no sign of cotton or other cultivated plants in the strata, so it seems that the Indians, even at this comparatively late date, still lived by hunting, fishing, and food-gathering. Their material belongings were very simple: shell-beads and pendants for ornaments, a few crude weapons, and such utilitarian

[1] The classification of periods is that of G. H. S. Bushnell, *Peru* (London, 1956). A more detailed classification is to be found in J. Alden Mason, *The Ancient Civilizations of Peru* (London, Penguin, 1957). Both books provide an excellent introduction to the archaeology of Peru.

objects as bone-needles, string, and netted bags. They had no
pottery. The bodies of the dead were wrapped in the skins of the
vicuña – which suggests that these very primitive folk must either
have come down to the coast from the highlands, or at least have had
contact with that area.

THE EARLY FARMERS (ABOUT 2500 B.C.–900 B.C.)

The turning point in the evolution of any primitive society is
almost always the development of agriculture – a discovery which
seems to have been made by many different people at different
times and in different parts of the world. In Peru a date of about
2500 B.C. is assigned to this important development.

It appears, however, that well over 1,500 more years elapsed before this innovation brought about much change in the life of the
people living on the Peruvian coast. During this long period of ges-
tation the cultivation of plants – at first confined to squash, beans,
gourds, and chilli peppers – was still very much of a side-line. Evidently, the valley bottoms, strewn with boulders, covered by scrub,
and liable to sudden floods, were too much for these primitive
farmers. They grew their crops where they could in small plots of
land on the edge of the valleys, building their settlements for preference close to the sea. Fishing was probably their most important
economic activity, supplemented by the hunting of sea-lions which
then abounded on the Peruvian coast.

The people lived in small, one-roomed subterranean houses, roofed
with beams of wood and covered by mud and stones. The range of
their tools, utensils, and ornaments was still very limited. There is no
evidence of a social organization above the level of the small village
community, or of an organized religious cult. Art was still rudimentary.

It is only after 1200 B.C. that there are some signs of material progress: a crude pottery makes its first appearance and a primitive
form of maize seems to have been added to the crops under cultivation. Even so, as late as the beginning of the last millennium B.C.,
civilization in Peru was still only in the chrysalis stage. It rather
looks as though it needed a jolt from the outside world to cause the
butterfly to emerge and stretch its wings.

THE FORMATIVE PERIOD (900 B.C.–A.D. 200)

The next important step forward was taken by the Peruvians in
about 900 B.C. It is marked by the appearance at a number of sites,
mostly in northern Peru, of imposing buildings and an elaborate
form of pottery for ceremonial use, indicating the diffusion over a
wide area of an organized religious cult. This new religion was
centred upon a feline deity – an anthropomorphic jaguar or a puma
– whose monstrous features, in a highly stylized form, appear in both

the sculpture and the pottery of the period. This first important cultural horizon in Peru is known as Chavín, in view of its association with some ruins at Chavín de Huántar in the northern highlands.[1]

The origin and nature of the Chavín culture is still something of a mystery. The late Dr Julio C. Tello, the father of Peruvian archaeology, regarded Chavín as the earliest of the Peruvian civilizations. He thought that it had originated somewhere in the Amazonian region (hence the cult of the jaguar), and then spread over the highlands to the Pacific coast. But there are not many in the modern school of archaeologists who would agree with this diagnosis. For example, G. H. S. Bushnell suggests that this whole complex of the feline cult, ceremonial architecture, etc., may have originated in Mexico. He points out that already by 1500 B.C. agricultural people, at a considerably more advanced stage of cultural development than that of the Peruvians, were settled in villages in the Valley of Mexico, growing maize and making good pottery. In the middle of the Formative Period in Mexico a similar cult of a feline god, which had originated with the Olmec people on the tropical Gulf coast, became widely spread in Mexico, and there are indications that it may have percolated down through Central America to Ecuador and Peru at just about the time of the beginning of the Chavín culture in Peru.

Be this as it may – and it is doubtful if the last word has been said on this subject – there is incontrovertible evidence that in about 900 B.C. the Peruvians were at an important stage in their cultural development. Agriculture improved immeasurably and became the main source of food supply. Maize became the staple food on the coast. On the solid economic foundation of a viable agriculture it was now possible for social organization and the higher aspects of the culture to develop.

The Peruvian archaeologist Rafael Larco Hoyle likens the Formative Period to a crucible in which the various cultures which grew up subsequently on Peruvian soil were moulded in all their richness and diversity. In about 300 B.C. the pan-Peruvian cult of the feline deity seems to have suffered a decline. But if the second half of the Formative Period was characterized by the variety of religions and artistic expression in different areas, over-all it was a time of invention and discovery leading up by gradual evolutionary stages to the full flowering of Peruvian civilization.

[1] The site can be reached over a rough earth road from Huaraz in the Callejón de Haylas. The existence of such imposing buildings (with some interesting examples of early sculpture) in such a remote valley suggests a centre of religious pilgrimage.

CLASSIC PERIOD (A.D. 200–600)

The term 'Classic' (some writers prefer 'florescent') is used in America to describe the Indian civilizations of Mexico and Peru at what is regarded to have been the height of their cultural and material development. In both cases this culminating stage was reached at about the beginning of the Christian era – that is to say some 1,400 years before the rise to power of the Aztecs and the Inca who held the stage in their respective countries at the time of the Spanish conquest.

But although the Classic Period began almost simultaneously in the two areas (at the most the Mexicans may have been ahead by a couple of hundred years), there is no evidence to show that there was ever any close contact between the Old Maya empire, with its wonderful ceremonial centres built in the tropical forests of southern Mexico and Central America, or the majestic city of Teotihuacán in the Valley of Mexico, and the various civilizations – Mochica, Nazca, Tiahuanaco, and so on – of the Classic Period in Peru. Separated by wide stretches of country inhabited by more primitive people, it looks as though the Mexican and Peruvian civilizations, whatever contacts there may have been earlier in the Formative Period, evolved thereafter in isolation from each other.

The economic basis of the Classic civilization of Peru was an agriculture which had now been brought to the highest possible degree of efficiency, considering that the Peruvian farmer never had any more elaborate tools than the digging-stick and the hoe with which to do battle with one of the toughest environments in the world. Moreover, it was without draught animals or wheeled vehicles that the Peruvian engineers constructed the vast and intricate irrigation works in the coastal valleys. In the *sierra* where shortage of land rather than shortage of water was the problem many of the valleys were artificially terraced from bottom to top, a task which like the irrigation works must have involved a large amount of labour, and could only have been achieved by a mature and well-organized society.

By the time of the Classic Period all the known Peruvian food plants had been brought under cultivation – maize, beans, peanuts, potatoes, sweet potatoes, chilli peppers, manioc, pumpkins, gourds, cotton, coca, etc. – together with a wide range of tropical delicacies such as avocado, papaya, and pineapple. It is probably no exaggeration to say that by this time every acre of land in Peru which could be cultivated by the methods then available had been put to work, possibly a good deal more thoroughly than is the case today in many parts of the country. In the high Andes the grasslands of the *puna* were used to graze large flocks of llama and alpaca.

On this economic basis a number of separate nation-states developed in the different regions of Peru. Government was probably
theocratic in character; but to judge by their gorgeous attire as depicted in the pottery, the warriors too must have occupied an important place in the hierarchy as they did later in Inca times. In
short, once the essential needs of agriculture had been met, religion
and war were evidently the main preoccupations of the governing
élite. As in Mexico there was in Peru a large pantheon of anthropomorphic gods, and most of the surplus energy of the people was
devoted, or rather directed, to the erection of temples in their
honour, or to the furnishing of tombs worthy of revered ancestors –
ancestor worship being an important feature in Peruvian religion.
Animals and occasionally human beings were sacrificed to the gods,
but in Peru human sacrifice never became a bloodthirsty mania as
it did later with the Aztecs in Mexico.

Overshadowed by the great temples[1] and the palaces of their
priestly rulers, the people during the Classic Period lived simply
enough in thatched cottages grouped together haphazardly in small
villages. There do not seem to have been any large towns at this
time. Evidently, the standard of life of the peasants was not very
much above the level of bare subsistence, as indeed it has remained
to this day in the Indian communities of the *sierra*. The most remarkable characteristic of the ancient Peruvians is their great
manual skill associated with very simple apparatus.[2] They produced
wonderful pottery and textiles of which any nation of any age could
be proud; they were expert masons, enormous blocks of stone being
worked and fitted together with great accuracy, and they were
adept at metal-working and made the most beautiful ornaments of
gold and silver, although, apart from the use of copper and bronze
in some of their tools, their technology in most respects was still that
of the Stone Age. If their material and artistic achievements cannot
quite compare with those of the great agricultural civilizations of
the Old World, there are two good reasons for this – an inferior
technical apparatus and a much tougher environment. The wonder
is that the Peruvians were able to do so much with so little.

THE POST-CLASSIC PERIOD (A.D. 600–1532)

In Mexico, where things so often happen violently, the Classic
Period came to an end dramatically with the sudden abandonment
in about the seventh century A.D. of the cities of the Old Maya
empire and of the great city of Teotihuacán in the Valley of
Mexico. The reasons for this sudden collapse are unknown. It is

---

[1] For example, the Huaca del Sol, near Trujillo, a huge *adobe*-constructed
pyramid, 60 feet high.

[2] Bushnell, op. cit., pp. 29–30.

characteristic of Peru that nothing quite so drastic occurred, although in this area, too, at almost precisely the same time as in
Mexico, the end of the Classic Period was marked by a period of
unrest. On the coast this was a time of empire-building by three
aggressive states based on the most important valleys. There are indications, too, that for a time some of the coastal valleys may have
been invaded, and possibly temporarily occupied, by people from
the highlands.[1] However, by A.D. 1000 whatever temporary unity of
culture this highland influence may have produced in Peru had very
largely disappeared and provincialism was once more the order of
the day.

The population of Peru on the coast had now probably reached
its maximum, given the limited capacity of the irrigated valleys to
support life; society in each of the independent states on the coast
was highly organized; and in each of the coastal valleys there were
now towns of considerable size, so much so that some archaeologists
like to use the word 'urbanist' to describe this period.[2] In the highlands geography did not encourage such large concentrations of
population. By A.D. 1000 the civilization of Huari-Tiahuanaco was
in decline, and there does not seem to have been any dominant
power in this part of Peru. The *sierra* was rent by the dissensions of
warring tribes. No doubt pressure of population in a mountainous
region, whose agricultural capacity could not be further expanded,
was mainly responsible for this state of affairs.

The Inca, when they first appear on the borderline of history in
about A.D. 1200, were just such a typical highland tribe engaged in
constant feuds with their neighbours. Their story begins with a leg-
endary character called Manco Cápac, the founder of the dynasty.
He led his people (from where exactly, nobody knows) to the valley
of Cuzco, and there founded his capital. The accounts of the chroniclers are extremely vague and often conflicting about the reigns of
the first eight Inca rulers. But the picture they paint is one of a still
small-time local tribe engaged in border warfare with similar tribal
groups, such as the Lupaca and Colla in the south, who occupied
the region of Lake Titicaca, and the warlike Chanca to the north.
These wars were not, however, very productive. After eight reigns
covering about 200 years of almost perpetual warfare with neighbouring states, the Inca had not succeeded in extending their sway
over more than a radius of about 20 miles from Cuzco.

The expansion of the empire only began seriously in 1438 under

[1] This is suggested by the otherwise inexplicable spread of an art-style
known as Huari-Tiahuanaco.
[2] For example, the ruins of Chan Chan, the capital of the Chimu kings
(situated near Trujillo), cover an area of 6 square miles.

the Inca Pachacuti. It is clear that this Inca was not only a very good soldier; he was also a highly competent and original-minded administrator. His greatest achievement was to develop an ingenious technique for holding down conquered people and turning them into loyal subjects of the empire. This was something which the predatory Aztecs never achieved in Mexico. Moreover, Pachacuti was fortunate in having able successors in his son, Topa Inca (1471–93), and grandson, Huayna Cápac (1493–1527), who between them expanded the empire by further conquest to its final limits, and perfected the administrative methods for consolidating these gains. In the year that Huayna Cápac died word was brought to him that Pizarro's first expedition of exploration had touched at Tumbes.

By 1527, less than a century after Pachacuti launched his first campaign of systematic conquest, the empire of the Inca stretched from the northern borders of Ecuador to central Chile, a distance of about 3,000 miles as the crow flies. It covered an area of some 350,000 square miles along the length of one of the most formidable mountain chains in the world. Its population is estimated to have been about 6 million people.[1] In what is today modern Peru only the savage tribes of the Amazonian rain forest remained unconquered. Elsewhere proud and powerful kingdoms, like that of the Chimu on the Pacific coast, were vanquished and absorbed. For the first time the Indians of coast and *sierra* were united by the Inca in a single political and economic system. Peru had become a nation.

[1] John Howland Rowe, *Handbook of South American Indians* (Washington, 1946), Vol. 2, p. 185.

Chapter 3

The Structure of Inca Society

'It was not long before sunset, when the van of the royal procession entered the gates of the city. First came some hundreds of
the Menials, employed to clear the path from every obstacle, and
singing songs of triumph as they came.... Then followed other
bodies of different ranks, and dressed in different liveries. Some
wore a showy stuff, checkered white and red like the squares of a
chess board. Others were clad in pure white, bearing hammers or
maces of silver or copper; and the guards, together with those in
immediate attendance on the prince, were distinguished by a rich
azure livery, and a profusion of gay ornaments, while the large
pendants attached to the ears indicated the Peruvian noble.

'Elevated high above his vassals came the Inca, Atahualpa,
borne on a sedan or open litter, on which was a sort of throne
made of massive gold of inestimable value. The palanquin was
lined with the richly coloured plumes of tropical birds, and
studded with shining plates of gold and silver.... Round his [the
Inca's] neck was suspended a collar of emeralds of uncommon
size and brilliancy. His short hair was decorated with golden ornaments, and the imperial borla encircled his temples. The bearing
of the Inca was sedate and dignified; and from his lofty station
he looked down on the multitudes below with an air of compo-
sure, like one accustomed to command.'[1]

Such, in the words of William Prescott, was the impression made
upon the awe-struck Spaniards on the occasion of that first dramatic
meeting in Cajamarca between Francisco Pizarro, the Spanish conqueror of Peru, and Atahualpa, the living representative of the Sun
God and the last of the truly free rulers of Indian Peru. It is by no
means easy to sort out the exaggerations and contradictions of gul-
lible and impressionable Spanish and Indian chroniclers of the sixteenth century; even among modern scholars there is still a wide
diversity of opinion – not so much about the facts as their interpre-
tation – on the subject of this remarkable, and in some ways unique,
Peruvian state. For, whatever one may think about it, the Inca

[1] William H. Prescott, *The History of the Conquest of Peru* (Modern
Library, New York), p. 938.

40

empire had features which distinguish it from any other society known to history. The labels 'communist', 'socialist', and even 'fascist', have been used by different writers to describe it. But none of these modern terms quite fit a state which, while in some ways surprisingly sophisticated, in most other respects was still extremely primitive.[1]

Compared with many civilizations at a roughly similar stage of development in the Old World, there is nothing unusual about the military character of the Inca empire or the hierarchical structure of its society. Nor was there anything unique about the pretension of the Inca to be a god. Most of the ancient civilizations of the Orient had similarly rested upon the twin foundations of military and theocratic power. Like any oriental potentate of old, the Inca lived in great state in his palace in Cuzco, and his life was hedged in by taboos. Nobody could look him in the eye; he never wore the same garment twice; like the Ptolemies, he normally married his eldest sister, while at the same time enjoying the company of a seraglio of secondary wives and concubines. To his subjects he was an omnipotent god, the personification of the sun. Ruthless in battle against his enemies and merciless towards wrong-doers, he was held in great awe by his subjects. But the chroniclers are unanimous in saying that, mingled with the awe, there was a feeling of gratitude and love. Both as a god and as a human leader of a welfare state, he was regarded by the people as their protector and the provider of all good things. There were indeed some good reasons for the popularity of the Inca with his subjects. As an absolute monarch he was a law unto himself, but his regulations for the government of the empire were invariably grafted upon ancestral customs, making it easy for every Indian of whatever tribe or station in life to understand and accept them.

The primordial cell of Inca society was the *ayllu*,[2] which is the term still used in Peru to describe an Indian agrarian community. The *ayllu* has roots which go back far into the past. Originally it seems to have been a kin-group, made up of all the descendants of a common ancestor, real or supposed. But with the development of agriculture as the principal means of support of the population it seems that the importance of the element of kinship in the *ayllu* tended to decline (without, however, disappearing altogether) and

[1] A bibliography (ancient and modern writers) is provided by Rowe, op. cit., pp. 192–7.

[2] The earliest modern writers (e.g. Bandelier, 1910) assumed that the *ayllu* was a clan with the classical characteristics of matrilineal descent, exogamy, totemism, etc. But Rowe, op. cit., pp. 253–6, argues that it was a kin group, with theoretical endogamy, descent in the male line, and without totemism.

the concept of territory took its place – the communal ownership of land rather than blood being the principal bond which held the community together.

The physical environment in Peru is one which encourages co-operation in such matters as irrigation and terracing. It was, therefore, conducive to the development of a communal system of agriculture. Certainly by the time of the Inca it had become the custom in Peru for the land of the community to belong to the *ayllu* and to be worked in the following manner: first, a portion of the communal land was distributed annually among the heads of family, who were each given enough arable ground and pasture to support their families, but no more; secondly, certain fields were set aside for the upkeep of the village chief, or *curaca*, and for the support of the local religion. These community and church lands were worked in common by the people under the direction of the chief, the labour thus provided being equivalent to the payment of a tax. At other times of the year the use of communal labour was requisitioned, under a rota system known as the *mita*, for the upkeep of the irrigation system, the terraces, the roads, and other public works.

With this body of time-honoured custom to serve as the infrastructure, it was unnecessary for the Inca to make any drastic changes in the social organization of the village communities which they absorbed. It was a question rather of adapting and expanding the existing organization of the *ayllu* to meet the wider needs of the empire. The village *curaca* was normally retained in office; the communal land continued to be distributed annually among the heads of family; there was the same tripartite division of the land, with the only difference that the produce formerly reserved for the support of the local chief now went to the Inca (in other words, the central government); while that reserved for the purposes of religion now had to serve not only the needs of the local cult, but those of the state religion as well. The obligation of *mita* continued but became more onerous. Men who had probably never before left their native village might be sent far away to serve in the army which, like the Roman legions, had to defend the frontiers of the far-flung empire; others would be mobilized for hard labour in the mines, on the roads, or on public works. As cogs in the machine of empire, peasants who had previously only known their own little community and served a familiar chief of their own kith and kin, now had to work for the greater glory of a god-like Inca – a remote and terrifying (but much esteemed) potentate seated on his golden throne in Cuzco, whom most of the Indians would never see with their own eyes.

But the people would be only too conscious of the Inca's great army of officials who controlled every aspect of their life. At the base of the official pyramid the heads of family – that is to say men between the ages of twenty-five and fifty – were divided into administrative groups of ten under a decurion. This lowest of officials, who in army terms would rank as a non-commissioned officer, acted as a foreman directing the communal work of his group. The decurion was responsible to a head of fifty families, the latter responsible in his turn to a centurion, an officer occupying the lowest rank in the nobility. Above the centurion there was an ascending scale of officials each in charge of an even larger group – 500, 1,000, 5,000, and then 10,000 – culminating in a 'governor' in charge of four groups of 10,000. The governor, in turn, was responsible to one of the four 'viceroys', each in charge of one of the four quarters into which the empire was divided. The four viceroys lived in Cuzco, and, under the supreme authority of the Inca, constituted an informal upper council of the empire.[1]

The Inca himself appointed the viceroys and governors. The latter appointed the officials lower down in the scale, being careful, however, to follow local custom in the method of selection. In some communities the chiefs were elected; but there was a growing preference at this time in Peru for the hereditary principle to be employed in the filling of offices both high and low in the official hierarchy. The office of Inca[2] had always been hereditary to the extent that only persons born into the royal family could occupy the throne. But there was still an element of choice left, since the Inca was free to pick out from among the sons of his senior wife (usually his sister) the boy whom he thought would be most capable of succeeding him. Each Inca, when he died, became the founding father of a new royal *ayllu* consisting of all his sons and their descendants. Members of these royal *ayllus* belonged to the highest nobility in Peru and occupied most of the senior posts in the official hierarchy. As a special privilege the royal nobles, known collectively as the Inca, were permitted to wear enormous ear-plugs which earned them the nickname among the Spaniards of *orejones* (big-ears).

Such, however, was the tremendous expansion of the empire that there were soon insufficient royal descendants of the Inca to fill all the important posts. A few exceptionally able soldiers and adminis-

[1] Viceroy, governor, etc., are the terms used by the Spanish chroniclers to describe these offices. The Quechua words are *Apu* (viceroy) and *T'Oqrikoq* (governor).

[2] The term Inca is commonly used in three different senses: (a) as the title of the Head of State; (b) to describe members of the higher nobility; and (c) as a generic name for the empire.

trators were therefore admitted into the Inca nobility; and in the end the emperor Pachacuti was forced to decree that all Indians who spoke Quechua as the language of their birth should be given the rank of Inca.

To belong to the Inca élite carried great privileges (fine clothing, a host of retainers and concubines, and even sometimes grants of land), but it was no sinecure. Every young man born into the nobility had to pass through a rigorous course of physical training and schooling to test and develop his physique, character, and intelligence. Education was a privilege reserved for the élite, on the fascist principle enunciated by the Inca Roca that the common people should not be taught what only great personages should know. Thus in the customs and constitution of the Inca nobility we see two conflicting principles at work. In the rigorous training of the young men recognition was given to the need for merit in the holders of high office. But, working against this, there was an increasing tendency, as the empire became consolidated, to model the social structure on that of the stratified society of the old coastal kingdoms, as exemplified by the Chimu, where the hereditary difference between the nobles and commoners was so wide that the two classes were believed to have resulted from separate creations.

A lower nobility, the *curaca* class, included all other administrative officials down to the rulers of hundreds and their descendants. The members of this class, many of them the chiefs of conquered tribes and nations, were exempt from taxes and were supported from the government fields. They, too, like the higher nobility might be rewarded by the Inca for outstanding service by gifts of clothing, ornaments, servants, concubines, and grants of land.

As for the common people at the base of the social pyramid, a few lucky peasants became small office-holders in their villages (decurions and so on); others joined the ranks of the artisans (the smelters, silversmiths, gem-cutters, etc.); but the vast majority of the peasants just remained on the land in their native villages without any hope of ever experiencing any other kind of life. There was, however, in Inca times also a landless class of Indians, known as the *yanacuna*, consisting of persons who had been taken away from their villages in youth to become the house-servants of the nobility, or, if especially gifted or good-looking, to serve in the royal household. The sovereign distributed *yanacuna* as gifts to the nobles in the same way as he did with wives and chattels. Essentially the *yanacuna* was a slave, but for a few lucky individuals this could be a blessing. As in the Roman empire, the bright young man of this class who caught the eye of his master might be given the chance to break through the social barrier and achieve high office in the state – a chance which would never come to a peasant who stayed at home on his land.

As in most primitive societies women did not count for very much in the Inca empire. A peasant's wife was expected to work in the fields, cook, and spin. But she would be valued most for the number of children she bore. Children were an economic asset, since their number affected the size of the plot of land which the head of the family would be granted each year. However, then, as always, feminine charm was at a premium. The prettiest girl in the village would probably be taken away to become the concubine of some noble, or even to enter the household of the Inca. Other girls of outstanding quality would be honoured by being chosen as Virgins of the Sun – an order of nuns with vows of perpetual chastity, who made the beautiful robes of the priests and in other ways served in the temples of the sun.

Religion, like every other aspect of life, was highly organized in the Inca empire. A hierarchy of priests, almost as impressive as that of the government officials, served a large and varied pantheon of gods. Indeed, in Peru at this time there were religious beliefs and practices to cater for every need and taste. The national cult was that of the sun, personified by the Inca, who thus combined in his person the duties and status of Head of State, Pope, and Deity. For the sophisticated noble or learned man there was a higher god, Pachacamac, the creator of all things and the philosophical sum of all the perfections. The peasants, for their part, while doing their duty towards the Sun God, were left free to worship and propitiate their ancestors, both mythical and real, together with a host of locally venerated sacred objects, known collectively as *huaca*, which were believed to represent the powers of nature. But without any doubt the most remarkable feature of the Inca empire was its economic organisation. Upon the foundations of a typically hierarchical and barbarous agricultural society, such as might have been found almost anywhere in the East before the advent of the Greeks, there was established in Peru a comprehensive system of state socialism – and the modern term really does seem to fit more or less – by means of which virtually every aspect of the life of the people was planned and controlled in the interests of the state. The underlying policy of the economic plan was to ensure that all the resources of the empire, animal, vegetable, and mineral, should be exploited to the full; every man, woman, and child, if fit to work at all, should do his stint in accordance with his or her aptitude and capacity; and nobody in the land should go in want for essential food and clothing and a roof over his head. There was nothing lavish, however, about the standards of this welfare state. Freedom from want for the mass of the people meant two extremely frugal meals a day; clothes which could not be renewed until they were in tatters; no shoes; a one-room house without windows; a field and two llamas for each head of family; a life of toil only relieved by an occasional fiesta, when the *chicha* would flow freely and for a moment the peasant could forget the hard world into which he had been born.

For it was not part of the policy of the economic planners – and in this respect, they were not true socialists – to better the life of the common people. Like the herds of llama, human beings were considered by the Inca to be no more than cogs in a machine. Cogs have to be oiled; men and llama must be fed. But the essential purpose of the economy was to produce a surplus, over and above the bare needs of the people, to support the Inca and his nobles in suitable splendour and to sustain the military power on which in the last resort the empire depended.

The national economic plan began with the compilation of statistics.[1] Every man, woman, and child in the land was counted. Likewise, an accurate and comprehensive survey was made of the economic resources of the region. It was the duty of the regional officials from the decurions upwards to provide the raw materials for these statistics. Local statistics were assembled in the regional capitals, and global statistics covering the human and material resources of the whole empire were kept by a group of experts in Cuzco to serve as the basis of the Inca's imperial policy. Whole communities might be uprooted either for strategic reasons or to fulfil the economic plan – experienced farmers being sent to under-developed or under-populated regions; people of doubtful loyalty transferred to places where they would be powerless to do any harm; craftsmen recruited for this or that purpose and sent to the place in which they were most needed. But however brutal the uprooting might be from a sentimental point of view nobody was ever allowed to suffer unduly in a material way and indeed great pains were taken by the Inca's officials to avoid inflicting undue hardship. But there was no freedom for the individual in such a system. Having deployed the population to best advantage in relation both to economic resources and strategic needs, it was essential, in order not to spoil the plan, that everybody should stay in the place to which he had been allotted. Thus nobody in the Inca empire could travel without an official licence.

The surplus of food produced from the fields belonging to the Church and the state, as well as the wool from the Inca's vast herds of llama and the metal from the mines, was stored in official warehouses dotted about the country. The peasants kept for themselves only what they could grow on their own plot of land or could obtain

[1] The data were recorded on a device of knotted cords called a *quipu*.

by barter from some similarly placed neighbour. This local market-ing of home-grown products was the full extent of private trade per-mitted in an otherwise totally controlled economy. Part of the surplus in the official warehouses was used for the upkeep of the Inca and his nobles. Another part went to sustain the armies. The rest con-stituted a reserve at the disposal of the economic managers, who in this way were able to solve the problem, always difficult in a socialist state, of matching supply and demand. Thus, in an indirect way quite a lot of the product of the labour of the people on the Inca's land returned to the people. If there was a famine in some region the people would be helped from the central store. Those who were too old or sick to work would be assured of a bare living. To this extent the Inca really did maintain a welfare state; and from all accounts the system worked with great efficiency.

However, as always, the price which had to be paid for security was regimentation. As the French economist Louis Baudin[1] has pointed out in criticism of the system, the Inca banished the two great causes of popular disaffection, poverty and idleness, but by the same token they dried up the springs of progress, initiative, and a provident concern for the future. Like privates in an army the Indians did what they were told, knowing that if they obeyed the orders of the Inca's officials their basic needs for food, clothing, and shelter, at the bare standard to which they had always been accus-tomed, would be taken care of. They also knew that if they dis-obeyed their masters they would be severely punished. For the laws of the Inca were rigorous, with the death penalty as the normal fate of all but minor transgressors.

There are almost as many conflicting views about the Inca system of government as there are writers on the subject.[2] Each author tends either to praise or condemn the system in accordance with his own political beliefs or prejudices. The debate began in the six-teenth century and has been going on ever since. For example, in the early conquest period we find Garcilaso de la Vega painting a picture of an almost idyllic life under the benevolent rule of the Inca, whereas another early chronicler, Pedro Sarmiento de Gam-boa, described the Indians under the Inca as abject creatures totally lacking in ambition. In subsequent centuries the view taken of the Inca tended to depend upon the attitude of the writer towards Spain – those who wished to blacken the reputation of the Spaniards would depict the Indians as models of virtue, and vice-versa. In

[1] Louis Baudin, *A Socialist Empire – The Incas of Peru* (New York, 1961), p. 200.
[2] See Fredrick B. Pike, *The Modern History of Peru* (London, 1967), pp. 7–13.

eighteenth-century France it became fashionable for a time to paint
a romantic picture of the Inca as 'the good providers'. In the nineteenth and twentieth centuries, with increasing concern among intellectuals and politicians about the Indian problem in Peru, the
argument about the achievement of the Inca tended to be couched
in modern political terms; the conclusions reached depended very
largely upon the view, optimistic or pessimistic, which the writer
took about the possibility of rescuing the Indians from the state of
apathy and despair into which they have sunk.[1]

Louis Baudin[2] concludes his chapter entitled 'A Menagerie of
Happy Men' with the assertion that in Peru a 'so-called happiness
was obtained only through the annihilation of the human person-
ality'. This is no doubt fair criticism from a modern point of view.
But if judged by the standards of the time and the place in which
they lived, the Inca can hardly fail to come out well from any impartial examination of their record. A nation of warriors, living in
an age of war, they were not only highly successful soldiers, but they
had the wit as well to extend the empire by cunning and diplomacy
when this better suited their purpose. Like the other barbarous
tribes of Peru in the fifteenth century, the Inca made drums from
the skins of those who revolted against them, but they were sufficiently sophisticated to prefer to win over their enemies by gifts and
retain their loyalty by offering them jobs in the official hierarchy.
The conquered people were enslaved, but they were treated by the
Inca better than they had probably been treated before under their
own local chiefs; if the ant-heap character of Inca society shocks
the modern observer, it must be remembered that the Inca built
their social organization on the foundations of institutions which
had already existed in Peru for thousands of years. Environment
had already made the Peruvian peasant the man he was, and the
Inca's system of government seems to have suited admirably his
passive and philosophic character.

At the cost of regimentation the imperial system of the Inca
succeeded in bringing peace and unity to a large tract of country
which hitherto had been the battleground of hundreds of warring
tribes. For the first time in their experience the peasants had no
need to fear either famine or the ravages of tribal warfare. Roads,
in every way as good as those of the Romans and crossing the most

[1] For example, Alejandro Deustua (1849–1945), a leading writer and
philosopher, thought that the Indians had developed themselves to the full
degree of their limited potential, and could never evolve towards a higher
level. But the Marxist writer José Carlos Mariátegui (1895–1930) was filled
with enthusiasm for the socialist empire of the Inca, and found inspiration
in it his plan for the future of Peru (see below, pp. 148–50).

[2] Baudin, op. cit., p. 208.

formidable mountain barriers, now connected the four corners of the empire. Along the roads at regular intervals there were store-houses and inns, so that the traveller, or even an army on the march, would never lack for food and shelter. By means of a system of runners news could reach Cuzco from Quito in about ten days. The Quechua language became the *lingua franca* in a country which before had resembled the Tower of Babel. By these means coast and *sierra* (but not the *selva*) were united for the first time in a single economic and political system – a remarkable achievement, surely, by a people who did not know how to read or write, and in so many other respects were barbarians.

Chapter 4

The Spanish Colony

IT IS SCARCELY POSSIBLE to conceive of two peoples so utterly different in character as the Peruvian Indians and their Spanish conquerors. Whatever they may have been like originally, the harsh Peruvian environment had turned the Indian peasants into servile, mild-natured creatures of routine, apparently content to be ruled by a handful of clever men who controlled every detail of their lives. Even the members of the Inca ruling class, able warriors and administrators though they were, were the disciplined members of a rigid hierarchy, bound hand and foot by the ties of traditional custom. Their most striking characteristic was their farsighted prudence. The Inca bureaucrats and statisticians left nothing to chance; everything was planned down to the last detail.

What a contrast there is between this cautious approach to life of the Indians and the reckless gambler's spirit of the Spanish conquerors. To the Spaniards, endowed with a superabundance of initiative and daring, life was a lottery. The Inca established their empire step by step through a systematic combination of conquest and diplomacy. But there was nothing systematic about the Spanish conquest of the New World. The initiative came from a handful of remarkable individuals who as often as not acted in conflict with Spanish officialdom. An important motive of these adventurers was no doubt a thirst for gold and booty; indeed, a financial dividend was necessary in order to pay the expenses of the expedition and to obtain the interest and support of the Crown. But the conquistadores were far more than piratical merchant adventurers. Just as much as by greed they were motivated by a combination of missionary zeal — the desire to conquer and convert the infidel for the glory of God — and a love of adventure. As Louis Baudin puts it, 'conquest fired their imagination by its quixotic element'. They were 'in love with glory'.[1]

It may seem surprising that a well-organized military empire with an estimated population of some 6 million people should have surrendered almost without a fight to a small force of less than 200 Spaniards. Francisco Pizarro was lucky, no doubt, to arrive at a

[1] Baudin, op. cit., p. 210.

50

time when the empire was rent asunder by the dynastic quarrel between Huayna Cápac's two sons, Huáscar and Atahualpa.[1] The latter, having triumphed over his half-brother, the legitimate Inca, was not very secure upon his throne and this may in part explain his failure to drive the Spaniards back into their ships. Despite their technical inferiority in weapons the Indian armies were so vastly superior in numbers that a determined stand against such a small force of strangers could hardly have failed to succeed. But the sudden apparition of this fearsome race of white men from across the sea, with their magical ships, prancing horses, and ear-splitting guns, seems to have mesmerized the Indians. The strangers were received with dazed wonder by the people of the coast, and no serious opposition was made to their landing. More surprisingly, no attempt was made to defend the passes of the *cordillera* when Pizarro, with unbelievable daring, marched his small force up through the mountains towards the Inca's highland stronghold in Cajamarca. And most incredible of all, Atahualpa, although supported by a strong army, allowed himself to be lured into the Spanish camp – he had been invited to dinner by Pizarro – whereupon the Spaniards set upon and massacred his unarmed entourage, and the Inca himself was taken prisoner. In one blow the proud Inca empire lay at Pizarro's feet.

For even in captivity the word of the Inca was law throughout the empire. Instead of the outraged Indian warriors now rising up in arms against the intruders, the whole vast, bureaucratic machine of the empire was put to the humiliating task of collecting a roomfull of gold for Atahualpa's ransom. What followed is a sordid story. A vast pile of beautiful golden plate and ornaments was hurriedly collected from the four corners of the empire and melted down into bars. The Spaniards could hardly believe their eyes and immediately started quarrelling when they saw this huge pile of loot. But although he had fulfilled his part of the bargain, the Inca did not win his freedom as had been promised. On flimsy trumped-up charges he was hastily condemned to death by the Spaniards.[2] To add to the cruelty of his situation, the living representative of the Sun God on earth was offered the choice of being burned alive if he adhered

[1] Huayna Cápac divided the empire between two of his sons, Huascar, the son of his senior wife (and sister), who became the Inca in Cuzco; and Atahualpa, his favourite son by an Ecuadorian princess, to whom he left the kingdom of Quito. Subsequently Atahualpa seized the whole of the empire for himself and had his brother assassinated.

[2] There were twelve charges against the Inca. The most important was that he usurped the crown and assassinated his brother; the most frivolous that he was guilty of idolatry and of adulterous practices, indulging openly in a plurality of wives.

to his pagan faith, or the more merciful garotte if he became a Christian. Being human, Atahualpa chose the less painful way of dying and was baptized a Christian on the scaffold. After this crime, Pizarro marched upon Cuzco, and in 1533 the capital of the Inca was seized and sacked without any serious resistance.

There followed sixteen confused years during which the new colony was racked by civil war. After the execution of Atahualpa, Pizarro appointed as a puppet Inca a son of Huayna Cápac, Tupac Huallpa. But this young man died suddenly and mysteriously – he was possibly the victim of poisoning – during the march upon Cuzco. Yet another son of Huayna Cápac, Manco, was then appointed by Pizarro for this menial job of keeping the empire quiet for the benefit of its new Spanish masters. But the Inca Manco was a man of spirit. Tiring of the humiliations of his life in Cuzco, he escaped into the mountains where he organized an Indian resistance movement. For a while in 1536 both Cuzco and the new Spanish capital of Lima on the coast were besieged by large, well-equipped Indian armies, and things looked very black for the Spaniards. But when the time came for sowing the new crops, the Indian armies, as was their wont, melted away and the sieges were lifted. Manco lingered on as a guerrilla leader until 1544 when he was murdered by a party of dissident Spaniards who had taken refuge in his camp. With the death of this brave man there ended the armed resistance of the Indians. The Spanish colony suffered no further serious trouble from this quarter until the abortive Indian rebellions in the eighteenth century.[1]

Meanwhile, even before the Indian war had been won, the Spanish conquerors had fallen out among themselves over the division of the spoils. Francisco Pizarro's partner, Diego de Almagro, the conqueror of Chile, seized Cuzco and attempted to hold it as part of his southern domain; but he was defeated by the Pizarros in battle, tried, and executed. In revenge, in 1541, Francisco Pizarro, the ruler of Peru, was murdered at his house in Lima by the 'men of Chile'. Meanwhile, his brother, Hernando, had been imprisoned upon his return to Spain for the arbitrary way in which Almagro 'had been put to death.

In 1544 there arrived in Peru the first Spanish viceroy, Don Blasco Núñez Vela, armed with full powers to impose upon the colonists the 'New Laws of the Indies' which had recently been promulgated. These laws were designed to protect the Indians against the depredations of the colonists and were aimed in particular against the system of *encomienda*, whereby the leading conquistadores had carved out for themselves vast feudal estates. The viceroy was a

[1] See below, pp. 68–70.

man of autocratic temperament and so infuriated the settlers by his high-handed methods that he provoked an uprising by Pizarro's younger brother, Gonzalo. The viceroy was deposed, and when he attempted to return to Peru at the head of an army recruited in Ecuador, he was defeated, captured, and executed by the rebels. Thus, in 1546, Gonzalo Pizarro became the *de facto* strong-man of Peru. But his reign was short-lived. A new royalist army was assembled and this last of the Pizarro brothers to figure in Peruvian history was, in his turn, captured and executed. Under the firm but more tactful rule of the new Spanish commissioner, Don Pedro de la Gasca, the colony was at last pacified. Thus ended in a draw — since the system of *encomienda* was allowed to continue for another generation — the first round of the struggle between the forces of law and order, as represented by the king and his viceroys, and the unruly colonists.

It is to the great credit of Spain that throughout the three centuries of her colonial rule in the New World the official policy of the Crown, as represented by the swelling volume of the Laws of the Indies, should have been designed primarily to protect the Indians from the exactions of the Spanish colonists. This policy emerged as the result of a remarkable debate which took place in Spain during the sixteenth century between the lawyers and clerics who advised the king on colonial matters. The Indians had their most vociferous champion in the Dominican friar, Bartolomé de las Casas, who, having witnessed the ill-treatment of the native inhabitants in the Caribbean islands (he was then one of the settlers himself), entered the Dominican Order and spent the rest of his life denouncing these atrocities in books and pamphlets and in verbal testimony before the Council of the Indies. The Indians, Las Casas argued, were the natural subjects of the king and should enjoy, from the moment of their entering into Spanish obedience, all the guarantees of liberty and justice provided by the laws of Castile. The conquistadores, by deposing Indian rulers, seizing Indian lands, and distributing Indians in *encomienda*, had usurped the royal authority and invaded rights which the king was sworn to protect.

But these passionate, and not always coherently presented, views of Las Casas, and of the other liberal-minded clerics who had the ear of the king, did not go unchallenged at Court. As the principal leader of the opposition party in this dispute, the distinguished Spanish scholar Don Juan Ginés de Sepúlveda took what in the sixteenth century must have seemed to be the commonsense line. He argued that the law of nations was to be found only among the educated élite in any community, not among those on the fringe of civilization. He was an advocate, therefore, of the principle of 'natural aristocracy' (with its inevitable counterpart of 'natural servitude'). Government of the lower races must be by the higher, just as in each race the lower elements in the population must be ruled by the higher. Thus, in Sepúlveda's view, the Spanish colonists had every right to take the Indians under their paternal authority and put them to work.[1]

For the colonists themselves these academic arguments between lawyers and clerics in far-distant Spain had little or no relevance to the realities of their situation. These hardy adventurers had not risked their lives and fortunes for nothing. Whatever might be the rights and wrongs of the case in theory, Indian labour was essential to enable them to exploit the conquered territories and, indeed, for the survival of the colony. It was not in the tradition of the Spanish knight to soil his hands with menial toil, and indeed there was not a man in the expeditionary armies, however humble his status might have been at home, who was prepared to go back to being a peasant in the New World. The Indians, the settlers argued, belonged to them like the land by right of conquest. Let the friars convert the natives to the true faith by all means; for that had been one of the purposes of the conquest. But in return for this blessing the Indians must expect to work and pay tribute in order to support their new Spanish masters in a way fitting to the latter's newly-won dignity as nobles and gentlemen.

Under the system of *encomienda*, it was the practice everywhere in the New World for the leaders of successful expeditions to parcel out the land to the most deserving of their followers. The fortunate recipient did not, however, obtain the outright ownership of the territories so donated, but as a feudal lord became responsible for the good government and welfare of the Indians under his jurisdiction, and in return for this responsibility was entitled to receive tribute from them. The Spanish kings, who were becoming increasingly autocratic in their ideas, disliked a system which gave so much power to individual settlers, and therefore tended to agree with the friars, who, like Las Casas, objected to the system for humanitarian reasons. Nevertheless, however great the theoretical objections, the system of *encomienda* was in practice the only way of settling the country in the first years after the conquest and providing a rough and ready administration for the native population. Moreover, it helped to satisfy the ambitions of the conquerors and make them less likely to cause trouble in the new colonies.

After one or two generations, during which the original beneficiaries and their heirs were allowed reluctantly by the king to continue with their *encomiendas*, the system became obsolete and

[1] J. H. Parry, *The Spanish Seaborne Empire* (London, 1966), pp. 137–51.

Crown officials, called *corregidores*, were appointed as district commissioners to administer the affairs of the natives and collect the tribute. But while in theory Crown officials might have been expected to protect the interests of the natives better than the settlers themselves had done, the lot of the Indians did not improve under the new system; if anything it became worse. As had been the case during the time of the *encomiendas*, the collection of tribute was left to the Indian chiefs, or *curacas*, who had been allowed to retain their hereditary offices in the villages and acted as middlemen between their own people and the Spanish *corregidores*. These petty Indian officials, as well as the *corregidores* who controlled them, were often corrupt. The latter were usually only interested in collecting as much tribute as possible, with no questions asked of their subordinates about the method of collection. A number of lucrative rackets were developed. For example, the *corregidores* managed to obtain the monopoly for selling European goods to the Indians, on the argument that the ignorant peasants would be cheated by private traders. Instead, they were cheated by the *corregidores*. Using their position of power, these officials forced the unfortunate peasants to buy goods they did not want and could not afford. Loaded with debts which they could only pay off by work, the Indians, although technically free men in a free society, were virtually enslaved by this means.

But of all the exactions to which the Indians were subjected during the colonial period by far the most onerous and disruptive was the *mita*. We saw how in the Inca empire the *mita* was used as a device for obtaining by rota communal labour for the upkeep of the roads and other public works. But, while the Inca, with their gift for organization, had made great efforts to be scrupulously fair in the distribution of the burden of *mita*, there was little or no proper control exercised by the Spaniards over the demand for labour. Whole communities were denuded of their male population in order to fill the quota of labour needed in the great silver-mines of Potosí upon which the economy of the colony so much depended. Many of the Indians who set off on the long trek to upper Peru never returned to see their native villages again.

As the combined result of the *mita*, epidemics of European diseases, and the flight of many Indians to regions beyond the control of the Spaniards, there was a sharp decline in the Indian population during the first century of colonial rule. It became harder for the *corregidores* and the settlers to recruit the labour required to support the rapidly expanding economy of the colony. As a partial remedy negro slaves were imported to work in the coastal *haciendas*, thus adding to the racial complexity of an already complex society.

As a further remedy the fifth viceroy, Francisco de Toledo (1569–81), forced many of the Indians in the *sierra* to abandon their small isolated settlements and to be concentrated in towns where they could be more easily counted and controlled. Meanwhile, he made determined efforts to regulate the system of *mita* so that no more than one-seventh of the adult male population in any region should be called up in any one year. But in Peru a vast distance, both geographical and bureaucratic, separated even this diligent and well-meaning viceroy from his subordinate officials in the field. The orders were duly noted and filed, but as often as not ignored.

It would be a mistake, however, to subscribe altogether to the 'black legend' of Spanish colonial rule – a one-sided theory of history which blames Spanish cruelty and greed for all the ills which befell the Indians in the post-conquest period, and gives no credit to the Spaniards for their tremendous achievement in discovering, conquering, and civilizing the New World. Suffering and hardship were bound to result from the impact of two such dissimilar and unequal civilizations; and the sixteenth century was a brutal age. But, even so, the Indians could count a number of blessings.

In the first place, at all times during the colonial period they had friends and protectors in high places – the king, the viceroy, the judges of the *audiencia*, and, above all, the host of good friars who attended to their spiritual welfare, many of whom strove manfully to mitigate the harshness of colonial rule. The civil administration in the provinces might be harsh and corrupt, but, in theory at any rate, the Indians had the law on their side; and they took to litigation like ducks to water. In Mexico a special court was established to deal with the flood of Indian petitions and complaints about such matters as forced labour, tribute, and the injustice of the *corregidores*. In Peru the petitions of the Indians had to go through the complicated and dilatory procedure of the *audiencias*, and thousands of complaints probably never reached their destination. But the Indians could at least let off steam in this litigation, even if the machinery for the redress of their grievances was too cumbersome and distant to be effective.

As a second blessing, the Spaniards brought with them to the New World a number of material benefits which, potentially at any rate, enriched the life of the Indian peasants. The horse, the mule, and the donkey to some extent replaced the human beast of burden in the countryside. To the Indian farmer's meagre equipment of wooden hoe and digging-stick were added iron tools and the plough. Cattle, pigs, sheep, chickens, and a variety of new crops greatly expanded the possibilities of the agrarian economy. If the Indians, in their suspicious conservatism, were slow to take advantage of these blessings – and on the whole they preferred to stick to their old methods and diet – the Spaniards cannot fairly be blamed for this.

As a final but admittedly very marginal blessing, the Indians, by and large, enjoyed under the Spaniards a somewhat greater measure of personal freedom than they had done in the Inca welfare state. In Inca times, as we saw, an Indian could not move from his village without official permission. But now the highways, already falling into disrepair under the more negligent Spaniards, were thronged with travellers and vagabonds. The Inca had restricted private trade among the Indians to the minimum; but in the colony there was greater freedom. Village markets, so typical of the Peruvian countryside today, were able to flourish. Local arts and crafts – pottery, textiles, silverware, and so on – which had previously been controlled by the state, now became a legitimate field of private enterprise in each community. Regions became famous for their specialities, and the products of Indian skill were traded widely all over Peru. Added to the periodical excitement of market days, the old round of religious festivals, which had broken the monotony of the agricultural year in Inca times, continued quite happily and if anything became more colourful under the Roman Catholic Church. The friars on the whole showed considerable leniency in their toleration of the survival of many old pagan customs and beliefs, provided that they could be decently disguised under a Christian veneer. The saints were fitted easily into the village pantheon, and Christian churches and shrines were built on the sites of ancient *huaca* which the Indians had venerated since time immemorial. The Indians' love of pageantry was kept alive by such imported ritual dances as that of the Moors and the Christians but with subtle changes in the plot and the cast to give the story local significance. In short, although undoubtedly extremely hard from a material point of view – and with cruel treatment the lot of many – the life of the Indians during the colonial period was not necessarily always one of pure tragedy; it had its lighter moments. Although this was scarcely a blessing, it should perhaps be recorded in this context that drunkenness and coca-chewing – two Indian vices which had been strictly controlled by the Inca – became widespread under the more lax discipline of the Spaniards.

From a psychological point of view, no doubt the worst thing which happened to the Indians as a result of the Spanish conquest was to find themselves second-class citizens in their own country; and this change of status must have been particularly hard to accept by the members of the Inca nobility. Some brave spirits joined the Inca Manco in the wilderness and died fighting for their freedom.

The majority of the nobles, however, submitted peacefully to the rule of the Spaniards and allowed themselves to be absorbed into the fringe of upper-class colonial society. They took to wearing European clothes, learned to read and write in Spanish, and married off their daughters to the white settlers. Nor, as we have seen, did the lower Indian nobility, the hereditary *curacas*, do too badly out of the conquest. Many of them became rich men in their new, if not very dignified, role as middlemen between the *corregidores* and the peasants.

As for the Indian peasants, there was a choice between three possible paths for them to take. Those who were adventurous could join the footloose fraternity of the *yanacuna* and seek wage-earning work in the new Spanish towns. There were some relatively soft jobs to be found as servants in the houses of the rich. Yet the misfits and the unlucky who took this path might well end up as beggars or petty criminals. But no matter. The Indian who adopted European clothes, however tattered, and lived, however disreputably, in a town, ceased to be an Indian in the eyes of the Spaniards as also in his own eyes. However poor he might be, the city-dweller felt himself to be a cut above the Indian who remained in his village and he was so accepted in colonial society.

A less adventurous path for the peasant lay in leaving his own village and seeking work in one of the big Spanish-owned ranches or *haciendas*. By this means he would be assured of a bare living; if he were lucky in his master he might be reasonably well treated in a paternal kind of way. But, as in Inca times, the price he would pay for security would be almost total loss of liberty; under a bad master he would find himself in a position little better than that of the negro slaves on the coastal plantations.

The third path for the peasant was one simply of doing nothing – of staying where he was on what might remain of his communal land. Indians who chose this path – and especially those in the more remote regions – met the challenge of the conquest by retiring into their shells and shutting themselves off from Spanish influences. Such a policy of withdrawal, manifested outwardly by a suspicious and negative attitude towards the white man and all his works, is still widely spread among the Indians in the Peruvian Andes.

But however much the Indians might cling pathetically to what remained of their old ways and traditions it was impossible to put back the clock. For better or for worse, Peru was now an outpost of European civilization, or at any rate of that mediaeval brand of it which the Spanish conquerors brought with them from sixteenth-century Spain. In the alien soil of Peru the vigorous and hardy plant of Spanish civilization took root and was soon flourishing. The new order of society was symbolized in the shape of the new towns which were built immediately after the Spanish conquest in the coastal valleys and at strategic points in the mountains. In the tree-shaded central *plaza*, dominated by the Baroque cathedral or church and the more severe but imposing palace of the governor, were represented the twin pillars of the Spanish colonial administration. The economic and social structure of society showed itself in the contrast between the massive stone-built mansions of the rich settlers, the family life of their cool and pleasant patios within hidden behind heavy iron-studded doors, and the noisy populous streets and mean shacks of the native quarter.

The Spaniards were town-dwellers by preference. Even the owners of large landed estates and mines normally only paid fleeting visits of inspection to their properties in the hinterland, and preferred to spend most of the time with their families in their town houses. The Spaniard inclines to be gregarious. Not for him the wide open spaces, except occasionally as a field for sport, adventure, business, or war. What he liked best was to stay at home and gossip with his friends in the streets, ogle the ladies during the evening *paseo*, show off the paces of his horses, and attend the bull-fights and the Masses; in short, to enjoy to the full all the sporting, social, and religious life of the town.

Under a surface of frivolity and leisure, politics, closely linked with business, was an important preoccupation of the white settler. The new towns of Peru were organized on the traditional Spanish pattern with their councils (*cabildos*) of twelve councillors (*regidores*) who, in turn, elected the *alcaldes* or municipal magistrates. These municipal offices were much sought after by the white settlers both for their prestige and because of the local power and influence which went with these jobs. Thus, office-holding in the Peruvian provincial towns tended to be restricted to an oligarchy of the leading families who were also the most important owners of property. It was a convenient system for those who benefited from it. The same men who owned property were responsible in their capacity as *regidores* for allocating the available land between the Indians and the white settlers. The farmers who supplied food to the town as a private venture regulated its price in their official capacity. The mine-owners who desired to requisition labour, as *regidores* could influence, directly or indirectly, the administration of native labour under the *mita*. Of course, as private individuals they could be sued, but the municipal magistrates were usually in their pockets. Thus, for the wealthy settler the *cabildo* was a most valuable and cherished institution which gave him not only prestige, but enabled him to feather his own nest and to protect his interests against the policies and actions of the distant and not always friendly colonial government in Lima.

Of all the towns of Peru, the capital, Lima, founded by Francisco Pizarro in 1535, was by far the most important. It was both the seat of government and the mecca of society, centred upon the glittering viceregal Court. The viceroy, as the representative of the king, was surrounded by all the trappings of royalty, but his effective power was limited by an elaborate system of checks and balances. As governor and captain-general, the viceroy was the supreme executive authority in the colony in military and administrative matters, but in making important decisions he was required to consult both with the Council of the Indies in Spain and with the *audiencia*. This important judicial body, staffed by eminent lawyers appointed from Spain, was the supreme appellate tribunal in the colony. It had the power to hear appeals against the viceroy or make complaints against his administration. It also exercised a general supervision over the conduct of inferior magistrates and had an overall responsibility for Indian affairs.

Viceroy, *audiencia*, provincial governors, *corregidores*, together with the learned clerks (*escribanos*) who provided the nucleus of a civil service – these together constituted the machinery of colonial government. It is to be noted that there were no popular or parliamentary institutions of any sort in the colony above the level of the town *cabildos* – and, as we have seen, the latter very soon ceased to be democratic except in theory. As it had been under the Inca, Peru was still ruled by a bureaucracy. But while the Inca bureaucracy seems to have been highly efficient and rigorous in the enforcement of the law, the colonial government, although well-intentioned, was cumbersome and slow and, in the lower levels of the administration, corrupt. The viceroys were usually men of high calibre drawn from the Spanish nobility or the higher ranks of the Church. But in the lower levels, as was customary in Europe at this time, offices were bought and sold, being regarded as investments because of their perquisites rather than as positions of trust.

Closely allied with the official bureaucracy was the hierarchy of the Roman Catholic Church which, in Peru, acted virtually as a branch of government. In the early days of the colony the friars did splendid work as missionaries and defended the Indians against the depredations of the settlers. But as the Church got better established and itself became the owner of vast properties, the missionary zeal began to fade. Good living in the monasteries replaced the self-sacrificing austerity of the early days. The activities of the Church became increasingly concentrated upon the more comfortable job of catering to the educational needs of the upper-class Peruvians.

As early as 1551 Charles V granted his assent for the founding of
the two great universities of Mexico and San Marcos in Lima, and
other religious and educational foundations followed thick and fast
in later centuries. University education was dominated by the
Church until the late decades of the eighteenth century when the
ideas of the Enlightenment began to gain ground in intellectual
circles in Peru. But even then ecclesiastical authority was never
seriously undermined. To this day the Roman Catholic Church is
still an important prop, in a moral sense at any rate, of the Peruvian
Establishment.

Colonial society in Peru was rigidly hierarchical, the class system
being based on the three interconnected factors of social position,
wealth, and race. The upper class in the colony, with the viceroy at
the summit, consisted of peninsular Spanish officials and clerics who
occupied all the senior posts in the administration. Immediately
below them in social status, but nevertheless enjoying considerable
social prestige, were the creole descendants of the Spanish settlers.
Some of them had some Indian blood in their veins through inter-
marriage at the time of the conquest, but, nevertheless, they were
considered to be and considered themselves to be white. Many of
the creole settlers were rich and powerful in the community, but
even so, to their growing chagrin, they were seldom allowed to
occupy any of the senior posts in the colonial administration. The
poorer among the white settlers used the influence of their rich
relatives if they could to obtain lowly-paid but suitably honorific
offices in the governmental machine or in commerce. It would
never have done for a white man to work as a labourer in colonial
Peru.

Unskilled manual labour was the province exclusively of the Indians and the negroes, although even at this low level of society
there was social and racial discrimination. The bronze-skinned
Indian, who in Peru was legally a free man, considered himself to
be superior to the negro who worked as a slave on the coastal plantations. Between the two poles of society – white and coloured – there
was a wide range of people of mixed blood, each combination –
mestizo (Indian and white), mulatto (negro and white), and *zambo*
(Indian and negro) – being given its own derogatory nickname by
the Spaniards, and carrying with it an appropriate status in the
community; the general principle of classification being that some
white blood was better than none, while Indian blood was better
than that of the negro. Racial discrimination in Peru was not, however, of the absolute 'touch of the tar brush' kind to which Anglo-
Saxons seem to be addicted when they find themselves in the position of a dominant minority in a multi-racial society. In colonial

Peru birth and wealth were just as important as skin colour (given a reasonable minimum admixture of white blood) in determining social status. As in Spain during this period, and indeed in most of Europe, a great gulf separated the upper from the lower classes in Peru. To bridge the gap there was only a very small white or *mestizo* middle class doing white-collar work as clerks, shopkeepers, artisans, and so on.

For the more wealthy Peruvians of the upper class life during the colonial period was gracious and leisurely. Although a colonial outpost, Lima with its viceregal Court was quite a sophisticated and indeed a somewhat frivolous capital, much addicted to fiestas and the social round and famous for the beauty and the smart appearance of its society ladies.[1] Intellectual life was not perhaps very lively by contemporary European standards, being too heavily dominated by the clerical tradition. But the colony did have its writers,[2] a theatre, and some excellent, if traditional, art in the *Cuzqueño* school of painting – mostly religious subjects done by native artists who, although trained by Spanish masters, added their own characteristically Peruvian touch to their work.

Economically, the colony depended for its prosperity mainly on the export of silver and other minerals to Spain, which allowed the colony to import a wide range of manufactured goods from Europe. There was also, in later colonial times, a considerable amount of trade via Mexico with the Far East in which Peruvian silver was exchanged for imported oriental silks. Trade was rigidly controlled by the Spanish and colonial authorities. Both exports and imports to and from Europe had to take the hazardous, pirate-infested route via Panama, the goods being trans-shipped across the isthmus from ocean to ocean by mule. In Lima the merchants were organized into a guild known as the *consulado*. All goods intended for Peru and the outlying Spanish colonies to the south, had to be channelled through the port of Callao, which lies only a short distance from Lima. This was a very lucrative business for the Lima merchants and laid the foundations of the fortunes of a number of creole families. Other fortunes were made, no doubt, by smuggling goods into the colony from English, Dutch, and French privateers who, in the later part of the colonial period, made an increasingly success-

[1] The flavour of life in colonial Peru is best conveyed in the ten volumes of Ricardo Palma's *Tradiciones peruanas* (Lima, 1899).

[2] Letters were a serious concern in the colony. But it was a literature written for an élite, trained in the classics and much given to the cult of elaborate metaphors, recondite allusions, and stylistic virtuosity. It produced no great names (Stephen Clissold, *Latin America: A Cultural Outline* (London, 1965), pp. 69–73).

ful effort to break the Spanish monopoly of trade with the New World.[1]

To sum up: The advent of the Spaniards and the 300 years of colonial rule which followed transformed Peru from a self-sufficient Indian empire, belonging culturally to the Bronze Age and almost completely cut off from the rest of the world, into a multi-racial colonial society and an outpost of the Old World. Spaniards, Indians, and imported negro slaves – and, in due course, their multi-coloured offspring – found themselves thrown together in a single community and had to learn somehow to co-exist. The pattern of society which resulted was beneficial for the white men on the top, but tough in varying degrees for the Indians, negroes, and those of mixed blood in the nether regions. For better or for worse, the hierarchical and rigid traditional society of the Indians was brought into contact with the mediaeval and feudal but more fluid and immensely richer civilization of Spain. As an inevitable result of such an unequal confrontation the higher traits of the Indian civilization were destroyed and replaced by those of Spain. But neither culture prevailed completely over the other. The Indian peasant, retiring into his shell, clung tenaciously to his traditional way of life and on his own level succeeded very largely in preserving it. Colonial Peru, as indeed is modern Peru, was not only multi-racial; it was also multi-cultural – a country of two incompatible cultures which, like oil and water, do not readily mix.

[1] One useful route for smugglers was through Buenos Aires and the rivers to upper Peru.

Part Two

THE YOUNG REPUBLIC
(1821—1895)

Chapter 5

Independence

EVERY COLONIAL SYSTEM contains the seeds of its own destruction. However loyal he may be in sentiment to king and country the settler overseas will inevitably develop interests different from those of the mother-country. If there is a native population, a three-cornered struggle between the imperial government at home, the settlers, and the natives is almost bound to ensue, the natives demanding from the colonial government protection against the depredations of the settlers; the settlers clamouring to be allowed to run the country in their own way and to their own advantage. So it is in Southern Rhodesia today. So it was in Peru at the end of the eighteenth century after 300 years of colonial rule.

Perhaps the surprising thing about Peru (as indeed about the other Spanish colonies in the New World) is that it took so long for this quarrel between the creole settlers and the Spanish officialdom to come to a head. During the sixteenth and seventeenth centuries the creoles in Peru seem to have been reasonably well contented with their lot. True, they were resentful about being denied higher office in the colonial administration and seeing all the plums going to Spaniards; but, even so, they were able to exert a certain amount of political influence in the colony. More important, they could make a good living and enjoy considerable prestige by means of the municipal offices they held in the town *cabildos* and as feudal land-owners. Add to this the profitable monopoly in trade enjoyed by the Guild of Lima Merchants, most of them wealthy creoles, and it will be readily understood how the white settlers in Peru were able to retain a genuine and indeed deeply felt loyalty to the Spanish Crown, while resentful of, and often snapping their fingers at, royal authority when it came to matters directly affecting their own interests.

When, however, in the early eighteenth century, the Bourbons, with their new-fangled French ideas about efficiency, replaced the tired and decadent Hapsburg line of Spanish kings, the screws were tightened, and life became far less pleasant and profitable for the creoles. In 1784 a new and more efficient system of colonial government was adopted for Peru. The viceroyalty (which had been

67

greatly reduced in size with the detachment of Ecuador and Bolivia) was divided into eight regions each administered by an intendant; and each intendancy was further subdivided into smaller districts under the supervision of sub-delegates. To these officers, usually Spaniards born in Spain, were delegated powers covering the whole field of colonial administration. This new arrangement brought the colonial government into headlong collision with the vested interests of the creole-dominated town *cabildos*. More efficient government in the provinces, combined with stronger measures to protect the interests of the Indians, greatly reduced the power of the creole landowners to run things in their own way.

Nor was the Guild of Lima Merchants left untouched by the new Bourbon broom. In 1778 the old monopolistic control over trade which had been vested in the *consulados* was abolished and trade between Spain and her colonies became a free-for-all. While welcomed by many, this development undermined the favoured position of the former members of the Lima *consulado*. At the same time it whetted the appetite of a new generation of Spanish and creole merchants who were soon agitating to be allowed freedom to trade, not merely with Spain, but with the rest of the world. The liberal ideas of 'free trade' began to gain ground in Peru.

Meanwhile, to add to the mounting discontent of the creoles, the political ideas of the Enlightenment were beginning to seep into Peru. Books forbidden by the Church were smuggled into the country and read by eager students. Revolutionary ideas about the 'natural rights' of man were in the air, and the old dogmas – religious, social, and political – were increasingly subjected to rational analysis. In the universities scholasticism went into eclipse; even among the priests it became fashionable to take an anti-clerical line. Before the beginning of the nineteenth century few people talked seriously about independence from Spain, but there was a rising demand in creole intellectual circles, as indeed for different reasons among the businessmen, for greater local autonomy and a drastic overhaul of the outmoded and cumbersome colonial machine.

In parallel with the spread of liberal doctrines in Peru, and no doubt to some extent the result of it, there was a revival, but in a completely different form, of the great debate of the sixteenth century about the proper way to treat the Indians. But in the eighteenth century the champions of Indian rights were not the Spanish friars, who had by this time lost their missionary zeal, but romantically-minded Indian or *mestizo* hereditary *curacas*. These local chiefs, having become prosperous and locally powerful by collaborating with the Spaniards, began to look back nostalgically to the glory of the Inca empire and even dream in a vague way of its revival. It became fashionable at this time for Indian women to have their portraits painted in the costume of Inca princesses, and Inca art-styles were revived in local crafts. In some provinces the Indians took to wearing mourning clothes on suitable occasions in memory of their defeated rulers. Even among the creoles, who prided them-selves on being white, it became the thing to boast of a modicum of Inca blood, and elaborate family trees were constructed in order to substantiate these claims. The famous Quechua drama *Ollantay*, an epic tragedy in typical Spanish style of love and war in Inca times, belongs to this period. Not that this neo-Inca movement was only the result of nostalgic romanticism. There seems to have occurred at this time a genuine stirring of conscience among the *curacas* about the plight of the Indians and a growing feeling that some-thing should be done to improve their lot. The treatment of the Indians at this time was indeed extremely bad. Tribute was exacted from those under eighteen years-of-age and over fifty, contrary to the law. All the men in some districts were rounded up under the *mita* to work in the factories and mines, leaving only the women and children behind. Wages in the factories were often unpaid, hours worked incredibly long, and children of six or eight years made to work in them in defiance of the regulations.[1]

The first serious Indian revolt since the death of the Inca Manco broke out in 1737 and extended to seventeen provinces. It was savagely repressed. There followed a whole series of unco-ordinated minor rebellions in different parts of the Andes under local leaders. The most important of these uprisings took place in 1780 in the Cuzco region. Its leader was a well-educated and wealthy *mestizo curaca* who was descended from the Inca nobility. He assumed the title of Tupac Amarú II in memory of an earlier Indian chieftain of this name who had led an abortive revolt against the Spaniards in the sixteenth century. The first act of rebellion of the second Tupac was to seize and execute an unpopular *corregidor* who had persecuted and exploited the Indians in his district in the *sierra* of southern Peru. An Indian uprising of major proportions ensued and resulted in the indiscriminate slaughter of both *mestizos* and whites, becoming in the words of the Peruvian historian, Jorge Basadre, 'a movement of collective vengeance' – a blind rebellion against white civilization, without apparently having any very practical pro-gramme in sight for the betterment of the lot of the Indians, and certainly with no idea of winning independence from Spain. After Tupac Amarú's death – he was duly captured, hanged, drawn, and quartered in the main *plaza* of Cuzco – the struggle was carried on

[1] Clarence H. Haring, *The Spanish Empire in America* (New York, 1947), p. 72.

by two disciples. In upper Peru the fierce Aymara Indians from the Titicaca region besieged La Paz, the future capital of Bolivia. In the province of Huarochiti another Indian rebel claimed that Tupac Amarú had been raised from the dead and was still leading the revolution from the fastness of the Amazonian forest. Gradually order was restored by the Spaniards and stern measures were taken to stamp out this resurgence of Inca nationalism. The title and function of *curaca* were abolished. Portraits of the Inca, which the Indians had been accustomed to hang in their houses as evidence of their noble birth, were confiscated. Indeed, it was made a crime to claim Inca birth without specific royal authority, and many descendants of the Inca were either executed or deported to Spain. At the same time, however, measures were taken to correct the worst of the abuses of the *corregidores*, and later in the century, as we saw, these officials were replaced by the new and more efficient system of *intendencias*.

Tupac Amarú's Indian rebellion made a considerable impression on creole society in Lima. The alarmed landowners and businessmen gave their fullest support to the colonial government in the stern measures it took to put out this dangerous forest fire. Thus, at a time when creole discontent against the Spaniards was rising in most of South America, this event, if anything, strengthened the position of the Spaniards in Peru. But there were some dissident voices. A leading creole intellectual, José Baquíjano y Carillo, had the temerity to protest vehemently against the treatment of the Indians on the unsuitable occasion of his address of welcome to the newly arrived viceroy, Agustín Jáuregui (1780–84). His speech, larded with references to the political theories of the French encyclopedists whose books were banned in Peru, fell like a bombshell among the assembled dignitaries. The Spanish authorities in retaliation seized and destroyed all the copies they could find of the offending speech, and there followed a general witch-hunt and burning of forbidden books.[1] But, despite the persecution, the voices of the liberals could not altogether be silenced. Supported by a considerable portion of the creole clergy, the new doctrines of the Enlightenment continued to be preached by Baquíjano, Toribo Rodríguez de Mendoza,[2] and Hipólito Unánue,[3] to mention but three outstanding men of this time who may be considered the founding fathers of the liberal movement in Peru.

[1] Because of this incident Baquíjano lost his chance of becoming Rector of San Marcos University. The job went to a safe conservative.

[2] A priest of liberal leanings and an ardent disciple of Locke, Descartes, and Voltaire, he was appointed in 1785 Rector of the *Real Convictorio de San Carlos*, the principal college of higher studies in Lima.

[3] The moving spirit behind the liberal periodical *Mercurio peruano* and a professor of anatomy at San Marcos University.

However, until the end of the eighteenth century practically nobody in Peru, creole or Indian, liberal or conservative, was thinking
in such positive terms as seeking independence from Spain. The
Indians in their blind revolts wanted simply a better deal from the
white man. The creoles wanted greater freedom to run their own
affairs – the conservatives, so that they could make more money and
enjoy the plums of high office, while maintaining the traditional
structure of society; the liberals because they wanted – or claimed to
want – to put into practice their theories about the natural rights
and essential equality of man. In liberal thinking there could be no
doubt that the creoles were equal to the peninsular Spaniards and
should be so treated in the colony. But, rather awkwardly, it had to
be admitted that in logic this same 'equality' ought to be applied
also to Indians and *mestizos* and for that matter even to negroes and
mulattos as well. But, while such an extreme view sounded all right
in rhetorical discussion in avant-garde parlours, few among the
liberals of this generation were prepared to face up to the full implications of their doctrine when it came down to practical politics.
Most of them came from well-established creole families. As is not
unusual in such cases, instinct and family upbringing were stronger
than the conclusions of logic and rational thought.

Independence from Spain only began to become a live issue in
Peruvian politics when its possibility was forced into the consciousness of the creoles, liberals and conservatives alike, by a series of
world-shattering events – the successful rebellion of the British colonies in North America, the French Revolution, and, most devastating
of all in its emotional consequences, the invasion of Spain in 1808
by Napoleon. The Bourbon king, Charles IV, was forced to abdi-
cate, as also was his son, Ferdinand. Napoleon's brother, Joseph, a
middle-class Corsican, was placed on the proud throne of Castile.
To the creoles, who for 300 years had retained a sentimental loyalty
to the Spanish Crown, whatever they might have thought about the
colonial government, this came as the final blow. It fatally weakened,
if not immediately destroyed, the shackles binding them to the
mother-country.

An agonizing conflict of loyalties now tore at every Spanish or
creole heart. In Spain revolutionary *juntas* of citizens who remained
loyal to Ferdinand sprang up on every side, and after some difficulty, given the regional fragmentation of Spain, a central government of the rebels was formed in Aranjuez. This body assumed the
direction of the guerrilla war against Napoleon which, with powerful British help, now ensued. The rebel Spanish government, as
might be expected, was dominated by the liberals.

In the colonies of the New World conflicting instructions began to be received from the two rival governments in Spain. The viceroys, and indeed Spanish officialdom as a whole, continued to take their orders from Madrid, as the legitimate centre of government, although now dominated by Napoleon. But the majority of the creoles in South America, both for reasons of loyalty and because they saw in this development the chance to assert themselves, adhered to the cause of Ferdinand. In the years 1809 and 1810 revolutionary *juntas* on the Spanish model, initially at any rate claiming to be devoted to the cause of Ferdinand, but already sniffing at the heady air of independence, were established in a large number of colonial cities – in the north, Caracas, Bogotá, and Quito; in the south, Buenos Aires and Santiago; in upper Peru, Chuquisaca and La Paz. There were, however, no *juntas* formed in Peru itself, where the viceroy remained in control. The political map of independent South America was already beginning to take shape. In 1811, under the influence of the old Venezuelan revolutionary Francisco de Miranda and the young firebrand Simón Bolívar, the *junta* in Caracas declared the independence of Venezuela. Buenos Aires, at the other pole of the empire, had also become virtually independent by this time, after the repulse of a British attempt to seize the city. But at this stage of the revolution there was no orderly progression towards independence. The situation was one of almost complete chaos, with families torn apart by conflicting loyalties, neighbouring towns at war with one another, the liberals dreaming their dreams of a Brave New World, and the conservatives, intent on preserving their property, watching anxiously to gauge the direction in which the wind was blowing.

The Peruvian creoles found themselves in a particularly difficult position. The liberals among them were not lacking in revolutionary fervour. But a society which derived its wealth from its feudal domination of an Indian peasantry – Indians who had only recently been showing alarming signs of discontent – was naturally conservative in its attitude towards social change; its outlook was quite different from that of the cowboys of the Venezuelan *llanos* and the gauchos of the Argentine – tough, rough-riding individualists who had little to lose and a lot to gain by supporting the movement for independence from Spain. Apart from these local considerations, Peru was the main bastion of Spanish power in the New World. It was from Lima that the viceroy, Abascal, mounted the Spanish counter-attack against the revolutionaries. The royalist armies were officered to a considerable extent by creole and *mestizo* Peruvians – many of whom in later years were destined to play an important part in the affairs of the republic – while the rank and file consisted mostly of Indians recruited in the Peruvian Andes, who had no interest at all in this quarrel between white men and just did what they were told. In 1814 Ferdinand was restored to his rightful throne with the successful conclusion of the Peninsular War; and by 1816 the Spanish armies, based on Peru, had managed to restore order practically everywhere. Simón Bolívar took refuge in Jamaica. But while peace had been restored on the surface, the rumblings of revolution continued underground.

Ferdinand VII, a typical Bourbon, had learned nothing during his years of exile and he showed no gratitude to those who had supported his cause. At the earliest opportunity the liberal constitution of the rebel Spanish *Cortes* of Cadiz was torn up, the Inquisition reinstated, and the old system of absolute monarchy restored; it was as though nothing at all had been happening in the world. This may have pleased some of the conservatives in the New World, but it infuriated the liberals. From now onwards there was nothing vague about the revolutionary aims of the liberals in South America. They were quite simply independence from Spain and the implantation of democracy in the new republics which would arise when this had been achieved. If there was any argument among the leaders it concerned the form which this new democracy should take. But the immediate problem was to defeat the royalist armies in battle and remove the last vestiges of viceregal power which was centred upon Peru.

In 1816 Bolívar landed once more in Venezuela, and in a series of brilliant campaigns made himself master of the territory of New Granada, later to become the independent republics of Venezuela, Colombia, and Ecuador. In the south San Martín, a professional soldier trained in the Spanish army during the Peninsular War, was organizing an army of liberation based on the river Plate. He conceived the bold plan of attacking the Spanish forces on the west coast in the rear, by leading his men through the high, snow-clogged passes of the Andes into Chile. It was a feat in the best tradition of the Spanish conquistadores. In 1817, the royalist army having been taken completely by surprise and overwhelmed, Chile was declared an independent republic. Thus, like the two arms of a giant nutcracker, Bolívar in the north and San Martín in the south closed in inexorably upon Peru, the one remaining citadel of Spanish power in the New World.

San Martín got there first in September 1820, landing his forces on the coast at Pisco in southern Peru from a makeshift fleet organized and commanded by the British mercenary Admiral Cochrane. Having got his troops safely ashore San Martín did not hurry. He wanted first to see what reactions to his landing there would be in Peru. With his amphibious force he was secure so long as he stuck to the coast. But the Spanish armies were very powerful, and he was not strong enough to engage them in serious battle inland without Peruvian reinforcements. For the Peruvians, torn in their loyalties, and in any case until now prevented from doing anything very much by the sheer weight of the Spanish presence, the awful moment of choice had arrived.

True, from 1811 onwards, there had been a series of minor rebellions organized by provincial *caudillos*, but they had been quickly suppressed by the Spaniards. The most serious of these uprisings was one which broke out in Cuzco in 1814 instigated by two *Cuzqueño* brothers, José and Vicente Angulo, and led by a *mestizo curaca*, Mateo García Pumacahua, who took charge of the military operations. This revolt seems to have started, like all the other Peruvian revolts, as an attempt to redress intolerable local grievances; but as the movement spread, with important towns such as Ayacucho, Arequipa, and La Paz temporarily falling into the hands of the rebels, it began to assume the character and proportions of a bid for independence. As such it was joined by figures of national importance, such as the poet Mariano Melgar (who was subsequently captured and executed) and the well-born young creole priest Mariano José de Arce, who was to play an important part in the foundation of the republic.

Thus in a way this unsuccessful revolt of Pumacahua stands in the same relationship to Peruvian independence as Father Hidalgo's equally abortive, but more famous, *grito de Dolores* which the Mexicans still commemorate as the clarion call for their independence, although the independence of Mexico from Spain, like that of Peru, still lay some years ahead.[1] Nevertheless, Pumacahua, with his makeshift and ill-equipped revolutionary forces, was no match for the professional royalist troops of the viceroy Abascal. Like those before it this movement was soon suppressed. The Spaniards in the years immediately following clamped down vigorously on all revolutionary activities, actual or potential. They even went to the length of closing down the Convictorio de San Carlos, Lima's most illustrious centre of learning which had become a hotbed of liberalism. Its eminent director, Rodríguez de Mendoza, was hauled before the Inquisition with the accusation that he had been reading prohibited books. Thanks to these stern measures, all was quiet in Peru when San Martín made his landing in 1820.

But it was not now only revolutionary firebrands like Pumacahua

---

[1] On 16 September 1810, Father Miguel Hidalgo y Castillo, parish priest of Dolores in Mexico, exhorted his Indian parishioners to revolt with the battle-cry 'Death to the Spaniards'. A massacre ensued until the rebellion was crushed.

and José de Arce who were nursing the ambition to free Peru from the clutches of the Spaniards. The Peruvian conservatives, including many of the senior clergy, were also becoming restive for precisely the opposite reasons from those which animated the liberals. The ·conservatives had watched with growing alarm the rise of the liberal tide in Spain, and had come to the reluctant conclusion that Peru would be better off on her own, still linked to Spain if possible through the monarchy but with her own (conservative) government, which could be trusted to keep the Indians (and the liberals) in their place. In short, they wanted to preserve the social structure of the colony in everything except its subservience to the government in Madrid and the preference shown to peninsular Spaniards when it came to filling high offices in the state. These thoughts were no doubt in the mind of the marquis of Torre Tagle, a Peruvian aristo-crat who in 1820 occupied the important post in the colonial ad-ministration of intendant (governor) of northern Peru. He knew that San Martín, although dedicated to the cause of independence, was a man of sound conservative principles with monarchist leanings and decided to throw in his lot with the Argentine leader. It was a fate-ful decision not only for Torre Tagle himself, but for Peru.[1]

Now assured of ample Peruvian reinforcements, San Martín re-embarked his forces and landed in the north. The Spaniards, seeing themselves outnumbered on the coast, and after a royalist battalion had defected, abandoned Lima and retired to the mountains. Thus, San Martín was able to enter Lima in triumph without having to fight. On 28 July 1821, in front of a cheering crowd in the Plaza de Armas of the viceregal capital, he declared the independence of Peru. Thereupon, at the request of the leading citizens, he assumed dictatorial power with the title of Protector.

Yet, although celebrated with all the pomp and ceremony for which the Limeños were famous – and they still do these things very well – there was a faintly hollow sound about the patriotic and triumphant speeches, with a powerful enemy lying only a few miles away, strongly entrenched behind the barrier of the mountains. Real independence was still very far from having been achieved. Instead of bending all their energies to the prosecution of the unfinished war, the creole politicians who quickly surrounded San Martín, and in the following year became the members of Peru's first Congress, engaged in an acrimonious debate about what should be the political structure of the new country. A monarchy or a republic? A central-ized form of government or a federal system on the United States

[1] For similar reasons, the Mexican conservatives found their champion in a wealthy creole, Agustín de Iturbide, who in 1821 declared the indepen-dence of Mexico and assumed the title of emperor. He was shot in 1823.

model? The maintenance of a hierarchical structure in society, or the immediate wholesale application of democratic principles in a country to which they were completely foreign and for which no preparation had been made?

San Martín himself, supported by Torre Tagle and other conservatives, had no doubt about what the proper answer to these questions should be. He was sure that Peru must have a strong, centralized government and favoured the idea of a constitutional monarchy.[1] But the liberals, who dominated the new Congress, would have nothing of this. They wanted democracy here and now. As a foreigner, San Martín found himself in an untenable position. He decided to go to Guayaquil to consult with Simón Bolívar, the liberator of the north, in order to discuss with him the future of Peru and to obtain the latter's support for the continued prosecution of the war against Spain. During San Martín's absence from Peru, Torre Tagle was left in charge of the government.

The meeting of the two great liberators, which took place in the steamy heat of Guayaquil, a tropical port lying on the Equator, was a complete failure from San Martín's point of view. The taciturn professional soldier was no match, when it came to negotiation, for the voluble, theatrical, politically-minded, and brilliant Simón Bolívar. The latter, having only recently occupied Guayaquil, was determined to keep this important outlet to the Pacific as part of his recently created state of New Granada. He was deaf to the plea that this territory had originally formed part of the viceroyalty of Peru and ought therefore now to go to Peru. Nor was Bolívar, a confirmed republican (although a believer in strong government), prepared to listen to San Martín's arguments in favour of a monarchical government for Peru. San Martín departed from Guayaquil with nothing gained beyond the promise of Bolívar's support for the continued prosecution of the war against Spain. And when he got back to Lima he found that the Peruvian liberals had taken advantage of his absence to organize a palace revolution designed to weaken his conservative support. Thoroughly disillusioned and honestly convinced that there was nothing more he could do to help Peru, he decided to throw in his hand. On 20 September 1822 he placed his resignation in the hands of the new Peruvian Congress and departed in a ship bound for Valparaiso.[2]

[1] At a secret meeting of notables called by San Martín in December 1821 it was decided to establish a monarchy in Peru, and an agent was commissioned to go to Europe in search of a suitable prince. When it became public, the scheme was killed by the liberals, working through a body known as the *Sociedad Patriótica*.

[2] San Martín took no further part in South American politics. He died in France, a lonely exile, in 1850.

The destiny of Peru now rested in the hands of a caucus of creole politicians, brilliant men many of them, but none with any practical experience of government. This first Peruvian Congress consisted mainly of professional men, with lawyers and priests in the majority. It was dominated by the new generation of liberals, who had learned their lessons well in the Convictorio de San Carlos – men such as Manuel Pérez de Tudela, the author of the Act of Independence, the priest Francisco Javier de Luna Pizarro, and, perhaps the most brilliant advocate of the liberal cause, José Faustino Sánchez Carrión. To carry on the government after the departure of San Martín, the Congress appointed an executive committee of two civilians with a soldier, General José de la Mar, as its chairman. In the following year Peru was presented with her first constitution. Providing for a very weak executive arm of government controlled in every detail by a supposedly democratic Congress – the executive could neither initiate nor veto legislation – it was a hopelessly unpractical document, given the realities of the social and political conditions of Peru and the need to continue vigorously with the prosecution of the war against the Spaniards.

It is not altogether surprising, therefore, that later in the same year the Peruvian army leaders, faced with the problems of the war and having dismally failed in their first foray against the Spaniards, and getting what they thought was very little support from the Congress (the wages of the soldiers had not been paid), decided to take matters into their own hands. In Peru's first military *coup d'état* – and there would be many to follow – the triumvirate was overthrown by the garrison of Lima, and a nominee of the army, General José de la Riva Agüero, was appointed as the first President of Peru.

A creole of aristocratic family, Riva Agüero had been one of the first leading Peruvians to espouse the cause of independence and at one time had been deported by the Spaniards because of his revolutionary activities. He was reputed to be a good soldier. As Peru's first President he now made a great effort to organize a national army, laid the foundations of a fleet, solicited aid from neighbouring countries and raised a loan – the first in a series – from England. But the military campaign which he launched against the Spaniards was no more successful than that which General La Mar's triumvirate had attempted earlier in the year. In June 1823 the Spaniards counter-attacked and occupied Lima. Riva Agüero, after an acrimonious exchange with the Congress, retired with his government to Trujillo in northern Peru, but only a few of the deputies followed him there. The dissident rump of the Congress preferred to remain close to the capital in the port of Callao.

It is perhaps uncharitable to suggest that this was the moment of confusion for which Bolívar, biding his time in New Granada, had been waiting before plunging himself into the affairs of Peru. Not all the Peruvian historians are very friendly to the Liberator. Anyhow, as a first step he sent his principal lieutenant, Marshal Antonio José de Sucre, still then a young man of twenty-eight, to find out what was going on. Sucre landed in Callao a few days after Riva Agüero's departure for Trujillo and his ears were soon full of the recriminations of the dissident congressmen who had remained behind. When in July, for tactical reasons, the Spaniards evacuated Lima, Sucre entered the capital and, in the name of Bolívar, proclaimed the marquis of Torre Tagle (San Martín's old right-hand man) as the President of Peru. Peru now had two Presidents, and in the confusion which reigned even a devoted liberal like Sánchez Carrión came to the sad conclusion that the only sensible thing to do was to invite Bolívar to come to Peru in person and clean up the mess; and so it was decided by a majority of the Congress. Simón Bolívar, the liberator already of three South American republics, stepped ashore in Callao on 1 September 1823, with the not very promising task of liberating yet another. In fact, in only just a little more than a year, he had added two more republics – Peru and Bolivia – to his collection.

Torre Tagle and the Congress immediately invested Bolívar with full command of the armed forces, Peruvian as well as Colombian, and shortly afterwards conferred upon him dictatorial powers as well. Within little more than a month after his arrival, Riva Agüero, the rival Peruvian President in the north, was betrayed by one of his own staff officers, General La Fuente (whom he had sent to Lima on a peace mission to Bolívar), and was captured and exiled. Freed of internal political preoccupations, Bolívar was now able to concentrate his whole attention – and he was a man of considerable military aptitude – on what should always have been the priority task for Peru, that of defeating the Spaniards. In this Bolívar, in a remarkably swift campaign, was completely successful. In 1824 a mixed Colombian and Peruvian force under his command defeated the Spaniards in the battle of Junín. After this action Bolívar left the army in charge of Marshal Sucre, and at Ayacucho, on 9 December 1824, this officer inflicted a crushing defeat on the Spanish forces, which put an end to the power of Spain in Peru. Marshal Sucre then proceeded to upper Peru and in a very short time overcame all Spanish resistance in that area. In 1825, to the enormous annoyance of the Peruvians who considered upper Peru to be a part of their territory, Sucre was proclaimed as the first President of an independent Bolivia, as the territory was renamed in honour of the Liberator.

Peru was now free of the Spaniards – only a small garrison of Spanish troops held out for two years more in the fortress of San Felipe in Callao. In the first flush of his great victory Bolívar was the hero of the hour and was warmly acclaimed by the Peruvians who extended his dictatorship for another year. It was not long, however, before many Peruvians began to have second thoughts about the Liberator and to resent his continued presence on their soil. His plan for a Confederation of the Andes, within which what are now the republics of Venezuela, Colombia, Ecuador, Peru, and Bolivia would be incorporated, was highly unpopular. In 1826 the Peruvians accepted under duress his equally unpopular constitution, through which, as executive for life – a monarch in all but name – Bolívar had hoped to govern his proposed confederation of five co-equal republics. But this arrangement was opposed vigorously by the liberals under the leadership of Luna Pizarro. And it was not only the liberals who were getting tired of the Liberator, with his much disliked entourage of Venezuelan and Colombian advisers, and behind them the solid phalanx of his victorious Colombian troops. The Peruvian generals, who had taken an honourable part in the battles of Junín and Ayacucho, were now nursing political ambitions of their own. They looked forward to the day when there would be no more Colombian troops on Peruvian soil, and they could call their country their own.

No doubt sensing all this and with urgent business awaiting him in his own country, Bolívar in 1826 said farewell to Peru, appointing Andrés Santa Cruz, a general from upper Peru, as President of the Council of Ministers and Commander-in-Chief of the Armed Forces.[1] Theoretically, under the new constitution, Bolívar, although absent from the country, continued to be the President of Peru for life, but he must have known in his heart that in Peru his day was done.[2] In the following year the Colombian troops which had been left behind in Peru mutinied and had to be withdrawn. The liberals took this opportunity to tear up the hated constitution. General Santa Cruz, trimming his sails to the new wind of Peruvian nationalism, convened a new Congress, hoping that this body would express their gratitude by confirming him in the presidency. But he was disappointed. The liberals in Congress disliked 'strong' generals, especially one who had been appointed by Bolívar. So, instead, they

[1] A talented and colourful young soldier of fortune, descended on his father's side from Spanish and on his mother's from the Inca nobility.

[2] Bolívar got back to Bogotá to find that his original creation of New Granada was fast breaking up into its component parts – Venezuela, Colombia, and Ecuador. Shortly before his death in 1830 he complained: 'America is ungovernable. He who serves a revolution ploughs the sea'.

elected their own nominee, General La Mar,[1] to become the constitutional President of Peru. The Peruvians were now at last truly on their own.

[1] See above, p. 77.

Chapter 6

Growing Pains

IN TERMS OF SIZE, population, and standing in the world the new republic of Peru was but a shadow of what the country had been in the great days of the Inca empire, or during the prime of the Spanish colony.

Cuzco had been 'the navel' of the civilized Indian world, governing an empire of 6 million people. From Lima the Spanish viceroys had ruled the greater part of Spanish South America until the Bourbon kings in the eighteenth century, acting in the interests of efficiency, had hived off the *audiencia* of Quito (now Ecuador) from Peru, and had transferred upper Peru (now Bolivia) to the *audiencia* of Charcas and placed it under the jurisdiction of the viceroy in Buenos Aires. These changes had been a bad enough blow to Peruvian pride. But now, after independence, the proud city of the kings had sunk even further in the world. Politically Lima had been downgraded by Bolívar into the capital of a republic of only 1,200,000 people – one co-equal republic among the five which the Liberator hoped to join together in his Confederation of the Andes. Moreover, it had lost a great deal of its commercial importance. Enjoying a monopoly of the South American trade with Spain during most of the colonial period, Lima's port of Callao now had to compete with Buenos Aires, Valparaiso, and Guayaquil. In comparison with Buenos Aires which faced the south Atlantic, Callao suffered the great disadvantage of distance from the centres of world trade. It did not matter whether the goods were trans-shipped across the isthmus of Panama or took the long-haul by sailing-ship around Cape Horn. In either case, the distances were immense and the freight charges correspondingly prohibitive.

In the question of her frontiers Peru, as the last of the Spanish colonies to be liberated, came out particularly badly from the partition, or at any rate this is how it looked to the Peruvians. In general, the frontiers of the new republics of South America were based upon the jurisdictional and administrative areas of the Spanish empire as they existed at the time when the War of Independence began. This rough and ready method of dividing up the territory was in accordance with what the Latin American lawyers call the principle of *uti possidetis* based on the frontiers as they existed in 1810. But unfortunately for the future peace of the continent this plan was not followed systematically. When it came down to detail, many areas adjoining the old Spanish borders were incorporated within one or other of the republics, either because this was what the inhabitants wished (thus exercising the right of self-determination), or more often in accordance with the whim of some national or local *caudillo*.

The disputed frontier between Peru and Ecuador is an example of the confusion caused by the failure to follow any single method of partition. On the principle of *uti possidetis*, the important Pacific port of Guayaquil, with its rich tropical hinterland, should have gone to Peru. But we have already seen how Bolívar seized it for Colombia (from which it was inherited by Ecuador) and refused to listen to the pleas of San Martín on behalf of Peru. On the other hand, in fairness it must be said that at other points along the Ecuadorian frontier the Peruvians managed to obtain possession of the disputed territories of Tumbes, Jaen, and Maynas and likewise refused to give them up.[1] To the east, in the still virtually unexplored jungles of the Amazon, the boundary of Peru with Brazil was based on the Treaty of San Ildefonso of 1777 between Spain and Portugal. This boundary, because of the wild nature of the country, gave little trouble at first, but in the south an immediately explosive situation was produced when Bolívar allowed Marshal Sucre to create the independent republic of Bolivia out of the territory of upper Peru.[2] Before the reforms of the Bourbon kings this territory had come under the jurisdiction of the viceroys of Peru, and during the War of Independence it had been reoccupied and administered by the Peruvian-based viceroy, Abascal. Ethnically and economically Bolivia had a close affinity with southern Peru. But now an artificial line had been drawn across the waters of Lake Titicaca, cutting the new republic off from its natural hinterland of Cuzco, Arequipa, and the Peruvian coast. Later in the nineteenth century Bolivia's lack of an outlet to the sea was to be one of the causes of the disastrous war between Peru and Chile.[3]

Had it not been for feelings of hurt national pride, it was probably just as well that the Peruvians, untrained in government and lacking

[1] The disputed area consisted of the *Commandancia General* of Maynas, the *gobierno* of Jaen, and Guayaquil and Tumbes, all originally part of the viceroyalty of Peru. In the eighteenth century Maynas was incorporated into the viceroyalty of New Granada until it was reunited to Peru by royal warrant in 1802. Under the Mosquero–Monteagudo Treaty of 1822 Guayaquil opted for Gran Colombia, the rest of the disputed territory became part of Peru.

[2] See above, p. 78.
[3] See below, pp. 113–17.

in resources, did not have to take on the administration of a greater area than was contained within the borders of the new republic. The Bourbon kings had been wise to create smaller and more manageable administrative units at the expense of the vast unmanageable territory which had originally been entrusted to the viceroys of Peru. True, the Inca had managed to control an even greater territory. But they had had the great advantages of an efficient central bureaucracy, a docile Indian population, and, above all, excellent roads – in particular the great longitudinal highway along the ridge of the mountains which connected Cuzco with Quito. But under the colonial government the Inca's road system had been allowed to fall into disrepair. At the time of independence the roads were so bad it took twelve days of hard travel from Lima to reach Cuzco, or, in the other direction, an equal time to reach the northern city of Piura. In these circumstances it is not surprising that provincial loyalties were at first a good deal stronger than any feeling of devotion to the new republic. In southern Peru, in particular, there was no love felt for the central government in Lima. Even in colonial times Arequipa and Cuzco had been hotbeds of discontent and revolution. Now there were many people in the south who were seriously thinking of creating a separate southern Peruvian republic with Arequipa as the capital – an aim which was actually achieved for a short time (1835–42) during the ill-fated Peru-Bolivian Federation.[1]

In social structure the new republic of Peru was very similar at first to that of the former colony. No waving of a democratic wand could bridge the yawning gap between the Indian peasants and the creole upper class. According to figures published in 1826, of the estimated population of about 1,200,000 inhabitants, well over half (673,000) were pure Indians, mostly living as peasants in the *sierra*. In addition there were some 50,000 negro slaves working on the coastal plantations. Most of the rest of the population were classified as having mixed blood (the figures no doubt reflect the tendency for anybody, however humble his status in society, to claim some white blood if he possibly could); but only a mere 150,000 of privileged people in the upper class were able to claim to be of pure European stock on both sides of the family.

One of San Martín's first acts on assuming the government was to issue decrees designed to free the negro slaves on the coast and to abolish the tribute paid by the Indians. But in neither case was it found possible, for economic reasons, to put these generously conceived measures into practice; and in one form or another both slavery and the payment of Indian tribute lingered on in Peru until the middle of the nineteenth century. Bolívar, in his turn, also

[1] See below, p. 89.

wanted to help the Indians. Inspired by the liberal ideas of his time, he swept away the paternalistic regulations of the colonial government which had made it illegal for Indian communities to dispose of their land. His aim was to turn the Indians into free men in a free society, each in outright possession of his own plot – in short, to create a society of small landowning farmers. But it did not work out in that way. The idea of private property, in the European sense, was foreign to the Indian mentality.[1] Bolívar's measure merely served to undermine the time-honoured system of communal land-ownership and put the individual Indian peasants at the mercy of the big white and *mestizo* landowners. These gentlemen (and who can blame them since it was now legal?) were quick to gobble up, plot by plot, all the land they wanted from uneducated Indians who could easily be persuaded to sell. The result of these well-meaning decrees was therefore the precise opposite of Bolívar's purpose – the power and wealth of the feudal landowners was increased, while more and more Indians became reduced to a state of serfdom. Thus, on the whole, the conditions of the Indians deteriorated during the nineteenth century. The only progress made, if it can be called such, was by those Indians who drifted into the cities – many of them as the result of conscription into the army – and in this way added themselves to the fringe of the growing urban working class.

Essentially, however, the War of Independence was a creole revolt against Spanish rule. It had no revolutionary implications for the Indians. In colonial times the Peruvian establishment had rested upon the three pillars of the peninsular Spanish bureaucracy, the Roman Catholic Church, and the creole settlers – the latter enjoying considerable wealth and social prestige, but possessing very little power. The result of the war was to send the Spanish officials and bishops packing, leaving the field to the creole oligarchy and the republican army as the only elements in the new society capable of filling the power vacuum. The Church still remained, of course, and continued to exercise a great moral influence in Peru; friendly relations were quickly established between the Vatican and the republican government. But the Church in Peru was no longer the political force it had been in colonial times. The oligarchy and the army had now truly come into their own.

But it would be a mistake to regard the oligarchy[2] as being in any

[1] When the Inca made grants of land to deserving nobles, the beneficiary enjoyed no more than the usufruct during his lifetime.

[2] The word 'oligarchy' is very commonly used in the Latin American political vocabulary, without ever being closely defined. In Peru people often speak of 'the forty families' who are supposed to control the wealth of the country.

way monolithic. The interests of its individual members and their outlook on politics varied greatly. The feudal landowners were naturally inclined to be conservative and believed in strong government. As far as possible they wanted to preserve the structure of society as it had been in colonial times, with the sole important difference that power should now rest firmly in creole hands. They preferred on the whole, however, to exercise their power by remote control rather than by descending themselves into the political arena. Among the merchants and businessmen, however, a somewhat different point of view was to be found. Many of them were critical of the feudal structure of society and dreamed of a modern, efficient, capitalistic economy run on *laissez-faire* lines, with government strong enough to keep order, but keeping its hands off the money and affairs of the businessmen. Both sections of the oligarchy – landowners and businessmen – were content to leave the day-to-day business of politics to the Congress. This body, however, was something rather more than a mere extension of the oligarchy. True, many of the Congressmen had connections with the ruling families for which they acted as a mouthpiece. But the Congress also included a large number of professional men, many of them eminent intellectuals with sincerely held political beliefs which by no means always coincided with those of the oligarchy.

The fundamental problem which faced the Congressmen was to devise a system of government which would fill the power vacuum left by the departure of the Spaniards. The liberals, who dominated most of the early Congresses of Peru, wanted to implant at once some measure of democracy in the new republic, although it was obviously impossible to go the whole way with a popular franchise while the majority of the population was illiterate. Taking the United States constitution as their model, they sought to curb the power of the President. But democracy was totally foreign to the traditions of both Indian and colonial Peru, in which a strong centralized government had always been the rule. Almost inevitably in the turmoil and economic bankruptcy of the immediate post-war period, with anarchy lying only a little way below the surface, the eyes of almost everybody, except the most stubborn of the liberals, turned towards the new republican army as the only body capable of producing a strong enough government.

The army was a relatively new phenomenon in Peru. Indeed, until the Bourbon reforms of the eighteenth century there had been no standing Spanish army in South America. But during the War of Independence Peru had become, of necessity, the bastion of Spanish military power in the colonies. The Spanish forces had had to be built up with great speed by recruiting Peruvian Indians in

mass into the ranks and employing creole and *mestizo* 'gentlemen'
in the more junior officer grades. It was from these war-hardened
locally-recruited officers, most of whom eventually defected to the
republic, that there emerged the leaders of the new Peruvian army –
tough men who had won their spurs in battle. This new generation
of military *caudillos* had little in common with, or respect for, the
soft and highly civilized civilian creoles in the cities, perpetually
arguing in the Congress about political theory or worrying about
their money. In spirit and outlook the Peruvian generals were much
more akin to the original conquistadores – military adventurers on
their way up in the world and anxious to carve out private empires
for themselves. With their mixed blood (they were often of quite
humble middle-class origin), they symbolized the new Peru in many
ways better than the creole aristocrats. The difficulty, of course, for
the politicians was how to use the generals but at the same time
keep them under proper civilian control. The liberals tried to solve
the problem by choosing as their military Presidents amenable
generals like La Mar or, later, Orgeboso. But neither of these two
liberal soldier-politicians were strong enough to stand up against the
plotting of tough and unscrupulous characters like Generals Santa
Cruz and Gamarra, whose thirst for power and mutual jealousy
underlay much of the political history of the years immediately
following the departure of Bolívar from Peru. The story which follows is a tangled skein of foreign wars, internal revolutions, plots
and counter-plots, set against the background of an economy which
was very close to bankruptcy.

In 1827 La Mar[1] entered upon his period of office faced by the
imminent danger of a war with Bolívar, now back in Colombia and
thoroughly disgusted with Peru and its liberal-dominated Congress.
Nor could the new Peruvian President count upon the loyalty of the
senior generals in his own army. In 1828 one of these dissident Peruvian general, Agustín Gamarra,[2] the Commander-in-Chief of the
army in the south, took it upon himself without consulting La Mar
to invade Bolivia, where Marshal Sucre, Bolívar's favourite lieutenant, was still installed as President. The Peruvian invasion succeeded,
Marshal Sucre resigned his office, and a government subservient to
Peru was installed in La Paz. In taking this independent action
Gamarra was no doubt motivated by personal ambition, but he
could plead in justification that he had served his country well by
securing Peru's southern flank in the war with Colombia which now
inevitably ensued.

The war against the Colombians went well at sea, and the port of

---

[1] See above, p. 80.
[2] A *mestizo* from Cuzco.

Guayaquil was captured by the Peruvian fleet under the command of the British-born Admiral Guise. But on land La Mar was defeated by a Colombian army under the command of Marshal Sucre. This was the moment of weakness for which La Mar's powerful enemies in the Peruvian army had been waiting. Three generals – Gamarra, the victor in the recent successful invasion of Bolivia; Santa Cruz who, having failed to become the President of Peru, now aspired to be the President of his native Bolivia; and La Fuente, a turncoat soldier-politician who had already betrayed one President of Peru[1] and was now preparing to betray another – met together in Arequipa and hatched a plot for getting rid of La Mar. The plan worked perfectly. La Fuente, who had been ordered to bring reinforcements from Arequipa to the hard-pressed army of La Mar in the north, stopped off instead in Lima and seized the presidential palace. Gamarra, whose southern army had already joined La Mar's command in the north, had the President arrested in his military headquarters in Piura and assumed command of the Peruvian army; then, having concerted an armistice with the Colombians, he hurried southwards to be nominated President of Peru by a stunned Congress, with La Fuente taking office as Vice-President. Meanwhile, Santa Cruz, who had kept the south quiet for the conspirators, was duly rewarded by becoming the President of Bolivia. As for the unfortunate La Mar, he was bundled off into exile in Costa Rica, where he died in the following year.

Gamarra ruled Peru as a strong-man from 1829 until 1833. The leaders of the liberal opposition were exiled. A peace with Colombia was quickly patched up on the basis that Guayaquil was to be evacuated by the Peruvians and the boundary with Ecuador remained exactly as it had been before the war started. But Gamarra, as a *Cuzqueño*, was more interested in the situation on Peru's southern frontier. When plotting the downfall of La Mar both he and Santa Cruz had agreed that Peru and Bolivia must be joined together in some kind of a federation. But now these two ambitious men found themselves facing each other as Presidents of their respective republics. They both still wanted Peru and Bolivia to be joined, but only on their own very different terms. A new war between Peru and Bolivia was only averted thanks to Chilean diplomacy.

Gamarra completed his first term as President of Peru in 1833, and sought to 'impose'[2] upon the country a successor of his own choice, General Pedro Pablo Bermúdez. But the liberals, who always managed to come to life again at election times, had other ideas.

[1] Riva Agüero, see above, p. 78.
[2] The attempted or successful 'imposing' of a favoured successor by the outgoing President is a recurrent theme in South American politics.

Just as in 1827 they had put La Mar into the presidency against the wishes of the army leaders, so once again a liberal-dominated Congress flouted the wishes of Gamarra and selected for the presidency a more amenable general than Bermúdez, General Luis José de Orbegoso.

At first Gamarra seemed to accept this setback philosophically, and Orbegoso was installed in office. But Gamarra soon had second thoughts, and in a quick revolution Orbegoso was deposed and Bermúdez put into the presidency in his place. It was, however, only a temporary victory for the forces of military reaction. Orbegoso had some powerful friends in the army and the civilian population was mostly on his side. There now occurred the nearest thing to a popular revolution which Peru had experienced since the beginning of the republic. After some fighting, during which several of the generals who had originally supported Bermúdez changed sides, Orbegoso was restored to his uneasy throne. Gamarra and his friends retired into exile.

The liberals, as was their wont, celebrated their triumph by promulgating in 1834 a new constitution designed to restrict the power of the President, a limitation which Orbegoso, as their nominee, was prepared to accept. But not so the leaders of the army, the Roman Catholic Church, and a powerful section of the oligarchy. In 1835 these conservative elements found their champion in the young and debonair Inspector-General of the Peruvian army, General Felipe Salaverry. He revolted, and for a second time Orbegoso was overthrown.

These unhappy developments in Peru were watched with keen interest by the President of Bolivia, General Santa Cruz, who still nursed in his bosom the ambition of being master of a federation embracing both republics. He now found himself in the happy position of having two Peruvian ex-Presidents — Gamarra and Orbegoso — knocking at his door for help. His first inclination was to support his old friend and rival, Gamarra, and an agreement was reached between the two men for mutual assistance in the creation of a Peru-Bolivian federation more or less along the lines which Santa Cruz had always wanted. Then, distrusting Gamarra's good faith, the Bolivian President switched his support to the weaker and more malleable Orbegoso, who held the trump card of being the legitimate elected President of Peru.[1] Gamarra, left out in the cold, could do nothing else but offer his services to Salaverry. Santa Cruz then

[1] Orbegoso transferred to Santa Cruz all his powers as President of Peru, to be rewarded later by Santa Cruz with the title of Grand Marshal, the life-rank of President (without any of the powers), and a gratuity of 100,000 pesos.

marched into Peru at the head of an army and, after defeating
Gamarra in the south, advanced towards Lima. Salaverry came out
to meet him, but in February 1836 the Peruvian army was routed
and Salaverry himself was taken prisoner. He and his principal
officers were then lined up and shot by the unrelenting Bolivian
caudillo.[1]

Santa Cruz was now the undisputed master of both Bolivia and
Peru. In 1837, at a meeting of delegates at Tacna in southern Peru,
he was invested with the title of Protector of the newly created
Peru-Bolivian federation. This shaky structure consisted of three
component republics – Bolivia, Southern Peru, and Northern Peru –
with their capitals respectively in La Paz, Arequipa, and Lima. The
wily Bolivian had managed to reduce Lima to the status of a provincial capital. The balance of power in the Confederation lay in
the south. Each republic was to have its own local government and
legislature, but foreign and economic affairs, and, more important
still, the control of the armed services, would be in the hands of the
federal government, of which, it soon became clear to everybody,
Santa Cruz intended to be the autocratic master.

These arrangements for confederation pleased practically nobody.
The *Limeños* resented having their capital relegated to provincial
status; the *Arequipeños* would have preferred a purely southern
federation of which Arequipa would have been the natural centre;
the Bolivians disliked losing their independent sovereignty. Virtually
all the politicians, irrespective of region, were alarmed by the obviously dictatorial pretensions of their Protector. Even less was the
new federation popular in the neighbouring states of Argentina and
Chile, who viewed with concern the creation of a super-power in
the Andes under a hardened old warrior like Santa Cruz. And there
was still at large that somewhat discredited, but redoubtable, *caudillo,* Agustín Gamarra, now joined with other Peruvian exiles in
Chile in plotting his revenge.

The first attack by the Chileans against the Confederation in
southern Peru was a failure. But in 1838, under the command of
the Chilean general Manuel Bulnes, but with a number of Peruvian
generals such as Gamarra and La Fuente in important subordinate
commands, an expeditionary force was landed in Peru and Lima
was taken. In a final confrontation at Yungay, Santa Cruz was
decisively beaten and fled from the battlefield into exile. A grateful
Peruvian Congress in Lima then appointed Gamarra as President of
a restored Peru. The ill-fated Peru-Bolivian Confederation had
collapsed.

[1] Despite his dubious political record, Salaverry is now remembered as a
national hero in Peru.

During his second term as President, Gamarra ruled Peru uneasily from 1839 until 1841. He was not popular in Arequipa, where Santa Cruz, now in exile in Ecuador, still had his friends and agents. The opposition to Gamarra centred around the elegant figure of General Manuel Ignacio de Vivanco, a soldier much loved by the conservatives in Arequipa. But Vivanco's attempted revolt was crushed. In 1841 Gamarra, hearing rumours that Santa Cruz was organizing a come-back in Bolivia, decided to mount a second invasion of the neighbouring republic. He was determined this time to settle the sore question of Peruvian-Bolivian relations on his own terms. But his invading army was defeated by the Bolivians at Ingavi and Gamarra himself was killed on the battlefield.

Thus ended in tragedy the feud between the two *caudillos* – Gamarra and Santa Cruz.[1] But at the price of much bloodshed at least one important thing had been settled. Henceforth, for better or for worse, Peru and her neighbours, Bolivia and Ecuador, were to go their ways as separate republics within roughly speaking the same boundaries that had resulted from the War of Independence. Bolívar's grand design of a Federation of the Andes was finished.

These wars left Peru impoverished and exhausted. The economy was in ruins; most of the mines were closed; and with many of the Indians conscripted into the armies of the rival *caudillos*, agricultural production had fallen drastically. Externally, the existence of Peru as a separate republic had been threatened. Internally, dangerous separatist tendencies had been fostered by the temporary division of the country into two republics based on Lima and Arequipa. In short, the situation could hardly have been worse. Even so, this did not prevent the military *caudillos* from continuing with their senseless quarrels. With the disappearance of the strong hand of Gamarra, they proceeded to battle among themselves for supremacy within the ravaged and demoralized country, not hesitating to make use of the rivalry between north and south to further their narrow and sordid ends.

Thus, General Menéndez, who took over the presidency after the death of Gamarra, was soon ousted from his post by the commander of the northern armies, General Torrico; whereupon our old friend General La Fuente, who now commanded the southern troops, ousted Torrico, imposing in his stead a friend, General Vidal. Meanwhile, in Arequipa, General Vivanco had made himself master of southern Peru and, advancing upon Lima, succeeded in deposing Vidal. It was like a game of musical chairs.

For a time it seemed that General Vivanco, a cultured dandy of

[1] After Gamarra's death Santa Cruz played no further part in South American politics.

autocratic tendencies, would be able to restore order. He made a great effort to gather about himself all the best brains of the country. But the Peru of those turbulent times needed a firm hand rather than brilliance and brains. In 1845 the Supreme Director, as Vivanco styled himself, was in his turn thrown out of the presidential palace. A tough, practical-minded *mestizo* general, Ramón Castilla, who had distinguished himself in the battle of Yungay and later served as Gamarra's Minister of Finance, took his place. At long last order was restored throughout the republic.

We have now reached an important turning-point in the history of the Peruvian republic. It is almost as though the country suddenly stepped out of a sixteenth-century world of battling conquistadores in their glittering uniforms into the frock-coated respectability of the nineteenth century. There will still be plenty of revolutions, but the military *caudillos* will no longer have it all their own way. From now onwards the quill pen of the counting-house will be as important in Peru as the sword, even though the sword will still be unsheathed from time to time as a more effective instrument of political action than the ballot-box.

Chapter 7

Convalescence

IN THE YEAR 1860 the distinguished British traveller, Sir Clements Markham, paid a visit to Peru. His mission was to explore the tropical regions of the country, with a view to collecting specimens of the Peruvian quinine-yielding Chinchona tree – or Peruvian bark as it is usually called – and arranging for the introduction of this useful plant into the British Indian empire. But Sir Clements was a man of wide interests ranging far beyond the field of botany. He has left behind an excellent analysis of the 'present conditions and future prospects of Peru', as seen through mid-Victorian British spectacles.[1] He was able to give the now adolescent republic a reasonably encouraging report – after a very unsatisfactory start, Peru was now settling down quite well; not as well as Chile, he concluded, but a lot better than the unruly republic of Mexico, which was still, some forty years after independence, in a state of utter confusion.

This relatively happy state of affairs in Peru was the result very largely of the work of pacification of General Ramón Castilla, now, in 1860, in his second term as President, and close to seventy years of age. Here is Markham's pen-picture of this outstanding *mestizo* Peruvian *caudillo* who was undeniably the dominant political figure of his age.

'Castilla is a small spare man, with an iron constitution, and great powers of endurance. His bright, fierce little eyes, with overhanging brows, stiff, bristling moustaches, and projecting under lip, give his countenance a somewhat truculent expression, which is not improved by a leathery dried-up complexion; but he has a look of resolution and an air of command which is almost dignified. This remarkable man is an excellent soldier, brave as a lion, prompt in action, and beloved by his men. Uneducated and illiterate,[2] his political successes and management of parties almost amount to genius, while his victories have never been stained by cruelty, and his antagonists have seldom been proscribed for any length of time, generally pardoned at once, and often raised by him to posts of importance in the service of the Republic. His

[1] Clements R. Markham, *Travels in Peru and India* (London, 1862).
[2] Castilla was the son of a mining artisan.

firm and vigorous grasp of power has secured for Peru long periods of peace; faction has been kept under, while an incalculable blessing has thus been conferred on the country; and probably no other man had the ability and the nerve to effect this.'

So far so good; but Markham goes on in a more critical vein, remarking that 'Castilla, though a necessity, has been a necessary evil'. The price which Peru had had to pay for political and economic stability was the upkeep of a large standing army and a costly navy which she could ill afford. Nor was Markham impressed by the quality of Castilla's Ministers. The old man, he noted, preferred to have obedient clerks around him rather than independent Ministers. The more able and active-minded of the leading Peruvians who impressed Markham during his visit – he picks out for mention, among others, Felipe Pardo, Mariano Paz Soldán, Dr Francisco Vigil, and Domingo Elías[1] – were, he found, either leading unobtrusive literary lives, as they waited for better times, or engaged in their own private pursuits.

As regards the state of the economy, Markham's report was generally quite encouraging, although he saw some serious problems looming on the horizon. The economic recovery of the country since the state of near-bankruptcy of 1845 had been quite remarkable, revealing a natural buoyancy in the economy which, as we shall see, almost always comes to the rescue of Peru when things are at their blackest. True, in 1860, the *sierra* was still the economic backwater it had been ever since colonial times. The Indian peasants, with their primitive methods of agriculture, just produced enough to keep themselves alive. Mining, too, was still in the doldrums for lack of capital and adequate communications. The contribution of the *sierra* to the national economy consisted of no more than some modest amounts of silver and gold – a momentary hope that the Californian gold rush would be repeated in Peru had come to nothing – and the wool from the herds of sheep and alpaca which roamed in the high *puna*.

Nor did the vast tropical region beyond the barrier of the Andes contribute anything very much in the way of immediate wealth, although Markham, who explored a part of this region in search of his trees, came back feeling optimistic about the potentialities of this neglected and still mostly unexplored part of Peru. He noted some hopeful signs of progress. In 1858 a fluvial convention was signed between Brazil and Peru, establishing the conditions for free

[1] Pardo, an aristocratic creole, the father of President Manuel Pardo and grandfather of President José Pardo; Paz Soldán, an enlightened landowner with a passion for prison reform; Vigil, a theologian of liberal views; Elías, a wealthy landowner in the south, and leader of the Liberal Party.

navigation along the rivers of the Amazon basin. In February 1860 the Brazilian steamer *Tabatinga* arrived at Laguna on the Peruvian river Huallaga 3,000 miles from the mouth of the Amazon. Meanwhile, the Peruvian government had ordered steamers to be constructed to work on the upper waters of the Amazon in conjunction with the Brazilian line; and there were plans, too, to build roads connecting highland towns like Huánuco with the nearest navigable points on the tributaries of the Andes.[1] However, an attempt to settle some German colonists in one of the tropical areas had been a failure. The conditions were altogether too tough and the communications too poor to permit a European community to flourish. But at least in 1860 Belaúnde's dream of converting this wild tropical region into a rich garden was already beginning to take shape in the minds of the Peruvians.

It was on the Pacific coast that the most encouraging signs of economic progress were to be found. Castilla had successfully rounded up the bandits, and law and order had been restored to the coastal valleys, whose large irrigated, and on the whole well-managed, estates were now producing valuable export crops; of these sugar was the most important, but with cotton beginning to assume importance as more and more of the suitable land was devoted to satisfying the growing demand for this product from Manchester. The port of Callao was now joined to Lima by a railway – the first to be built in South America. And since 1840, when the British Pacific Steam Navigation Co. introduced the first steamer service to Peru, the steamship was replacing sail, enormously reducing the time of the journey from Peru to her overseas markets in the United States of America and Europe.

But the most remarkable source of new wealth – and one which for the next fifty years would revolutionize the economic life of the republic – was guano, the bird-droppings which over the ages had been accumulating on the desert islands off the coast of Peru, and were now suddenly discovered in Europe to be of commercial value as a fertilizer. For thousands of years millions of sea-birds had fed upon the abundance of fish in the cold Humboldt current and made their nests in the barren coastal islands. It is a wonderful experience to visit one of these islands at nightfall as the birds come home to rest. In the caves at the base of the cliff the sea-lions roar their welcome as formation after formation of birds – ungainly pelicans, streamlined cormorants, and gulls of every kind – circle the cliffs looking for their appointed place to land. The din is tremendous. But by nightfall all is quiet and every nook and cranny of the bare

[1] A road connecting Huánuco with the river port of Pucallpa has since been built.

rocks is covered by the sleeping birds. In the course of ages a sediment of guano, hundreds of feet thick and as hard as rock, was deposited on these barren islands. As the Inca had done in their time – but nobody bothered about it in the colonial period – it was only a question of landing men with the appropriate equipment in order to hack away, block by block, this almost inexhaustible supply of easily obtained wealth.

Markham reported that the three Chincha islands in the Bay of Pisco – and there were many other equally good sites – contained enough guano to last for at least twenty years at the rate at which it was being extracted in 1860, during which year as many as 433 vessels, with a tonnage of 348,554, loaded in this one group of islands. In that same year the guano monopoly brought in a revenue to the state of 14,850,000 dollars. And it was not only a question of guano. The coastal deserts of southern Peru, adjoining the frontier with Chile, were rich with borax and nitrate of soda. It was estimated that the available supplies of nitrate of soda were enough to last for a thousand years at the rate of export through the port of Iquique of some 1,370,248 cwts. a year.

A windfall of this magnitude did only harm to Peru in the long-term, creating an artificial prosperity which enabled the government to live by hand to mouth without any proper financial discipline. It also created a new class of local capitalists, who lived off the state and spent the proceeds from their guano profits either on urban land speculation or in ostentatious living. It became the practice of the state to sell the year's output of guano to one or two private firms of merchant bankers in London and on the Continent – and later as well to syndicates of Peruvian merchants – from whom loans were obtained at high rates of interest. By this means it was possible to pay off the arrears of pensions and other obligations that had accrued during the wars. But this was at the cost of putting the country into a chronic state of indebtedness to the guano consignees. No attempt was made to have a properly balanced budget. For example, in 1859 the total revenue of the state amounted to slightly less than 22 million dollars, of which no less than some 16 million came from the sale of guano. However, more than half this sum was spent upon the upkeep of the army and the navy. No wonder that Markham, with his tidy Victorian ideas about sound finance, was unhappy about the future of Peru – a feeling which was shared to the full by thoughtful Peruvians, such as Manuel Pardo,[1] who saw quite clearly that only disaster could come in the long run from such a profligate way of running the country's finances. True, the interest on the foreign debt had been paid, but otherwise, as Mark-

[1] A future President of Peru, see below, pp. 103–5.

ham noted, the windfall receipts from guano 'had either been embezzled or spent on immense and unnecessary armaments, and in jobbing salaries and pensions'. Thousands of families now lived on public money with the risk that if the guano receipts should fail, the ruin and suffering would be severe and widespread.

To turn now to politics,[1] Castilla's first term as President (1845–51) can best be described as a period of national convalescence. For the first time since the establishment of the republic a serious attempt was made to run the country in the democratic way laid down by the constitution, with both Congress and the executive performing their respective functions and managing peacefully to co-exist. The system creaked and groaned, of course. But Castilla, strong-man though he was, not only publicly proclaimed but showed by his actions his respect for the law, exercising considerable skill and patience in his relations with the often tiresome and sometimes irresponsible politicians.

Certain elementary reforms were long overdue and to these the President paid first attention. The law, mainly inherited from colonial times, required codification and certain features of it, such as the right to entail property in order to conserve the estates of the big landowners, were amended. Similarly, the old colonial educational system was hopelessly out of date and a new educational code was issued which was more in keeping with the times. Civil servants, to their surprise and gratification, were paid their salaries on time; and pensioners received their pensions, including San Martín, now in exile, but whose services to Peru were not forgotten by Castilla. Finally, even if Markham may have been right in criticizing its size and expense, the army, hitherto a mere revolutionary rabble, was placed on a more technical footing; and–important for Peru with her long vulnerable coastline–a beginning was made in building up a navy.

With Congress re-established after two decades of virtual suppression, the civilian politicians–both liberal intellectuals and conservative clerics–could once again lift their voices in public debate and the old arguments were resumed. During his first term Castilla managed to steer a middle course between the contending factions, and to keep the heat out of the political dialogue. But his successor, General Echenique (1851–54), who lacked Castilla's flair for politics, allowed himself to be captured by the conservatives, personified at this time by the priest Bartolomé Herrera, a dogmatic upholder of the hierarchical principle in society. Herrera was at least an

---

[1] A major source of information on the political history of republican Peru is the ten volumes of Jorge Basadre's monumental *Historia de la república del Perú* (Lima, 1964).

honest man. But the same could not be said about some of the
scoundrels whom Echenique, a man of good intentions but a child
in politics, brought into his Ministry. It was not long before his
government had become an open scandal. Huge profits were being
made by the guano consignees and there was widespread suspicion
of corruption in high places. Moreover, public money was being
handed out in a lavish way to private persons who presented claims
for compensation for damage suffered during the War of Independence under the scheme initiated by Castilla to consolidate the
internal debt. No less than 23 million soles were disbursed in this
manner. This sudden outflow of public money created almost overnight a new class of capitalists, many of whom, so the President's
enemies alleged, were persons who had family connections with
members of the administration.

In 1853 Domingo Elías, the liberal leader, published an open
letter in the newspaper *El Comercio* expressing in bitter terms the
public dissatisfaction with the government of Echenique. The President retaliated by casting Elías into prison and then deporting him.
Elías, though a civilian, attempted to organize a revolutionary
movement in Ecuador which was promptly squashed. Then, slip-
ping back secretly into Peru, he got into touch with ex-President
Castilla, who, although he had supported the candidature of Echenique, had now turned against him. With the political fervour of the
liberals and the military skill of Castilla combined in the opposition
camp the stage was set for civil war.

The ensuing struggle, which started in 1854 with revolts in Ica
and Arequipa, was long and bloody; for this was no mere battle between rival *caudillos*. Peru was now undergoing the rare experience
of a civil war in which ideological principles were involved. During
the campaign Castilla formed a government, and from his temporary
headquarters in Ayacucho and Huancayo issued decrees abolishing
slavery in Peru and the tribute which since colonial times the
Indians had been forced to pay to the government. After these
strokes of political warfare he then proceeded to outmanoeuvre
Echenique in the field of battle and after eleven months of arduous
campaigning captured Lima. The liberal cause had triumphed, and
Castilla for a second time became President of Peru.

Castilla's second term as President (1855–62) was almost entirely
dominated by the quarrel between the liberals and the conservatives.
With the liberals forming the backbone of Castilla's new Ministry, it
was not long before the politicians of this creed, now under the intellectual leadership of the Gálvez brothers, José and Pedro, once more
devoted themselves to their favourite pastime – the drafting of a new
constitution. There had already been three liberal constitutions, of

1823, 1828, and 1834, all of which had proved to be unworkable. Now a new constituent assembly was convoked and in 1856 yet another constitution was approved by the majority of this body.

In accordance with the orthodox liberal principles of that time, this new constitution was designed with a threefold purpose – to increase the power of the legislature at the expense of the executive; to decentralize authority to the provinces; and to curtail the power and influence of the army and the clergy. With these ends in view the presidential term was reduced from six to four years; the legislature assumed the right to approve all army promotions to ranks higher than that of major; military and clerical legal immunities were abolished; and a larger measure of local autonomy was extended to the departments, provinces, and municipalities. To the majority of the liberals this seemed to be quite a mild programme; the extremists would have liked to go much further, making it impossible for a military officer to occupy the presidency and with the complete separation of Church from state and the establishment of full religious freedom. But such advanced doctrines were not practical politics in colonial-minded Peru. As it was, the majority of the clergy, the soldiers, and conservative members of the oligarchy were filled with horror at this attempt to undermine their authority. Castilla himself, as a soldier, made it clear when swearing to the new constitution that he thought it unworkable and bound to cause trouble for the government.

He was right. Echenique, the ex-President, was still too discredited to provide a rallying-point for the outraged conservatives. But an ideal champion of their cause was to be found in the person of General Vivanco,[1] the autocratic *caudillo* who in 1844 had attempted to establish a government of brains and brilliance based on the authoritarian principle that the educated man knows better what the people want than the people know themselves. Vivanco had been deposed by Castilla and the time was now ripe for his revenge. Accordingly in 1856 he returned to Arequipa and in that clerical stronghold raised the standard of revolt.

The conservative revolt spread rapidly throughout the country, extending to the fleet whose support gave to Vivanco the command of the sea. However, an attempt by the revolutionaries to land an army at Callao was frustrated by Castilla, who forced Vivanco to retire to his base in Arequipa. There ensued a long siege of this city lasting from June 1857 to March 1858. At length Castilla took the city by storm in a severe and bloody battle, fought from street to street, in which most of the male population of Arequipa took part. Defeated, Vivanco departed once more into exile abroad.

[1] See above, pp. 90–91.

Castilla, with his prestige enhanced by his victories on the battle-field, was now ready to turn his attention to his opponents in the liberal-dominated assembly. Gone was the law-abiding President of his first administration; as a soldier he knew exactly what to do. The assembly was forcibly dissolved by the garrison of Lima. After this bloodless *coup d'état*, Castilla called elections in which – not unnaturally since he controlled the electoral machine – he was elected constitutional President. A year later similar methods were used to elect a new and more amenable constituent assembly in which the liberal representation was reduced to a mere handful.

In 1860 this body, under Castilla's guidance, approved a new constitution which, while in some respects representing a compromise between the views of the liberals and the conservatives, nevertheless gave the President all the powers which he felt were necessary in order to govern the country. Thus, Castilla by firm if unscrupulous methods got his way. His moderate, practical, middle-of-the-road political philosophy prevailed equally against the authoritarian concept of government advocated by the ultra-conservatives and the more democratic but, in the circumstances of the country, unpractical formula of decentralized authority put forward by the liberals.

This is not quite the end of the story of the liberal movement in Peru. In 1862 General Castilla's legal term as constitutional President came to an end. He was succeeded, peacefully, first by his old companion-in-arms General Miguel San Ramón and upon the latter's death a year later by General Juan Antonio Pézet, a worthy but somewhat colourless soldier who had been Vice-President during Castilla's second term. Pézet made himself unpopular because of his weak handling of a dispute with Spain[1] and handed over office to his Vice-President, General Díez Canseco; but before the latter had had time to settle into the presidency he in his turn was deposed by a popular uprising led by Colonel Mariano Prado, a member of the younger generation of army officers. In 1866 Prado became dictator of Peru.

The liberals, as always on the popular side in politics, had enthusiastically supported Prado's revolution. When, therefore, in 1867 the dictator called together a Constituent Assembly, this body, like that of 1856, was dominated by the liberals who true to their old form immediately set about drafting a new constitution. Two features of this document, designed to curtail the power of the Roman Catholic Church, were particularly unpopular with the conservative clerical party. One provided for freedom in education, which meant in practice that the state would support non-Catholic

[1] See below, pp. 112–13.

schools and colleges; the other, providing for complete liberty of the press, removed previous legal restrictions upon the public discussion of religious dogma. These features of the new constitution, coupled with conservative disapproval of the reforming zeal of the Prado government, had the inevitable effect of rallying once more the scattered forces of the opposition.

Arequipa, always a clerical stronghold, was once again the centre of conservative revolt. General Díez Canseco took charge of the troops there and declared against the dictatorship. At the same time Colonel José Balta, who was jealous of Prado for purely personal reasons, revolted in the north. Having suffered the indignity of seeing his constitution torn up by the liberals, that stout campaigner General Ramón Castilla, now a very old man, mounted his horse and rode with the revolutionaries. But the going was too hard for him and he died, quite literally in the saddle, in the middle of the campaign. He did not, therefore, live to see the defeat of Prado and the restoration in 1868 of his constitution of 1860. But he had left his indelible mark upon his country's future. Henceforth, thanks to Castilla, the Presidents of Peru would be relatively strong; power would be concentrated in the central government with but little provincial and departmental autonomy; and the state and the Roman Catholic Church would work together, as they still do, in close harmony.

This was the end of the road for the liberals in Peru. Although a Liberal Party continued to play some part in Peruvian politics until the early part of the twentieth century it was no longer of much importance. Nevertheless, in some aspects the liberal doctrines so passionately put forward in the nineteenth century did succeed in leaving a permanent mark upon the political thought of the country. In the coming years, as a result of the spread of liberal ideas, there would be an increasing prejudice against militarism, a growing preference for government by civilians, and a strong belief in the virtues of *laissez-faire* in economics – doctrines which were to find political expression in the *civilista* movement, which under the leadership of Manuel Pardo now makes its first appearance on the stage of Peruvian history.

Chapter 8

Boom and Bust

DURING THE NEXT DECADE economic problems took precedence over those of a purely political nature. The supply of guano began to dwindle, as did the national revenue which had depended for too long on this single source of wealth. Owing to short-sighted, hand-to-mouth methods of government finance – from which the local and foreign guano consignees profited at the expense of the state – the country was faced with increasing budgetary deficits and an ever-mounting internal and external debt.

The new President, Colonel José Balta (1868–72), was a simple, crude-mannered soldier. He entered the presidency at a time when a grounding in business and economics would have stood him in better stead than his acknowledged skill as a leader of revolutionary armies. Nor was he perhaps very fortunate in his choice of a Minister of Finance. José Nicolás Baltasar de Piérola,[1] who occupied this post, was a dynamic and determined man with a business background. But his critics regarded him as being too much of an optimist to be a good Minister of Finance in a country which was flagrantly living above its means. He ignored the pleas of Manuel Pardo and his business associates for a policy of retrenchment. Confident that the immense untapped riches of Peru in guano, nitrate, and minerals would somehow see him through – he had an almost visionary belief in the future of his country – he plunged cheerfully into a programme of expansion and development, at the expense of mortgaging the future and putting the country, already saddled with debts to the guano consignees, even further into the red.

In 1869 he signed a contract with the firm of Dreyfus of Paris, who undertook to purchase 2 million tons of guano in exchange for the exclusive rights on the sale of Peruvian guano in Europe and other parts of the world. Dreyfus undertook to advance immediately 2 million soles to the Peruvian government, and thereafter would pay into the national treasury 750,000 soles a month until March 1871. In addition, the firm would assume responsibility for covering the service of Peru's foreign debt, amounting to 5 million soles a year. This arrangement went a long way towards solving the

[1] A future President of Peru (see below, p. 129).

immediate problem of the budget deficit. It had, furthermore, the great advantage of improving the country's credit abroad. As against these benefits it was a great blow to the pride and pockets of the local businessmen to see this rich source of wealth handed over to a single foreign firm.

Under the leadership of Manuel Pardo, there was a great public outcry. The contract was challenged in the Courts and in the Congress. But thanks to the control which the government exercised over both these bodies the arrangement was upheld. For a time the danger of national bankruptcy seemed to have been averted. But politically the country was split into two hostile camps. Piérola never forgave Pardo and the two men became deadly enemies.[1]

It was not long before new pressure was being placed upon the hard-pressed economy. This was the age of railway-building in South America. President Balta, quite rightly, saw what a boon it would be for Peru to have a series of railways connecting the Pacific coastal ports with points in the interior, thus opening up to commercial exploitation the still untapped mountainous hinterland. Where he went wrong was in trying to do the job too fast. Through Dreyfus a large sum of money was raised in 1870 by floating a loan in Paris, which was eagerly taken up thanks to the improved credit which Peru now enjoyed. The services of an American engineer, Henry Meiggs, who had already proved his worth in building the Chilean railways, were contracted by Peru. A second loan was floated in 1872. As a result of these transactions Peru's public debt increased from some £4 million in 1870 to £50 million in 1872.

To build railways in Peru, which have to climb from sea level to some 15,000 feet, is no mean undertaking; but thanks to the drive and skill of Meiggs the job was done. The Central Railway running from Callao to La Oroya – one of the most dramatic railroads in the world – was almost completed at this time, as also was the greater part of the Southern Railway running from Mollendo to Arequipa and from Arequipa to Puno and Juliaca. Both these railways were destined to be of the greatest long-term value to the Peruvian economy, providing the foundation for the large-scale development of mining by foreign capital which took place at the beginning of the twentieth century. But since they ran mostly through wild undeveloped country, there was no immediate prospect that they would pay their way. Meanwhile, the republic was unable to support the crushing burden of debt with which it was

[1] Piérola, who had been educated in the seminary of San Toribio in Lima, was a devout Roman Catholic; he believed in the conservative doctrine of authoritarian government. The aristocratic Manuel Pardo was essentially a liberal in his political ideas.

saddled. The sudden inflow of capital caused an artificial and un-healthy boom in which some quick fortunes were made, but this soon collapsed, leaving the country upon the verge of bankruptcy.

It was thus against the sombre background of economic collapse that the elections for a new President were held in 1872. Colonel Balta, by his economic policies, had made many enemies, especially in the influential circle of the guano exporters. He had no political party behind him, apart from his friends in the army, and could think of no better candidate to support for the presidency than the conservative ex-President Echenique, who was now far past his prime.

Opposed to the 'official' candidate was Manuel Pardo, cam-paigning vigorously on a platform favouring competent government by civilians. He had the support of most of the business community, but because of his radical views – radical, at any rate, in Peruvian terms – he was not popular with the Church and the army. The *Civilista* Party at this time, although consisting mostly of members of the oligarchy, represented the new forces of progress – a progress based materially on *laissez-faire* capitalism; its programme also had other features derived from liberalism, such as the desire to do away with militarism and replace it by competent civilian administration; a healthy respect for sound government finance based on a balanced budget and an adequate system of taxation, and a realization of the importance of public education, free of church control, as the basis of a modern democratic society.

As Minister of Finance during Colonel Prado's short dictatorship, Pardo, although a businessman himself, had battled against the vested interests in an attempt to put the government's finances upon a proper basis, with a broadly distributed system of taxation which would have reduced the dependence of the state upon guano royal-ties. Later he made a very good name for himself as a competent mayor of Lima. Little wonder then that when the time came to choose a new President the majority of the electorate cast their votes in favour of the new forces represented by the *civilista* move-ment.

But the military were not prepared to give up their position with-out a struggle. The election had been a disorderly affair and Balta, using this as an excuse, declared it null and void. A new election was held, with a civilian, Antonio Arenas, standing as the 'official' candidate in place of General Echenique. But the results were just the same. The *civilistas* triumphed at the polls for a second time.

The military (without Balta's support, however) then resorted to direct action. Colonel Tomás Gutiérrez, the Minister of War, sup-ported by his three brothers who were also army colonels, seized

the presidential palace, imprisoned Balta, and declared himself
dictator. But he failed to gauge the strength of public support for
Pardo's policies of reform. Something quite unprecedented in the
history of Peru now occurred. An angry mob of civilians lynched
and killed one of the Gutiérrez brothers; whereupon the dictator,
believing the imprisoned President to be responsible, had him shot.
The navy declared in favour of Pardo, as did part of the army,
while armed civilians patrolled Lima. Finally, the mob stormed the
barracks in which the dictator had taken refuge. He and the remaining Gutiérrez brothers were slain and their mutilated bodies hung
from the towers of the Cathedral for all to see. Thus, by means of
an outburst of mob violence, provoked by an attempt of the military
to go against the will of the people as expressed in two successive
elections, the *civilista* movement triumphed over militarism, and
Manuel Pardo became the first civilian President of Peru.

He could hardly have entered office at a worse moment. Government receipts from guano were now only sufficient to cover the
service of the external debt; all other revenue was mortgaged up to
50 per cent of its value, while government expenditure on wages
and pensions had increased by 25 per cent. Nine million soles were
owing on account of the public works programme and Meiggs was
without money to pay the workers engaged on building the railways.

A heroic, if forlorn, attempt was made to remedy this desperate
situation. Government expenses were ruthlessly cut. The tax-
gathering machinery was made more efficient and higher customs
duties imposed. A new contract was negotiated with Dreyfus which
permitted a partial return to the old system of exporting guano on
a royalty basis. Finally, an attempt was made to create a new source
of revenue by setting up a government monopoly for the extraction
and sale of nitrate of soda, of which there were rich supplies available in southern Peru.

Side by side with these financial measures, the educational system
was improved. An effort was made to reduce the size and increase
the technical efficiency of the army. A National Guard was created
as a check against militarism and a scheme of administrative decentralization, involving the setting-up of departmental and municipal councils, undertaken. This last measure – a relic of the old
liberal programme – remained in force until 1880, but was never a
success because of the poor quality of the people who took part in
provincial politics.

This ambitious programme of reform was carried through bravely
despite the economic depression and the political unrest which this
caused – unrest which took the form of sporadic military revolts.
The most serious of these rebellions was led by Pardo's old enemy,

Nicolás Piérola. The President, although a civilian, took the field in person at the head of a mixed army of regular troops and the new National Guard in order to crush this revolt. Piérola was defeated and fled to Bolivia.

Pardo's constitutional term as President came to an end in 1876. In default of a suitable civilian candidate he was succeeded in the presidency by General Mariano Prado (1876–79), the former dictator under whom Pardo had served as Minister of Finance. In 1878 Pardo, while still quite a young man, was assassinated on the steps of the Senate by a disgruntled army sergeant.[1] Thus there ended in tragedy the life of a man who perhaps more than any of his contemporaries represented in Peru the modern spirit of progress based on the Anglo-Saxon concept of capitalistic democracy. However, Pardo did not live and die altogether in vain. From now onwards the army would only intervene in politics in times of crisis, or if there was no suitable civilian candidate for the presidency. Military government would now represent a fall-back position – a kind of insurance policy – to be used only if the civilians proved themselves to be incompetent and made a mess of things.

In 1876 the situation was so utterly bad that it made little or no difference whether a soldier or a civilian occupied the presidential chair. Under Prado, the economic crisis continued unabated, with the government reduced to printing paper money in order to pay for the construction of the railways. There were constant attempts at revolution, with the irrepressible Nicolás Piérola still acting as the principal troublemaker. But these internal troubles were soon overshadowed by a more serious crisis on the southern frontier. In 1879 Peru found herself engaged in a disastrous war with Chile, which resulted, among other things, in her losing the rich nitrate province of Tarapacá.[2] Thus, as both Sir Clements Markham and Manuel Pardo had so clearly foreseen might happen, the precarious financial edifice built upon the insecure foundations of guano and nitrate of soda collapsed.

[1] The crime had no political motive. The assassin, Melchor Montoya, was nursing a grievance because he had not been promoted to officer rank in the army.

[2] See below, pp. 113–17.

Chapter 9

Peruvian Diplomacy in the Nineteenth Century and the War of the Pacific

IN PERU'S FOREIGN RELATIONS during the nineteenth century it is possible to discern two conflicting tendencies. On the one hand, as a poor, weak, and unstable country dependent on the Great Powers for credit and markets, there was a feeling of solidarity with the sister republics of Latin America, who were all to a greater or lesser extent in the same predicament. On the other hand, working against the centripetal tendency towards unity, were the bitter rivalries and disputes with neighbouring states over such matters as boundaries, the location of natural resources, and the harbouring of political refugees – the latter often using the protection of a neighbouring republic to mount subversive operations in their own country. It was as though Peruvian foreign policy rested on a see-saw; there would be a sudden upward surge in the direction of continental unity, but with the balance always weighted on the side of dissension. Such Latin American unity as was achieved in the nineteenth century was ephemeral, representing an ideal rather than an actuality.

During this period Great Britain was by far the most important of the powers with which Peru maintained relations. She was the principal provider of credit and offered the best market for Peruvian exports. She was also at this time in the first place as an exporter to Peru of cotton goods, machinery, and indeed almost every kind of manufactured product which at this stage of Peru's development could only come from abroad. But the relationship was not without its difficulties. It had been with high hopes of the long-term commercial advantages to be gained that the British Foreign Secretaries Castlereagh and Canning had given all the support they could, short of armed intervention, to the Latin American republics in their struggle for independence. It was one of those fortunate cases where democratic principles and economic advantage went hand in hand. In 1823, under pressure from the City of London, Canning appointed Consuls to most of the new Latin American republics, including Peru.[1] In the same year, not to be outdone by the unilateral

[1] The United States of America had recognized most of the Latin American republics in the year before.

pronouncement by the United States of America of the Monroe Doctrine, Canning affirmed the British determination to protect the republics of Latin America from foreign intervention – a determination which was backed by the unrivalled supremacy of the Royal Navy on the high seas. Under the protective umbrella of sea-power, British capital flowed into Latin America, and British merchants exploited the opportunities of trade which opened up in the New World after the departure of the Spaniards. But by the middle of the nineteenth century enthusiasm in the City of London for Latin America as a field for British commercial enterprise had cooled. Several of the republics, including Peru, had defaulted on their foreign debts. It seemed in London as though the Latin American republics, with only a few exceptions, were incapable of governing themselves and providing the necessary guarantees for British subjects who did business in those troubled parts.

In some European countries, for example the France of Napoleon III, the idea gained ground that the solution to Latin America's political problem was to do away with the unworkable republican system of government and replace it by monarchy. Spain, too, observed the mounting chaos in her former colonies; the hope was kindled that in some way or another the opportunity might be found to re-establish, if not her former authority as a colonial power, at least something of her former influence. In the case of Great Britain, however, although she wanted, like everybody else, to see strong governments in Latin America capable of maintaining order, it was a cardinal principle of her foreign policy *not* to intervene in the internal politics of the several republics. The aim of British policy, even in the days of Palmerston, was never more than to ensure that British trade should receive fair and equal treatment, and that the persons and property of British subjects should be adequately protected.[1]

But even this limited objective was difficult to achieve in the chaotic conditions of most of the republics, including Peru, in the first half of the nineteenth century. This was a time when the Great Powers took a more robust view than would be acceptable today on how to support the claims of their subjects who had suffered personal outrage or damage to their property. One authority[2] cites forty examples for the period 1820–1914 of what he calls 'coercion' by Britain in Latin America to avenge outrages against British Consuls or the British flag, to protect British lives or property, or to enforce the claims of British subjects. No British marines or

[1] D. C. M. Platt, *Finance, Trade and Politics in British Foreign Policy 1815–1914* (Oxford, 1968), Chapter 6.
[2] Ibid.

soldiers were ever landed in Peru; but there were a number of occasions during the revolutionary turmoils when the Royal Navy took strong action to protect British merchant shipping. For example, during the civil war between Castilla and Vivanco, in 1844, the British merchant ship *Peru* was seized. In retaliation the Royal Navy captured and embargoed Castilla's squadron. In the same year a British warship, which had been denied facilities by the local authorities, bombarded the Peruvian port of Arica. These incidents gave rise to diplomatic exchanges in which Peru was forced to eat humble pie.[1] As for the claims large and small of British subjects, these, as elsewhere in Latin America, were a regular preoccupation of the British Legation in Lima; similar claims were made by the diplomatic representatives of all the principal countries, especially the United States and France, who maintained a substantial trade with Peru. The constant presentation of these claims by foreign envoys was the cause of considerable bad blood between Peru and the powers with whom she did business.

In her relationship with the United States there was already in the nineteenth century, as there is today, a certain ambivalence in the attitude of Peru. As political realists the Peruvians, like other Latin Americans, were well aware of their ultimate dependence upon United States goodwill and protection. Nor was there any lack of admiration in Peru for the United States as the pioneer in the struggle for American independence. But there was little real love for the *gringos* of the north. To the Spanish mind their Anglo-Saxon culture was uncouth. The Monroe Doctrine was regarded as a unilateral statement of United States policy, about which the Latin American governments had not been consulted. Might it not contain the seed of a new imperialism – a policy of shutting out Europe in order to permit the United States to exploit the weak republics in the south? At this time the United States was too busy with her own internal expansion to threaten to dominate Latin America economically, as she was destined to do in the following century. But by her war against Mexico she had already shown herself willing to use armed force in pursuit of her national ambitions. In this unequal contest Mexico had lost to the United States the vast territories of Texas, Arizona, New Mexico, and California. Where would this process of expansion stop? Mexico and the Central American and Caribbean republics felt themselves to be overshadowed and threatened by their powerful northern neighbour. In a much less acute form suspicion, if not fear, of the United States had percolated down to far-distant Peru by Castilla's time.

This tough *caudillo* was determined that Peru should not be

[1] Basadre, op. cit., Vol. 2, pp. 735–8.

pushed around by any foreign power, European or American. He complained about the grave lack of respect shown to Peru by great 'international potentates'. The main plank of Castilla's foreign policy was therefore to work towards the unity of the South American republics, in order that they should have sufficient power to stand up for themselves internationally, and more particularly to require foreign businessmen to abide by the local laws and refrain from appealing to their home governments for protection. Shortly after taking office as President in 1845, he reorganized and strengthened the Peruvian diplomatic service, establishing legations in Great Britain, the U.S.A., Chile, Bolivia, and Ecuador, and despatching a diplomatic mission to Nicaragua. In 1846 he sought to put some teeth into his foreign policy by a law regulating the conditions under which diplomatic agents in Peru could support private claims on behalf of their citizens. The Peruvian contention was that foreigners resident in Peru must first submit their claims to the appropriate Peruvian Courts or authorities. They should only appeal to their own governments if it was considered that there had been a miscarriage of justice, or undue delays.

In support of this policy Castilla, in 1846, had the temerity to demand, and obtain, the dismissal of the United States Chargé d'Affaires because of his alleged high-handed attitude when dealing with American private claims. On a later occasion – at the end of his second term – he quarrelled with the British and French diplomatic representatives over the same issue. The latter had been pressing the claims of their countrymen without getting anywhere with the Peruvian government. As a means of demonstrating their displeasure they feigned illness and absented themselves from a diplomatic dinner being given in honour of Castilla. The President was not, however, a man who could be publicly snubbed in his own country with impunity. During his speech to the assembled diplomatic corps he lashed out savagely at the two absent envoys, the representatives of Peru's two most powerful creditors, remarking bitterly that he hoped that all patriotic Peruvians would likewise find themselves to be too ill to attend any functions to which they might be invited in future in the French and British Legations.[1] These diplomatic incidents are not important in themselves, but they demonstrate the strength of Peruvian nationalistic feeling and sensibilities when dealing with the Great Powers.

In 1845 Castilla's policy in favour of Latin American unity was put to a practical test. General Juan José Flores, the first President of Ecuador, was thrown out of office, whereupon he proceeded to Europe and began plotting with the French and Spanish Courts for

[1] Basadre, op. cit., Vol. 3, p. 1229.

the establishment of a monarchy in Ecuador. His plan was to place a son of the Queen-Regent of Spain, María Cristina, on the throne in Quito, and for this purpose expeditionary forces were to be organized in Spain and Ireland. No sooner did Castilla get wind of this plan than notes of protest were addressed to Spain and Great Britain. The Peruvian minister to the Court of St James got a dusty reply from Lord Palmerston who, having disclaimed any knowledge of the plot, took the opportunity to lecture the Peruvians about their failure to protect British interests.[1] To strengthen his diplomatic hand, Castilla convoked a meeting of American republics in Lima, at which Bolivia, Chile, Ecuador, Colombia, and Peru were represented. At this inter-American assembly – the second of its kind to be held[2] – far-reaching plans for a defensive alliance and for eventual confederation were agreed, although not subsequently ratified by the governments concerned. Nevertheless, a common front against European intervention had been established, and the plans of Flores came to naught.

But it was not long before the see-saw had swung in the other direction and Peru found herself once more engaged in quarrels with her neighbours. A new war with Bolivia was only averted because of the simultaneous outbreak of Castilla's revolution against Echenique which kept the Peruvian army too busy at home for it to undertake a foreign war at the same time. There was also renewed friction with Ecuador. Surrounded by arch-conservatives, some of whom had monarchical leanings, Echenique undid all the good work of Castilla by allowing Flores to visit Peru, where he was fêted by the *Limeños*. This incident was greatly resented by the liberal governments of Ecuador and Colombia.

But in 1856 there was another swing of the see-saw towards Latin American unity when an American adventurer, William Walker, seized the presidency of Nicaragua with the backing, if not of the United States government, at any rate of powerful business interests in that country. Castilla was now back in power and responded to this new threat against Latin American unity with his usual vigour. On Peruvian initiative meetings of Latin American diplomatists were held, first in Santiago and later in the Peruvian Embassy in Washington, to discuss the project for a new continental treaty of alliance. On this occasion Peru, Mexico, Colombia, Venezuela, Costa Rica, Guatemala, and El Salvador met round the table. Once again, however, nothing of lasting value was achieved.

[1] Ibid., Vol. 2, pp. 768–9.
[2] Bolívar organized a Congress in Panama in 1826, but it was a failure. Only four Latin American republics (one of which was Peru) attended. The U.S. representative died on his way to the conference.

Only three years later, in 1859, the see-saw had swung the other way, and Peru found herself engaged in a second war with Ecuador. It was the old question about the disputed boundary. In an effort to settle outstanding claims with British creditors, Ecuador had ceded to the latter a large tract of land in the Amazon basin, which, according to the Peruvian map, belonged to Peru. Having achieved nothing by diplomatic negotiations, Castilla blockaded the port of Guayaquil and later occupied the city without bloodshed. Ecuador at the time was rent asunder by revolution, and it was difficult for Castilla to find either an army with which to fight or a government with which to make peace. Eventually an agreement more or less satisfactory to Peru was reached with an Ecuadorian general who at that time was in possession of Quito, and the war came to an end. But it had been fought to no purpose. The agreement was torn up by a subsequent Ecuadorian government. Despite a third war with Ecuador, fought in 1941, the boundary remains a cause of friction to this day.

From dissension yet another swing back towards continental unity. This time it was Napoleon III who was threatening an American republic. In 1861, taking advantage of the American Civil War which prevented the United States from fulfilling her normal role as continental watchdog, a small combined force of French, Spanish, and British troops was landed at Vera Cruz in an effort to force the Mexican government to settle outstanding claims. (For many years Mexico had been torn apart by internal revolutions, to the detriment of the commercial interests of the three countries.) Great Britain, to do her justice, had made it clear from the beginning that her only interest in the expedition was to protect British interests – she had no intention of interfering in the internal affairs of Mexico. Both Britain and Spain withdrew their forces when it became clear that Napoleon III intended to mount a full-scale invasion of Mexico with the object of ousting the liberal and strongly anti-clerical government of Juárez and placing the Austrian Archduke Maximilian on the throne.

The Peruvian reaction to these events was in keeping with her now established foreign policy. She addressed notes of protest to the three aggressors and circularized sister republics through diplomatic channels in an effort to rally Latin American support for Mexico. A special Peruvian envoy[1] was sent to Mexico with an offer of help – there was even some talk of sending Peruvian troops. When the French army was defeated by the Mexicans at the battle of Puebla there were great public rejoicings in Peru. The society ladies of Lima organized sewing circles in order to raise funds for Mexican

[1] Nicolás Corpancho, a poet.

relief. But it was all to no avail. Backed by French bayonets the ill-fated Maximilian became Emperor of Mexico. He reigned there uneasily for three years until Napoleon deserted him. He was then defeated by the insurgent armies of Juárez, captured, and shot.

Meanwhile the Spaniards, having backed out of the Mexican adventure, went on a rampage of their own in the New World. In 1861, to the great consternation of all the Latin American republics, Santo Domingo was reincorporated as a Spanish colony. In 1863 a powerful Spanish fleet arrived off the coast of Chile, ostensibly on a good-will mission but with the real intention, it was obvious, of re-establishing Spanish influence along the west coast of South America.

On their first cruise up the coast the Spanish sailors were fêted in Valparaiso and Callao. But it was not long before the Spanish general in command, Luis Hernández de Pinzón, began to show his teeth. A quarrel was picked with Peru over a question concerning Peru's debt to Spain, which dated from colonial times, and a minor incident on an agricultural estate in which Spanish immigrants were employed. These matters could easily have been settled by negotiation, but that was not the Spanish intention. Having failed to get satisfaction from the Peruvians through diplomatic channels – the Peruvians, perhaps rashly, objected to the colonial-style title of the Spanish envoy who described himself as a 'commissioner' – the Spanish fleet occupied the Chincha Islands, the main source of guano and of Peru's national revenue.

This unwarranted action naturally caused great indignation in Peru. Ex-President Castilla urged President Pézet to declare war. But Pézet, aware of the military and naval weakness of Peru, was not prepared to take such a drastic plunge. An attempt was made by the diplomatic corps in Lima to act as peacemakers: a delegation of foreign representatives, headed by the British minister, gallantly undertook the sea journey to the Chincha Islands in order to interview the Spanish general. (One can picture these dignitaries clutching their lace handkerchiefs to their noses as they climbed aboard the Spanish flagship in the odiferous anchorage of the guano isles.) But on their return they were not thanked by the Peruvian Foreign Minister, who contemptuously rejected their peace plan. However, when in 1865 General Vivanco was commissioned by Pézet to try his hand at peacemaking, the plan he brought back was even more humiliating to Peru than that which the foreign diplomatists had proposed. In exchange for the restoration of the islands, Vivanco agreed not only to most of the original Spanish demands, but also to the payment by Peru of a heavy indemnity. A wave of shame and indignation swept across the country. Castilla stormed once more into the presidential palace and delivered a vehement protest, only to be exiled for his pains. Thereupon a hitherto unknown colonel, Mariano Prado, revolted in Arequipa and seized power.

Meanwhile the Spanish fleet, having evacuated the Chincha Islands in accordance with the agreement with Vivanco, now turned its attention to Chile. Arriving off Valparaiso, the Spanish general delivered a protest to the Chileans, alleging that they had actively instigated Peruvian hostility to Spain; but the Chileans refused to meet the Spanish demands. The Spaniards retaliated by blockading and then bombarding Valparaiso, an undefended port. Meanwhile the Chilean navy managed to capture one of the Spanish warships, whereupon General José Manuel Pareja (who in December 1864 had replaced Pinzón as Commander-in-Chief of the Spanish fleet), in an excess of Castilian pride, withdrew to his cabin and shot himself through the head.

Prado, the new dictator, wasted no time in concerting an alliance with Chile, and in 1866 Peru formally declared war on Spain. A short time later Peru's two old enemies, Bolivia and Ecuador, adhered to the allied cause, combining to form a quadruple alliance. As always when faced with a threat from outside the continent, these four countries found that unity could be stronger than the more habitual state of dissension. But even now the Spaniards did not read the writing on the wall: they stubbornly bore down on Callao and bombarded that port from the sea. But thanks to good shore artillery the Peruvians defended themselves with vigour. Having suffered considerable damage the Spanish ships retired from the battle. Shortly after this humiliating defeat they set sail on the long journey back to Spain.

The glorious Second of May (1866) is still commemorated as a red-letter day in Peru.[1] The principle of continental unity, of which Castilla had been the champion, had been splendidly vindicated; but this was the last of the upward swings of the see-saw. Only thirteen years later, in 1879, Peru in alliance with Bolivia found herself engaged in the most disastrous war of her history with her erstwhile ally, Chile.

The cause of this new struggle, in which Peru allowed herself to become involved, was a long-standing dispute between Chile and Bolivia over a strip of desert country adjacent to the Pacific coast known as Atacama. Nobody had bothered very much about this arid, neglected, and apparently worthless region until in the 1840s the commercial possibilities of guano were discovered, the nitrate fields opened up, and a valuable silver-mine found in the area.

[1] The author had the honour to sit on the platform, under the same guns which had resisted the Spaniards, when the centenary of this event was celebrated in Peru.

Commercial exploitation was carried out almost exclusively by Chilean manpower and capital.

In 1866, after many years of Bolivian protests against this Chilean occupation, a treaty between the two countries was signed. This agreement set the boundary between Bolivia and Chile at the 24th parallel of south latitude, and provided that the zone lying between the 23rd and 25th parallels should be subject to the common jurisdiction of both governments for the exploitation of the guano deposits and mined products, the revenue from these sources to be equally divided. Bolivia agreed to make the Bay of Mejillones the only port through which traffic in guano should be permitted, with the condition that Chile should nominate an official to intervene in any matters concerning Chilean interests. On paper this arrangement looked sensible enough; but it did not work in practice and the friction between the two countries continued.

In 1873 Peru, by now also vitally interested in the guano and nitrate possibilities of her southern provinces of Tarapacá, Tacna, and Arica, bordering upon the Atacama region, decided to take a hand in this diplomatic game. Fearing encroachment upon Peruvian preserves by the energetic, businesslike Chileans, President Manuel Pardo signed a secret defensive pact with Bolivia; subsequently the diplomatic influence of Peru was used to stiffen the resistance of the Bolivians against Chilean penetration in the region.

As a result of the war with Spain a more friendly spirit prevailed for a time among the three powers and in 1874 a new treaty was negotiated between Chile and Bolivia, by which Chile agreed to renounce the zone between the 23rd and 25th parallels and to resign her claim to a share of the duties collected under the treaty of 1866. For her part Bolivia accepted the proposal that export duties on mined products from this zone should not be increased and that Chilean capital, industries, and persons should not be subjected to higher taxation than was in force at the date of the treaty.

This arrangement, like that of 1866, proved to be unworkable. In 1878 the Bolivians, contrary to the agreement, levied a tax of 10 cents on all nitrate of soda exported from the region. When the Chilean manager of the nitrate company in Antofagasta refused to comply with this provision he was imprisoned and his property confiscated. In February 1879 the Chileans, having failed to get any satisfaction from the Bolivians through diplomatic channels, broke off relations; four days later a Chilean force occupied Antofagasta. On 1 March 1879 Bolivia declared war on Chile.

These events placed the Peruvian government in a very awkward predicament. President Prado, knowing the naval and military weakness of the country, had no desire for war. He therefore sent an emissary, José Antonio de Lavalle, to Santiago with the offer that Peru should mediate in the dispute – a hopeless gesture because the Chileans were fully aware that Peru was bound to help Bolivia under the secret treaty between the two countries.[1] When finally Lavalle was asked outright by the Chileans to state whether Peru would remain neutral, he could only wring his hands and confess that this was impossible as his country was bound by Pardo's secret alliance with Bolivia. Thereupon, on 5 April 1879, Chile declared war on Peru.

The war which ensued falls into four main phases. The first phase was little more than a mopping-up operation in which the Chilean forces, using the captured port of Antofagasta as their base, completed the occupation of Atacama. The Bolivians, who put up but a slight resistance, retired into the mountains and thereafter played very little further part in the war. The Chileans now stood on the frontier of Tarapacá.

The second phase of the war was fought at sea, in which element the Chileans had the advantage of a superior fleet. To obtain complete command of the sea was an essential strategic objective for the Chileans; for this would open up the long Peruvian coastline to their attack, whereas to advance overland along thousands of miles of coastal desert would be extremely difficult, if not impossible. Although outnumbered and outgunned, the Peruvian fleet put up a gallant fight. Finally, after most of the major units of the Peruvian fleet had been sunk, Admiral Grau, in command of the monitor *Huáscar*, was brought to action by a superior Chilean force; after a desperate struggle, in which he and most of his senior officers were killed, this ship, the pride of the Peruvian navy, was captured.

The way was now clear for the third phase – the invasion of the Peruvian provinces of Tarapacá, Tacna, and Arica. Chilean troops were landed at Junín and Pisagua on the Peruvian coast, advanced across the desert, and, despite a successful Peruvian delaying action in the town of Tarapacá, succeeded at length in capturing Tacna and Arica. In the latter city a Peruvian force of 2,000 men under Colonel Bolognesi put up a desperate resistance, their leader before he was killed urging his men to 'fight to the last cartridge'. But Bolognesi's heroism was of no avail. By June 1880 the occupation of the three Peruvian provinces had been completed. The Chileans were now in complete possession of the southern portion of the country, where they controlled the nitrate of soda industry and the deposits of guano, the two principal sources of revenue on which Peru relied for the financing of her war effort.

[1] According to Basadre, Lavalle himself was unaware of the existence of the secret treaty when he originally set out on his mission.

In Lima the news of these defeats was received with consternation and there was a growing clamour among the people for a change in the government. The man to whom they turned in this crisis was Nicolás Piérola, the romantic revolutionary, who, after ten years of exile, could with justice disclaim any responsibility for the disaster into which the country had fallen. President Prado, who from the beginning had had no enthusiasm for the war, suddenly announced that he was departing for Europe in order personally to supervise the purchase of urgently required war equipment.[1] This left the door open for Piérola. In a swift *coup d'état* he seized the presidential palace, ousted Vice-President La Puerta, in charge of the nation in Prado's absence, and assumed office as Supreme Chief of the republic.

The stage was now set for the fourth and last phase of the war. After a preliminary bombardment by the Chilean fleet of Callao and a landing in northern Peru in the region of the Payta valley, a strong force of 30,000 men, put ashore at Pisco and Curayaco, marched on the Peruvian capital. Piérola was at his best at this time, full of fighting spirit and urging his troops to resist until the end. Fierce battles took place at Chorillos and in Miraflores on the outskirts of the capital, but nothing could now stop the victorious Chileans. With his armies shattered, Piérola fled into the mountains to carry on the fight from the interior. Early in the morning of 6 January 1881 Rufino Torrico, the mayor of Lima, tendered the formal surrender of the capital to the Chilean Commander-in-Chief, who took possession of the city the next day.

The war was now virtually over, although for the next two years General Cáceres, one of the Peruvian generals who had fought throughout the campaign, carried on a guerrilla campaign in the mountains against the Chilean army of occupation. With Nicolás Piérola also in the mountains the problem of the Chilean commander was to find somebody with whom he could negotiate a peace. An approach made by Piérola was rejected and this stalwart, realizing that his continued presence in the country could do no good, resigned as dictator and left once more for exile abroad.

Meanwhile in Lima a Congress had been called together and a government acceptable to the Chileans – and recognized by the United States – was set up under Dr Francisco García Calderón, a leader of the *Civilista* Party. But when it came to negotiating a peace it was found that Calderón's hands were tied by a decision of the Congress which prevented him from agreeing to any terms based

[1] Prado's extraordinary action has been much criticized by the majority of Peruvian historians.

on a permanent alienation of any section of Peruvian territory.[1] Inasmuch as the Chileans were determined to keep the captured provinces of Tarapacá, Tacna, and Arica in their own hands the negotiations broke down and President Calderón was exiled to Chile.

The Vice-President, Admiral Montero, then took over, retired to Arequipa which had not been occupied by the Chileans, and there set up a new government. He then began busily to collect men and arms in order to carry on the fight against the Chileans. With General Cáceres also still at large in the mountains, Admiral Lynch, the Chilean Commander-in-Chief, determined upon strong measures. A force was despatched to Arequipa, the city occupied, and Admiral Montero deposed; at this time also a relentless but unsuccessful campaign was waged against General Cáceres in his mountain stronghold.

At length, realizing that the situation was hopeless, General Iglesias, an army leader in the north, called together a convention, and, upon being approached by the Chileans, agreed to form a government. On 23 October 1883 a peace, known as the Treaty of Ancón, was signed by the two countries. Under this agreement the province of Tarapacá was ceded outright to Chile, as also, but for a period of ten years only, the provinces of Tacna and Arica. At the end of this ten-year period a plebiscite was to be held to determine whether these two provinces would remain as a part of Chile or be returned to Peru. The loss of these rich nitrate- and guano-producing provinces was a grievous blow to Peru and the Tacna-Arica question was to remain for many years as a sore spot in Peruvian-Chilean relations. But at least the war was over and at long last the Chilean army of occupation embarked and returned home.

[1] In 1880 and the following year Great Britain offered her good offices to Peru as a peacemaker, but they were rejected (Basadre, op. cit., Vol. 5, p. 2477 and Vol. 6, pp. 2556–7).

Part Three

THE MODERN ERA
(1896—1969)

Chapter 10

The Golden Age of the Oligarchy

THE WAR OF THE PACIFIC was a disaster for Peru, both moral and material; but it was a disaster from which the country would derive considerable benefits in the long run. Politically, after the first shock of defeat had worn off, it served to discredit the nineteenth-century cult of military government and led to a long and relatively peaceful period of civilian rule. Economically, it forced Peru away from an unhealthy dependence on guano and nitrate of soda and encouraged the development of her many other resources. Socially, it led to a critical reappraisal by Peruvian intellectuals of the still essentially colonial structure of society and a growing demand for social reform. In retrospect, then, this disaster can be seen as the watershed which separates the old strife-ridden, hierarchical Peru of the nineteenth century from the more modern type of state into which in the twentieth century it is beginning to evolve. But there was no sudden transition from the old order to the new. To the average educated Peruvian, contemplating the ruin of his country in 1883, there was indeed little to encourage optimism and a good deal to induce a feeling of despair.

Thus, in internal politics, the immediate aftermath of the war was a return to a period of arid, and at times corrupt, military rule under three generals who successively occupied the presidency: General Miguel Iglesias (1883–85) who was unpopular from the beginning for having signed what most Peruvians regarded as a shameful peace treaty; General Andrés Cáceres (1886–90), the hero of the resistance, who seized power from Iglesias; General Morales Bermúdez (1890–94) who was a man of straw, with General Cáceres pulling the strings behind the scenes.

During this decade of renewed military government – a political phenomenon which Basadre has described as a militarism of defeat – the members of the oligarchy, many of whom had been impoverished by the war, and the civilian politicians were for the most part in no mood to seek to grasp the reins of government. They were content to leave it to the soldiers – and Cáceres after all was a national hero – to clean up the mess.[1] But as with its accustomed

[1] Contrary to their traditions, the *Civilista* Party supported Cáceres. He was opposed by Piérola's Democratic Party.

buoyancy the economy of the country began to recover, so too did
the morale of the politicians. The turning-point came in 1895 when
General Cáceres tried to manipulate an election to get back into
the presidency for a second term. By this time the gold braid on the
uniform of the war hero was beginning to look tarnished. Public
feeling, already running strongly against Cáceres, was outraged to
the point of revolt by his cynical attempt to perpetuate his military
régime.

Ranged against the dictator were not only his erstwhile supporters, the *civilistas* (representing the new and more conservative generation of the party which Manuel Pardo had founded), but also the
'democratic' supporters of that arch-rebel, Nicolás Piérola. Having
escaped from prison disguised as a sailor, he was now in Chile and
back at his old pastime of hatching revolutionary plots. Armed resistance could not be expected to come from the comfortable professional and businessmen of the *Civilista* Party. But Nicolás Piérola
belonged to an older and more warlike tradition. The two parties
decided to forget their old enmity and work together against the
common enemy, the one providing money, the other reckless people
who were prepared to fight. Piérola was the acknowledged leader
of the coalition.

The revolution which ensued is unique in Peruvian history. All
over the country the people took to arms and, setting out in small
guerrilla bands, harassed the government forces wherever they could
be encountered. Piérola sailed from Chile in a small sailing-vessel
with a crew of four men, landed near Pisco, and put himself at the
head of the revolutionary movement. Then, advancing upon Lima
with a ragged force of *montoneros*, and assisted by armed civilians
in the city, he gave battle to the troops of the regular army. After
two days of fighting in the streets of the capital a truce was called.
Realizing that the people were against him, General Cáceres stepped
down voluntarily; a provisional *junta* was then established and new
elections held. Nicolás Piérola, the hero of the hour, became the
President of Peru.

In this dramatic fashion there was inaugurated a new political
era which can perhaps best be described as the golden age of the
oligarchy. From 1895 until 1919, with only one short military interlude, Peru was ruled by a succession of civilian Presidents. For
twenty-four years the government passed out of the hands of the
soldiers and was conducted in the interests essentially of an oligarchy
consisting of comfortably situated business and professional men
and the owners of the great landed estates. Compared with the
stormy days of the past there were few internal disturbances during

this time, with no very fundamental ideological issues in dispute between the members of the ruling class. The oligarchy was, however,
split between the two main political parties – the Democratic Party
of Nicolás Piérola and the *Civilista* Party, of which José Pardo, the
son of its founder, became the head. As is usually the case in Peru,
these rival parties were based more on personal loyalty to a leader
than on any real difference of policy or political outlook.

On the face of it, then, conditions were ideal for the development
of a two-party parliamentary system of government on the British
or U.S. models. This hope was not realized, however. The popular
basis of the electorate was too narrow – less than 10 per cent of the
people had the right to vote – for the development of anything like
real democracy; at best the system which evolved can be described
as one of pseudo-democracy. Moreover, the members of the ruling
class, although they possessed the right to vote, proved unwilling to
abide by the spirit of the constitution and conduct elections honestly.
Successive governments could not resist the temptation to use their
control over the electoral machine in order to impose upon the
country candidates of their own choosing.[1] In 1919 the two-party
system finally broke down altogether when Leguía made himself
civilian dictator of Peru. But if during this period the oligarchy was
firmly in the saddle, it was by no means a time of social or economic
stagnation. The country badly needed a breathing spell. With peace
reigning both at home and abroad, conditions were conducive to
economic recovery and expansion; these in their turn produced the
necessary conditions for social change.

When Cáceres took power in 1886 the country was bankrupt.
Urgent steps were taken to stabilize the currency, whose value had
been depreciated as the result of the reckless wartime issue of paper
money, to balance the budget, and to re-establish the shattered
credit of the country abroad. Towards this end, an arrangement was
made in 1889 with the British bond-holders, who, forming themselves into a company, established the Peruvian Corporation. The
Peruvian government agreed to hand over to this British company
the management of the railways for a period of sixty-six years,
together with deposits of guano up to the amount of 3 million tons.
In addition, the government was to pay the corporation in yearly
instalments the sum of £80,000 for the next thirty-three years. In
return for these concessions the Peruvian Corporation agreed to

---

[1] Peruvian Presidents are elected by direct suffrage (see below, Chapter 21).
But 90 per cent of the population were illiterate and therefore disfranchised.
Under the electoral law of 1896, the *Junta Electoral Nacional* was so composed that the majority of its nine members were invariably supporters of
the government and manipulated the results accordingly.

liquidate the British loans of 1869, 1870, and 1872 and to complete
the construction of the railways. This arrangement was criticized at
the time by Peruvian politicians as a sell-out of the national patrimony to a foreign corporation. But without a doubt it was beneficial to Peru. The Peruvian Corporation duly completed the construction of the railways as contracted and by this means opened up
for exploitation the immensely important mining region of Cerro
del Pasco in central Peru as well as some other important areas in
the south.

During this period, too, a beginning was made to exploit the oil
which had been found in the Lobitos-Talara region near the northern Pacific coast. In 1890 a company of mixed British and American
capital was formed in London, called the London and Pacific Company Ltd., and a contract was signed under which this enterprise
undertook to export to California a million and a half gallons of oil
during the next five years. Subsequently, the exploitation of these
important oilfields passed from the hands of the British company to
the International Petroleum Company, a subsidiary of Standard Oil
of New Jersey. At the time when they were negotiated these oil
concessions, favourable though they may have been to the conces-
sionaires, brought much-needed relief to the hard-pressed Peruvian
economy. But today, in a more nationalistic age, they are a subject
of passionate controversy in Peru.[1]

Thanks to these and other measures the Peruvian economy was
well on its way to recovery by the turn of the century. Indeed, it
was much stronger than it had ever been in the past, as a result of
the diversification brought about by the development of large-scale
exports of cotton, sugar, coffee, and oil, which now replaced guano
and nitrate of soda as the principal sources of the country's wealth.
Britain was still Peru's best customer at the beginning of the twentieth century, but from this time onwards her relative share of the
trade in both Peruvian exports and imports began to decline, while
the United States share steadily increased. Moreover, American
capital began to pour into the country; New York and Washington
replaced the City of London as the principal source of foreign credit.
Local capital, too, was increasingly put to productive use. With an
increasing domestic demand for consumer goods of all sorts, especially in the rapidly expanding coastal cities (apart from the mining
districts, the *sierra* continued to be a backwater), the economic basis
was created for the development of local industries – first, the textile
shoe, food, and beverage industries; later, glass, paper, electrical
goods, and light-metal fabrication. In short, an incipient industrial
economy came into being.

[1] See below, pp. 194–6.

These important economic developments inevitably had their repercussions on the social and political structure of the country. According to a census taken in 1876 the population of Peru towards the end of the nineteenth century had grown to 2,699,106 – about twice as many inhabitants as were counted shortly after Independence. The economy was still predominantly rural and agricultural, with 57·6 per cent of the population classified as pure-blooded Indians. At least 90 per cent of the people were illiterate. But from the turn of the century onwards there were two important changes in the pattern of population growth. In the first place, with a decreasing death-rate caused by improved sanitation, but with no decrease in the birth-rate among the untutored Indians, there occurred – and it is still going on – what can only be described as a population explosion. By 1940 the population was estimated to have increased to some 7 million inhabitants; by 1961 it stood at 11 million; today it must be well over the 12 million mark. The fundamental change which has been taking place relates not only to its size but also to the racial composition of the population and its manner of life – two factors which it is not easy to separate in Peru, since the term 'Indian', as used in the official statistics, and as understood by the people themselves, is employed rather loosely to designate both racial and cultural characteristics. As the combined result of population pressure and industrialization there began to take place a massive migration of Indians to the coastal cities in search of work in the new factories. The extent of this migration and the resultant process of racial miscegenation and cultural assimilation, show up clearly in the census figures of 1940 which classified 52·9 per cent of the population as being 'white or *mestizo*' as compared with only 38·5 per cent in 1876. Meanwhile the percentage of so-called 'Indians' had dropped from 57·6 per cent to 45·8 per cent in the same period.[1] In social terms, what these figures reveal is a decline in the relative size of the Indian peasantry in the *sierra*, accompanied by the growth, mainly in the coastal cities and more especially in Lima, of *mestizo* urban working and middle classes. Although this may not have been apparent to most of the members of the oligarchy at the turn of the century, this evolution of the social structure in the direction of a modern industrial society was destined to have a profound effect upon the politics of Peru in the years which were to follow.

One immediate political effect of incipient industrialization was the development of trade unions. These were very weak at first and had little bargaining powers with the factory-owners because of the unlimited supply of cheap labour. If the workers in a factory went on

[1] Robinson, op. cit., p. 83.

strike their jobs would quickly be filled by black-legs. But the workers soon learned that union means strength. If they could not intimidate their employers by withdrawing their labour, they could and did successfully intimidate the government by organizing mass demonstrations in the streets. In short, in the conditions then prevailing in Peru, political action was found by the workers to be more effective as a means of bettering their conditions than industrial bargaining. Strikers, deprived of their livelihood, increasingly resorted to violence. The government was then drawn into the dispute willy-nilly, if only to protect life and property and maintain public order. There were clashes between police and workers in 1906, 1908, 1912, and 1914, and in 1919 the first general strike was organized, with the support of the university students. This demonstration of strength intimidated the government of José Pardo to the extent of forcing him to decree the legal establishment of the eight-hour day – a major victory for the workers. However, a second attempt to organize a general strike in the same year was broken up by force and the strike leaders were jailed. There was a limit to the forbearance of the oligarchy when it came to labour troubles.[1]

The action of the university students in support of the general strike of 1919 was symptomatic of the new age. Traditionally the student body in Peru has always been radical. In the twentieth century student demonstrations began to be a political force which governments could not safely ignore. Nor was radical thinking confined to the students. In the university faculties, and among the intellectuals and writers generally, there was a good deal of new thinking at the turn of the century about the country's problems. In particular, Peruvians were seeking earnestly to discover the reason for their humiliating defeat at the hands of Chile. Why were the Chileans so much more advanced economically, socially, and politically than their cousins in Peru? The inescapable conclusion was that Peru's fundamental weakness lay in the rigid hierarchical structure of her society. How could she hope to compete for a place in the modern world when 90 per cent of her inhabitants were illiterate, and the majority of the people doomed to live a hopeless life as Indian peasants, with no effective part to play in the life of the republic?

The pioneers in the Peruvian reform movement of this period were intellectuals such as Javier Prado, Manuel Villarán, and Mariano H. Cornejo,[2] three professors at San Marcos University

[1] James L. Payne, *Labour and Politics in Peru* (New Haven, 1965), Chapter 2.
[2] Prado, son of President Mariano Prado, occupied the chair of philosophy; Villarán taught law; Cornejo occupied the first chair of sociology.

whose thinking had been influenced by Auguste Comte's doctrine of positivism, which was very popular for a time in Latin America. They believed in the empirical approach to all problems and were scientific rather than passionate in their approach to politics. However, unlike the more crusty conservatives of the time, who regarded the Indians as being little better than animals, this new generation of Peruvian reformers believed wholeheartedly in the possibility of redeeming the Indian masses and assimilating them into society. Their remedies were education, agrarian reform, and industrialization; also the protection of workers through the enactment of a wide variety of labour and social security laws. They were, however, essentially reformers, not revolutionaries. They did not, like the more radical Manuel González Prada, who had a following among the left-wing students in the universities, aspire to liquidate the oligarchy, in which, indeed, many of them had originated.

A somewhat later group of reformers – the generation of 1900 – were known as the Arielists after the famous book *Ariel* by a Uruguayan writer, José Enrique Rodó. Víctor Andrés Belaúnde, the uncle of President Fernando Belaúnde, and the historian José de la Riva Agüero were the leading lights in this new movement. The Arielists took a more high-minded and moral view of social problems than did the scientifically orientated positivists. They regarded spiritual values as taking precedence over economic considerations. They sought to find in a study of the Peruvian past – Indian, colonial, and republican – elements which were worthy of being incorporated into plans for the development of the nation. They were against a blind imitation of foreign intellectual fashions and especially hostile to those emanating from the United States of America. The essence of their message was that Latin America should work out her own destiny in her own way. For the first time it became fashionable among Peruvian intellectuals to take a pride in their own country and seek to understand the realities underlying the political problems of the day.[1]

Because of their moderation these ideas of the intellectuals were able to secure a certain following among the more enlightened members of the oligarchy, and indeed some of the specific proposals for social reform were taken up in a practical way by the politicians. It should be noted, however, that this first round of social reform in Peru was confined mainly to improving the lot of the urban workers – better working conditions for women and children in the factories, the eight-hour day, and so on. It is understandable why this was so. The urban workers could create disturbances: they were potential voters – potential members of the new middle class.

[1] Pike, op. cit., pp. 159–68 and 203–9.

The politicians had to begin to take them seriously. Although much was written about his problems, little was done about the Indian peasant at this time, since he was illiterate and lacked a vote. Any trouble in the *sierra* – and there were some quite serious Indian uprisings in southern Peru in the 1920s – could be dealt with by the army. However, insofar as Indians were trickling down steadily to the coastal cities in search of work in the new industries, thus becoming assimilated into the urban proletariat, there was progress of a sort even on this front.

In Peru's foreign relations, the most important change during this period was the growing predominance of the United States, both political and economic, in the affairs of Latin America. Britain and the other European powers began to loom less large. In 1889 the first comprehensive international conference of American states met in Washington, D.C., on the initiative of Secretary of State James G. Blaine, and resulted in the establishment of a permanent inter-American organization, at first known as the Commercial Bureau of the American Republics, later, in 1910, designated as the Pan-American Union (PAU). In its early days this inter-American organization was very largely dominated by the U.S.A., especially in the Caribbean where U.S. imperialism was rampant.[1] However, in South America, although likewise regarded in Washington as a U.S. sphere of influence, an attempt was made by Argentina, as the most powerful country in the southern hemisphere, to contest the leadership of the U.S.A. in inter-American affairs. Peru found herself caught between two fires. Her natural sympathies no doubt lay with Argentina as a fellow Latin American republic, but her need for development capital and diplomatic support in her disputes with neighbouring states made it essential for her to cultivate good relations with the Colossus of the North.[2]

For although some of the institutions of inter-American co-operation were established at this time, dissension rather than unity was still the prevailing tendency in Latin America. Great bitterness continued to be felt in Peru towards Chile. There were renewed border disputes with Bolivia, Ecuador, Colombia, and Brazil, but even if tension became high from time to time, war was averted. Most of the disputes related to undemarcated boundaries in the forest of the Amazon basin, for this was the time of the great boom in natural rubber. The hitherto useless jungle suddenly became a potential

[1] The U.S.A. moved troops into the Dominican Republic (1916–24), Haiti (1915–34), Nicaragua (1912–24); bombarded Vera Cruz, Mexico, in 1917; intervened four times in Cuba (1906, 1912, 1917, and 1923); detached Panama from Colombia (1903).
[2] See below, pp. 143, 145.

source of great wealth. There were occasions when the rubber-tappers of the rival nations came to blows. It was also the time when Sir Roger Casement was writing his famous report about the scandalous treatment of the native labour and imported negroes in the Putumayo region of Peru. Not that conditions on Peruvian territory were probably any worse than anywhere else in the region. The Amazon was a frontier where fortunes were being won or lost by unscrupulous adventurers. There were virtually no means by which the authority of governments could be exercised from far-distant capitals such as Lima, Rio de Janeiro, La Paz, and Bogotá.

These then were some of the underlying forces at work in Peru at the end of the nineteenth century and during the first twenty years of the twentieth century. The time has now come to introduce briefly the men, all but one civilians, who successively occupied the presidency between 1895 and 1919.

Nicolás Piérola (1895–99) requires no introduction. We have already seen this dapper little man, with the fine Victorian beard, in a number of roles: as President Balta's rather too optimistic Minister of Finance; as the outcast leader of desperate, sometimes almost single-handed, attempts to overthrow his rivals; and for a brilliant moment in his career as the symbol of national resistance when the Chileans were advancing upon Lima. We can now see him in the somewhat surprising role, given his fiery temperament, of a sober and competent leader of a civilian government which was determined to do away with the evil of militarism and heal the wounds of the past. Both as economic doctor and as political peacemaker he succeeded magnificently in his task. Not only did he manage to put the economy back on its feet with a balanced budget, but he was also successful in stimulating a programme of public works. Politically, his main achievement was to restore the principle of civilian government, without (as Manuel Pardo had done) falling foul of the army whose conditions of service were improved.

His chosen successor, Eduardo López de Romaña (1899–1903), who was a member of Piérola's Democratic Party, carried on the good work of national reconstruction. Born in Arequipa and educated at Stonyhurst and London University, he was a man of solid worth rather than brilliance, being an engineer by profession. His term of office was bedevilled by a series of tiresome border disputes. But, as an engineer, his natural bent lay towards economic development. During his time, in 1902, the Cerro de Pasco Company was formed with American capital, inaugurating a new period of mining development after a long period of neglect. There was also a tremendous increase in the output of agriculture: sugar exports, in particular, went up by leaps and bounds and accounted in this period for more than a quarter of the world sugar exports.

In the bitterly disputed election of 1903 power passed from the hands of the Democratic Party to those of the *Civilista* Party, and Manuel Candamo (1903–04) became the next President; but he died after less than a year in office. He was succeeded by José Pardo.[1] Although a man of aristocratic background and wealth, the new President was by no means a typical member of the oligarchy. He possessed all his father's passion for educational and social reform, as well as being an expert on international law and thus particularly well equipped to deal with the border disputes in which Peru continued to be involved. During his first term as President (1904–08), Pardo pushed ahead vigorously with his plans for educational reform: the administration of the schools was taken over from inefficient municipal councils and placed in the hands of the central government; primary schooling was made compulsory. The number of schools in Peru almost doubled during the four years of his administration.

He was less immediately successful as a social reformer, although equally zealous in this field. He appointed a professor of San Marcos University, José Matías Manzanilla, one of the leading exponents of neo-positivism in Peru, to be chairman of a committee to prepare a labour code. This committee put forward a number of far-reaching proposals covering such matters as sanitary and safe conditions of work, the regulation of child and female labour, compensation for industrial accidents, the right of workers to organize and strike, the eight-hour day, and so on. But, in spite of the strong support of the powerful newspaper *El Comercio*, these proposals were blocked by the upholders of business interests in the Congress. It was not until after 1911 that the fruits of Manzanilla's labours began to be enacted into law.[2]

Pardo's successor, Augusto B. Leguía (1908–12), although a leading light in the *Civilista* Party and, apart from Pardo himself, by far its most able member, was a man of comparatively humble origin who had worked his way up in life by sheer ability. He was born in the provinces, received his education in an English school in Chile, and, on returning to Peru, had worked successively as a clerk, a sergeant in the army during the war with Chile, a cashier, and a book-keeper. He did not go to a university, but he was a hardworking man of great acumen and drive, and soon rose in the business world, becoming the representative of an insurance company, a banker, and the General Manager of the British Sugar

---

[1] The son of President Manuel Pardo, the founder of the *Civilista* Party.
[2] Pike, op. cit., p. 193.

Company. Appointed Minister of Finance in the governments of Candamo and Pardo, he quickly acquired a national reputation as a coming man of outstanding administrative ability.

As Pardo's right-hand man in the Ministry of Finance, he threw himself with much energy into the task of putting the country's finances onto a sound basis. A French mission was invited to Peru in order to carry out much-needed reforms in the administration of the customs, and a new agreement was negotiated with the Peruvian Corporation, which provided among other things for some further extensions of the railways. As President of the Republic, Leguía continued to give earnest attention to the development of sound economic conditions and pushed forward vigorously with public works of every kind.

As a politician he was rather less successful. Piérola's Democratic Party strongly resented the domination of the *civilistas* in Congress and their control over the electoral machine. In 1909 the brother and two sons of the now aged democratic *caudillo* staged one of the most fantastic attempted revolutions in Peruvian history. With only a handful of followers, they seized the palace, killed the guards, and made President Leguía a prisoner, and then paraded him through the streets of Lima, shouting 'Viva Piérola', to the amazement of the onlookers. Leguía was only saved in the nick of time by a squad of soldiers and his own cool handling of the crisis. One might have thought that this incident would have consolidated the *Civilista* Party behind their President. But the middle-class upstart Leguía was not popular with the aristocratic conservatives who now formed the backbone of that party. And Leguía himself never felt at ease in their company. Thus almost everything which Leguía tried to do was blocked in Congress. When, in 1911, the President was discovered in a plot to interfere with the elections in an effort to pack the Congress with his own supporters, he found himself thereafter in a state of open warfare with the majority of the party which had put him into power. That Leguía managed to remain in office for his full constitutional term is a tribute to his determination. But the iron had entered into his soul. Never again would the future dictator of Peru allow himself to be pushed around by the oligarchy, or indeed by politicians of any political creed.

For the elections of 1912 the *civilistas*, believing themselves to be secure in their control over the electoral machine, put up a safe, but not very exciting, candidate in the person of Antero Aspíllaga, a wealthy landowner. But the people were now tired of the *civilistas*. A radical member of the Democratic Party, Guillermo E. Billinghurst, decided to stand as the opposition candidate in the hope that, by appealing directly for the support of the urban masses in Lima and Callao, he could successfully give battle to the well-entrenched but now divided *civilistas*. In the event he was swept into power on the crest of a wave of popular enthusiasm. It was the first time in the history of Peru that the urban working class had played a significant part in the choice of a President.

Guillermo E. Billinghurst (1912–14) is an interesting example of a man whose political thinking was a long way ahead of his time. The grandson of an English soldier in the War of Independence, he was a businessman of substance, with nitrate and guano interests in southern Peru. Although advocating progressive policies, which alarmed his fellow businessmen, he was a firm supporter of capitalism. But he believed that capitalism would be doomed to eventual destruction unless it was prepared to take a benevolent interest in the plight of the working class and take the initiative in doing something to remedy it. These advanced views might have been more acceptable to the oligarchy if they had been expressed in moderate terms. But Billinghurst was incapable of moderation.

He was soon to discover, however, that it is easier to make promises of far-reaching social reform as an irresponsible member of the opposition than it is to keep these promises when faced with the responsibilities of office. When he failed to fulfil his promises his working-class supporters quickly deserted him. Thus one of the first events of Billinghurst's stormy presidency was a strike of stevedores in Callao – one of the first major strikes in the history of Peru – in which the President was forced to give way, granting to the dockworkers an eight-hour day.

It was not long, too, before Billinghurst, who lacked the diplomatic touch, had fallen out with ex-President Leguía, whom he had defeated, and the *civilista* members of the Congress, who in 1914 refused to pass his budget. The President retaliated by trying to dissolve Congress. This was too much for the oligarchy. At the instigation of one or two influential civilians,[1] Colonel Oscar R. Benavides, the Chief of Staff, took possession of the presidential palace and forced the resignation of the President, who was then exiled from Peru. Congress then named Benavides as provisional President.

This intervention by Colonel Benavides (the Marshal Benavides of later times) exemplified the new political role of the army as a kind of insurance policy which could be used to protect the interests of the oligarchy in a time of crisis. The *coup d'état* was inspired by the civilian members of the Congress, not by the army itself. Benavides at this time does not appear to have had any presidential

[1] The Prado brothers, Jorge and Manuel (sons of the former dictator, Mariano Prado), seem to have been the ringleaders. Manuel, who was twice President of Peru, remained a lifelong friend of Benavides.

ambitions. Indeed, not feeling comfortable on the presidential seat, he remained there only long enough for new elections to be held. The *civilista* candidate, José Pardo, was then elected President for a second time.

The second term of José Pardo (1915–19) was not happy. The European war, while profitable for Peruvian exporters, was the cause of inflation and food shortages in Peru and therefore of considerable hardship to the working class. In 1919 strikes occurred in Lima and Callao, the last of which was only broken by the use of armed force. During this time Pardo did, however, manage to push through some of the social legislation which he had planned during his first term. Meanwhile he found himself in trouble, too, with the university students. The latter had not only come out into the streets in support of the workers, but they were also vigorously agitating at this time for university reform,[1] demanding the right to censure incompetent professors and to have a say (*cogobierno*) in the government of the universities. Rather surprisingly, in view of his close interest in education, Pardo turned a deaf ear to these pleas and more or less told the students to mind their own business. He thus played into the hands of his political rival Augusto Leguía who, on his return to Peru in 1919, was hailed by the students as the 'Mentor of Youth' and received their enthusiastic support in the presidential election. It rather looks as though the aristocratic Pardo, although a man of progressive views by oligarchical standards, was out of tune with the stormy times through which the world was now passing.

In his attitude towards the 1914–18 war Pardo, like the majority of his circle, favoured a policy of neutrality, his main concern being to safeguard the interests of Peru in the disturbed economic conditions which resulted. However, when in 1917 President Wilson, on behalf of the United States, declared war against the Central Powers and sought the support of the Latin American states, it became necessary for Peru to define her attitude. Argentina, under the energetic leadership of President Irigoyen, asserted her independence of the U.S.A. by remaining neutral, and Chile, Mexico, and Colombia followed the Argentine example. But Peru needed the moral support of the U.S.A. in her quarrel with Chile over the lost provinces of Tacna and Arica. Accordingly, after the Peruvian ship *Lorton* had been torpedoed by a German submarine, the Peruvian government somewhat tardily followed the U.S. lead to the extent of severing relations with the Central Powers. In recommending this policy to the Peruvian Congress in a speech on 5 September 1917, the Peruvian Foreign Minister, Tudela Varela, justified it in terms of 'pan-American solidarity, founded on the principles of

[1] The movement had started in Argentina in the University of Córdoba.

international justice as proclaimed by the President of the U.S.A.'
But although this decision may have been dictated very largely by
considerations of self-interest, it was with genuine rejoicing that the
Peruvians celebrated the Allied victory in 1918. To the man in the
street, for so long dominated by the oligarchy, it seemed like the
triumph of democracy. Emperors and kings were being toppled
from their thrones in Europe and there was a new spirit of freedom
and even revolution in the air. The noble principles of international
justice so movingly enunciated by President Wilson suggested that
a new deal was in the making for small countries. If applied to the
affairs of Latin America, they must surely lend support to Peru's
claim against Chile for the return of Tacna and Arica. Indeed, just
in case this matter should escape the attention of the busy American
President, a group of private Peruvian citizens published in the
Lima press an 'Open Letter to Wilson' and had the text telegraphed
to Washington.[1]

As for Peru's wartime relations with Britain, these remained quite
friendly in spite of the dislocations to Peruvian trade caused by the
naval blockade of the Central Powers. Britain, like France, had her
quota of passionate Peruvian supporters, some of whom went to the
length of volunteering for service in the British and French armed
forces. But for most Peruvians it was the commercial rather than
sentimental links with Britain that mattered. During the war years
there was a mounting criticism in the Peruvian Congress of the
terms of the oil concession which had been granted in 1890 to the
London and Pacific Co. Ltd., but President Pardo (at some cost to
his popularity) took the sting out of the controversy by agreeing to
submit the dispute to international arbitration. Shortly after the close
of hostilities a British goodwill mission to South America, headed
by Sir Maurice de Bunsen, was cordially received in Peru by
President Pardo.

In 1919 the time arrived for new elections. The contending candidates were Antero Aspíllaga, who once again was chosen to represent the *Civilista* Party, and ex-President Leguía, who had now
returned to the country where he proceeded to form his own 'Independent' Party in opposition to the *civilistas*. During his exile, the
middle-class Leguía had come to be regarded by the masses as their
champion. Like Billinghurst, he won the election with a landslide.
Then, fearing that the *civilistas* might seek by fraudulent means to
annul the elections, he seized the presidential palace and placed
President Pardo under arrest.

This was the end of the *Civilista* Party as such; for no sooner
was Leguía in power than the leading members of this party, in-

[1] Basadre, op. cit., Vol. 8, pp. 3841–7.

cluding Pardo, were deported. It was also the end of the golden age of oligarchy. The wealthy families would continue to be a force in politics, as indeed they are to this day, but from now onwards the oligarchy would not have it all its own way. A new force had begun to play its part in Peruvian politics – the urban working and middle classes. Their growing influence could no longer safely be ignored either by the men of wealth or the soldiers. Thus, although still very backward by European standards in a social, economic, and political sense, Peru by 1919 had already taken a first important step into the modern age.

Chapter 11

The Dictatorship of Augusto B. Leguía

IT MAY SEEM IRONICAL that Leguía, the apostle of the new Peruvian middle class, and the people's choice for President, should have set about his task of national renovation by plunging his country into the most nearly absolute dictatorship that it had ever experienced. But just as the Mexican dictator, Porfirio Díaz,[1] contemplating the chaos in his country after the revolution which had unseated him, remarked in self-justification while in exile in Paris, 'I knew my Mexico', so Leguía thought that he knew his Peru. He was determined to modernize the country from top to bottom; but he had bitter memories of the power of obstruction of the conservative oligarchy in Congress. At the other extreme he had before his eyes the dreadful examples of the Mexican and Russian revolutions. No doubt he was quite genuine in his desire to improve the lot of the common people and regarded himself as their champion. But they must behave themselves. What Leguía regarded as 'communism' – in other words any form of left-wing agitation – would not be tolerated in his new Peru.

Leguía's approach to the problems of his country was essentially that of the practical businessman. He saw clearly that the most immediate need was large-scale economic development. He realized, however, that this could not be brought about without a massive injection of foreign capital. In those days there was, of course, no foreign aid – in the great financial centres of the world there was then no altruistic desire to promote social change in Latin America, such as is now an essential part of the philosophy of the Alliance for Progress. Private capital or foreign loans could only be attracted to an underdeveloped country like Peru if there was a solid guarantee of political and economic stability. This guarantee the dictator was prepared to provide for his foreign backers by the ruthless suppression of political liberty. Suppression finally became a habit and a means of perpetuating himself in power.

Leguía's first task was to consolidate his position, and this he set

---

[1] With one four-year interlude, Porfirio Díaz ruled Mexico as a dictator from 1876 to 1910. In many respects his policies were strikingly similar to those of Leguía.

about to do with characteristic thoroughness. An assembly of hand-picked adherents was called together to draft a new constitution in which the presidential term was increased from four to five years and provision made for the election of a new Congress which would remain in being for the same five-year period. Under the earlier constitution one-third of the Congress had been renewed every two years – a system which would have allowed the *civilista* opposition to retain a majority in that body. Now, by a clean sweep, his enemies were eliminated from the legislature and the newly elected Congress was filled with his friends.

At first the *civilistas*, who had not yet taken the measure of the new dictator, were inclined to resist, and there were a number of abortive rebellions. But these disturbances, which were of a minor nature, never seriously worried Leguía.[1] By means of constant arrests, imprisonments without trial, summary deportations, and the suppression of hostile newspapers all opposition was finally crushed. Henceforth the only voices raised were those in praise of the dictator. Thus, when in 1924 Peru celebrated with much pomp and cere-mony the centenary of the battle of Ayacucho which had secured her position as a free, democratic, and sovereign republic, those liberal idealists who framed her first constitution must have turned in their graves. Except on paper, there was little of either freedom or democracy to be found in the country.

In 1924 the President's five-year term of office, as stipulated in Leguía's own constitution, came to an end. But the dictator had provided for this contingency by pushing through Congress an amendment which permitted his re-election for the following term. This measure was opposed by Dr Germán Leguía y Martínez, the Minister of the Interior, who had been nursing presidential ambi-tions of his own. Discovered in a plot to overthrow the régime, this cousin of the dictator was deported, leaving the field clear for Leguía, who was re-elected President for the next five years without opposition. In 1930, by means of a similar tampering with the con-stitution, Leguía was elected for yet another term – a term which he was not, however, destined to complete.

It was thus by strong-arm and arbitrary methods that President Leguía secured for himself both the time – eleven uninterrupted years – and the internal tranquillity which he deemed necessary to

[1] On 10 September 1919 a number of leading *civilistas* were arrested, and in the subsequent disturbances the houses of Antero Aspíllaga and Antonio Miró Quesada were sacked by a mob. In August 1921 the garrison in Iquitos, under Captain Guillermo Cervantes, revolted. In August 1922 there was a military revolt in Cuzco in which Major Luis Sánchez Cerro (see below, p. 146) was involved.

carry out his ambitious projects for the modernization and economic development of the country. Anticipating President Belaúnde's policies by thirty years, Leguía gave a high priority to the development of communications and agriculture. An important beginning was made in opening up the interior of the country by building during the eleven years an estimated 11,000 miles of new roads and adding 600 miles of track to the railway system. He also pioneered the irrigation of the coastal desert, bringing 100,000 acres of new land into cultivation in the regions of Cañete, Olmos, and Lambayeque. The cultivation of rice was introduced in the departments of Cajamarca, Ancash, Junín, and Huancavelica, and model cattle-breeding farms established in Puno and other cities in the *sierra*. An agricultural university, still a flourishing institution, was founded at La Molina on the outskirts of Lima, and agricultural experimental stations were established in Lambayeque, Piura, and Tumbes. No previous President of Peru had done so much to help the farmer. As a result very largely of Leguía's efforts agricultural production in Peru was tripled between 1919 and 1930.

Nor were the cities ignored. Lima was transformed almost beyond recognition during the time of Leguía. Before 1919 most of the life of the capital had been concentrated in the area immediately surrounding the Plaza de Armas, with its old Spanish-style mansions, crumbling churches, and narrow congested streets. The Pardos and the Prados and other leading families of the oligarchy still lived at this time in this central area in their original town houses, some of which, although no longer used as residences, can still be admired today, with their typical Peruvian wooden balconies (from which the girls courted their lovers in the street below), massive iron-studded gates, and inner courtyards. Now suddenly, under the stimulation of Leguía's development plans, the city began to spread outwards. The old mansions in the centre were abandoned and degenerated into office-buildings or tenement slums as the members of the old oligarchy and the new prosperous middle class moved out and built themselves palatial modern houses in the Californian and other exotic modern architectural styles. A splendid tree-lined avenue named in honour of Leguía (but re-named Avenida Arequipa after his downfall) connected the centre of the city to the prosperous suburb of Miraflores and a new motorway (the first cars were just beginning to make their appearance) joined the capital to the port of Callao. Real-estate operators were making money hand over fist as the new suburbs or *colonias* began to take shape, with their pleasant parks and gardens adorned with fountains and statues, and with every other modern amenity. Nor was the older part of the city neglected. The main shopping streets were cleaned up; the

Plaza San Martín was adorned by colonnades; with the *Bolívar* Lima was provided with her first decent hotel; a few blocks away there arose the now familiar building of that Holy-of-Holies of the oligarchy, the *Club Nacional*; nor did Leguía neglect his own comfort – the presidential palace which had been badly damaged by an earthquake was rebuilt on a more grandiose scale. On a more practical level, Lima and its suburbs – as well as provincial cities like Arequipa, Mollendo, and Cuzco – were provided with modern drinking-water and sewage facilities, and for the first time the roads were properly paved. Similar works were under way in Iquitos, Puno, Ayacucho, Pisco, and Cañete when Leguía was overthrown in 1930.

Referring to these many great enterprises in one of his annual messages to the nation, President Leguía likened himself to 'one of those devoted builders of Cathedrals who have planted in mother earth the stone pillars upon which later will rise the mystic spires until they lose themselves in space'. Certainly, he laid some solid foundations for the future economic progress of Peru, especially in his development of agriculture, irrigation, roads, railways, and ports and no doubt also in some of his plans for urban development. But many of his schemes were wildly extravagant for a country as poor as Peru, and they could only be financed by means of a massive inflow of foreign capital. As one Peruvian critic put it: 'Leguía was like the bartender who gave unlimited alcohol to the alcoholic.' He convinced the Peruvians that their country could painlessly become as great as England. Peruvian society lived for a few years in a dream of 'A Thousand and One Nights'.[1]

The dictator, with his English educational background and after his years of exile in London, would have liked British capital to have had a substantial share in these enterprises; but the City of London, which in the nineteenth century had had a long and bitter experience of Latin American finance, showed little enthusiasm for these vast projects, with the result that most of the business went to American firms. Between 1918 and 1929, Peru's foreign debt rose from approximately $10 million to $100 million, mostly raised in the U.S.A. The loans were not government-to-government but made by private U.S. merchant banks, often on onerous terms. In 1931, after Leguía had fallen from power, the U.S. Senate conducted an investigation into the operations of the U.S. banks which had been lending money to the Latin American countries on such a lavish scale – for Peru was by no means the only beneficiary from the estimated $1,894 million which were poured into this area between

[1] The Peruvian social reformer, Dora Mayer de Zulén, quoted Pike, op. cit., p. 229.

1918 and 1930. These enquiries revealed that the lending banks had exercised little or no control over the way in which the money was spent in Peru. Quite often it had been used for unproductive purposes, sometimes, for example, simply to make good a budgetary deficit. Meanwhile, with little regard for the future, the Peruvian government had earmarked specific items of revenue for the servicing of these loans, making it more and more difficult for the Ministry of Finance to raise funds to cover the normal expenses of government. There was also, it seems, a good deal of graft in high places. For example, it transpired that Juan Leguía, the President's son, had received a rake-off of $415,000 in connection with one of the loans.[1]

Under these somewhat dubious circumstances a veritable American economic empire came into being in Peru. It included, among other great enterprises, the Cerro de Pasco Copper Corporation, with its 40 million-dollar investment, the International Petroleum Co., which controlled the major part of Peru's oil production, and the W. R. Grace Company, conducting a wide variety of business activities in Peru. The majority of the railways remained in the hands of the British Peruvian Corporation, but the construction of new lines, undertaken on a large scale at this time, was mostly given to American contractors, as also was the building of the new port-works at Callao. A large part of the work involved in sanitation and town-planning was entrusted to a single U.S. firm, the Foundation Company of New York, under a succession of contracts which amounted to $50 million or more. This company, however, suspended its operations in Peru on 1 December 1929, when hit by the World Depression, and the Peruvian government was left to pick up the pieces.

Along with the money came foreign experts and technicians of every kind. This was probably all to the good. Leguía was determined to overhaul drastically the country's antiquated system of government and was not too proud to put foreigners into some of the key positions. U.S. missions were assigned to the navy, the customs service, and the Department of Education, and an American expert was appointed to run the newly created Central Reserve Bank. A French mission was attached to the army, a Spanish mission to the Civil Guard, and the administration of the postal and telegraphic services of Peru was entrusted to the British Marconi Company.

While economic development was the keynote of his modernization plans, Leguía was well aware of the need for improved social services. A large number of schools were built during his time in office and the school system was overhauled by an American educa-

[1] Basadre, op. cit., Vol. 9, pp. 4118–19.

tional mission.[1] He also built a children's hospital in Lima. It was Leguía, too, who introduced the principle, now firmly established in Peruvian law, that compensation must be paid to employees and workmen when they are dismissed from their jobs, an idea which seemed very revolutionary to the local business community when it was first mooted.

Towards organized labour Leguía's attitude was ambivalent – his policy a mixture of carrot and stick. Having come into power as the result of the popular vote, he wanted to be regarded as the workers' friend; but he was not prepared to suffer any nonsense like the general strikes which had caused so much trouble during his predecessor's time. One of his first acts on taking office was to release the labour leaders who had been imprisoned by President Pardo because of the general strike of 1919. But by 1922, when a committee formed in 1919 to agitate for the reduction in the cost of living began once again to make demands on the government, he jailed the leaders and outlawed their organization. In the years which followed there were many more arrests and deportations of the leaders and propagandists of the labour movement.[2] Even so, by 1929 the unions had become sufficiently organized to have formed their first national labour centre, the *Confederación General de Trabajadores Peruanos* (C.G.T.P.). By 1930 this body had fallen under the control of the recently formed Communist Party of Peru.

There was a similar ambivalence in the dictator's attitude towards the problems of the Indian peasants. Since 1918, after a long period of quiescence, there had been some serious riots among the Indians in the southern highlands, caused by the encroachment upon their ancestral lands by unscrupulous white and *mestizo* landowners. Leguía at first seemed to be sympathetic towards the plight of the Indians. With the approval of Congress, he appointed a commission to investigate their grievances. At the same time, he created within the Ministry of Development a section for Indian affairs, appointing as its chief a man who was known to be an enthusiastic supporter of Indian rights, Hildebrando Castro Pozo. The commission duly reported its findings and presented to the President some far-reaching proposals for the protection of Indian rights and the development of education in the Indian communities. By this time Leguía, under pressure from the landowners and no doubt with the fear of 'communism' always present in his mind, had lost his reforming zeal. The commission was dissolved, its report pigeon-holed, and Castro

[1] More than 800 new primary schools were constructed between 1921 and 1929.
[2] Payne, op. cit., pp. 39–40.

Pozo sent into exile. In the end, instead of doing anything to redress Indian grievances, Leguía sent in the army to restore order.[1]

There was similar back-sliding in Leguía's attitude towards university reform, which was increasingly being demanded by the students. During his election campaign he had posed as the students' friend and he fulfilled his election pledges to the extent of pushing through Congress a much-needed University Reform Law. But when Marxist doctrines began to become popular with the student body, he took alarm and jailed or deported the leaders. Nor was it only the students with whom he quarrelled. Among the professors there was much criticism of Leguía's attempts to muzzle the press and sympathy for the many distinguished journalists and writers who were languishing in jail. So strong were these feelings that Víctor Andrés Belaúnde,[2] perhaps the leading intellectual of this time – and he was certainly no radical – was provoked into uttering a public condemnation of the government's policies in a lecture delivered in San Marcos University. Leguía retaliated by having Belaúnde deported, whereupon the San Marcos professors went out on strike. The 'Mentor of Youth' had succeeded by his action in closing down the university.

And so inevitably Leguía lost his popular following. The workers, the students, and the intellectuals, who had supported his election with such enthusiasm, felt increasing disillusionment when it became clear that, apart from economic development – and most of that was in the hands of foreigners – he had nothing to offer the country in the way of social change. All they could see was the rich getting richer, and some new men of the middle class – men of the same stamp as Leguía – also making money. But the fundamental structure of society remained unchanged. The new rich were simply absorbed into an enlarged oligarchy. 'Establishment' was probably now a better term to describe the ever-widening, distinct, but interconnected circles of prosperous men, some of them aristocratic, others nouveaux riches, who between them owned most of the land and occupied the most important positions in business and the professions. But otherwise the gulf between the classes remained as wide as it had always been. Thus, increasingly, as Leguía consolidated his position, and allowed his fear of 'communism' to gain the upper hand, the nation became divided between the 'Establishment', which generally supported the dictatorship (apart from those members of the oligarchy who had quarrelled with Leguía and were in exile abroad), and the rest of the voting population who had become thoroughly disillusioned with his policies. If any social

[1] Pike, op. cit., pp. 221–2.
[2] The uncle of President Fernando Belaúnde.

revolution was taking place in Peru at this time it was underground in the trade unions and among the students and the intellectuals.[1] Leguía himself was never in any doubt that the only proper way to deal with 'communism' was to repress it ruthlessly; and in this he had the full support of the vast majority of the business community.

In foreign affairs Leguía continued to follow, to the point of subservience in the view of his critics, Peru's now traditional policy of maintaining especially friendly relations with the U.S.A. This policy was dictated in part by the country's growing dependence on U.S. capital, but perhaps even more – and this had been President José Pardo's hope as well – by the expectation that, if Peru showed solidarity with the U.S.A. in Pan-American and world affairs, she would be rewarded by U.S. support in her disputes with neighbouring states. For it was these local vendettas, rather than world-wide issues, which were the bread and butter of Peruvian diplomacy. Leguía, with his practical businessman's outlook, was determined to put an end to these tiresome and unprofitable problems of the frontiers, which were still, a hundred years after Independence, no nearer to any solution.

The most urgent problem in Peruvian eyes was to obtain a satisfactory settlement of the dispute with Chile over the territories of Tacna and Arica, which the Chileans had seized from Peru during the War of the Pacific. In the Treaty of Ancón, which Peru had signed under duress in 1883, it had been agreed that ten years later, i.e. in 1893, a plebiscite would be held to determine whether these provinces should remain under the Chilean flag or return to Peru. But no plebiscite had been held; and, as the occupying power, Chile had now consolidated her position to an extent which made it unlikely that the verdict would be favourable to Peru if the matter were put to the popular vote. Accordingly Leguía's policy was to try to reach a negotiated settlement with Chile, using the good offices of the U.S.A. It was therefore hailed by his supporters as a triumph for Peruvian diplomacy when, having reached an impasse in direct talks with Chile – the Peruvian contention being that a plebiscite was no longer practical – it was agreed, under the Washington Protocol of 20 July 1922, to submit the question to the President of the U.S.A.

But three years later, on 5 March 1925, there was consternation in Peru when President Calvin Coolidge announced his decision that the Tacna-Arica matter should after all be settled by a plebiscite, to be held under U.S. supervision. The widow of Admiral Miguel Grau, the Peruvian hero of the War of the Pacific, led a protest march of 20,000 women through the streets of Lima, and

[1] See below, Chapter 12.

there was a good deal of muttering in the press and on street corners about the perfidy of the U.S.A. One does not have to dig very deep under the surface in Peru to find plenty of anti-American feeling; but in this instance the U.S.A. did not do too badly by Peru. The two successive U.S. arbitrators, General John Pershing and General William Lassiter, very quickly realized that conditions in the provinces, where the Chileans were in full control, were such as to make it impossible to expect a fair vote. In 1926 General Lassiter decided that a plebiscite was impracticable.

Having won this important point, Leguía persevered with his efforts to reach an agreement by direct negotiation, still using the good offices of the Americans. Finally, in the neutral atmosphere of Washington a compromise was reached: Tacna should return to Peru with Arica remaining under the Chilean flag. The treaty arranging for final settlement was signed by Peru on 3 June 1929. Thus the hatchet was buried in the midst of much official rejoicing. But the settlement was not popular in Peru; and although few dared to raise their voices against it in public, there was much murmuring against the dictator, who was accused of truckling to the Americans.

Nor was the agreement which Leguía reached in 1922 with regard to the Colombian frontier any more popular; for here again the negotiations were conducted under American auspices and a considerable area of land was ceded to the Colombians, including the entire left bank of the Putumayo river and a corridor leading from this river to the Amazon, where Colombia obtained an outlet at Leticia. All attempts subsequently made by the Peruvians to persuade the U.S. government to sponsor a more favourable treaty failed. The U.S.A. at this time was anxious to mend her fences with Colombia, still resentful about the way in which Panama had been detached in order to give the Americans control over the Canal, and this consideration seems to have overridden any debt of gratitude that Washington may have felt it owed to Peru. Leguía, up to his neck in negotiations for loans from U.S. bankers, was in no position to make a fuss. He was thus finally obliged in December 1927 to induce the Peruvian Congress to ratify the treaty, this being done – it was probably a coincidence – only a few days after he had obtained a considerable loan from Messrs. Seligman and Co. of New York. This Colombian settlement not only sowed the seeds of the 'Leticia Incident',[1] but it added fuel to the flames of Peruvian resentment against the U.S.A., to which, so it seemed to many, Peru was being sold by Leguía, at cost to her national dignity and without anything very much to show for it in the way of political or economic benefits.

[1] See below, p. 161.

1   Megalithic Inca architecture (Sacsahuamán, near Cuzco)
2   Funeral of the Inca Atahualpa (from an oil painting by Lepiani)

3　San Martín proclaiming the Independence of Peru in Lima, 28 Jul 1821 (from an oil painting by Lepiani)

4　The defeat of the Spaniards at Ayacucho, 1824

5 Marshal Don Ramón
Castilla, President 1845–51,
1853–62

6 Manuel Pardo y Lavalle,
President 1872–6

7 The battered Peruvian monitor *Huáscar* after her lone fight aga[i]
an overwhelming Chilean force, 1879

8 Peruvian dead after the battle against the Chileans in Miraflore[s]
1881

9   Don Nicolás de Piérola,
President 1895–9

10   Guillermo E. Billinghurst,
President 1912–14

11 Augusto B. Leguía y Salcedo, President 1908–12, 1919–30

12 Marshal Oscar R. Benavides (President 1933–9) in the state coach accompanied by Manuel Prado y Ugarteche (later President 1939 1956–62)

13 General Luis M. Sánchez
Cerro, President 1931–3

14 General Manuel A. Odría
President 1948–56

15 Madame María Delgado de Odría, President of the *Asistencia Social*,
on a visit to a children's clinic

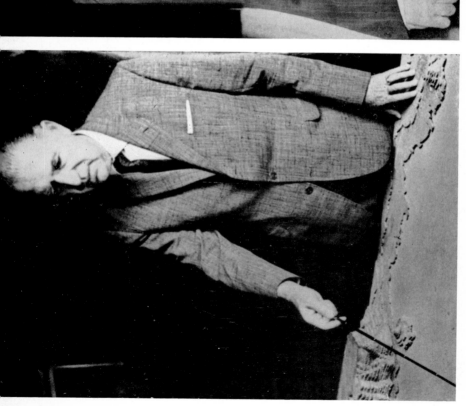

16 Ing. Fernando Belaúnde Terry, President 1963–8

17 APRA leader Víctor Raúl Haya de la Torre

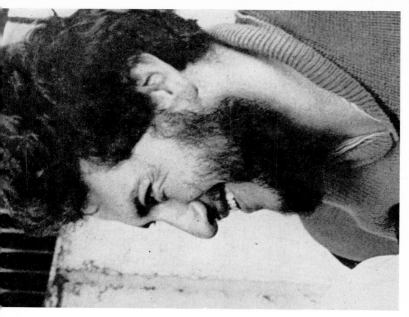

19 *Guerrillero* Hugo Blanco

18 General Juan Velasco Alvarado, President 1968–

20 Cuzco

21 Plaza de Armas and Municipal Palace, Lima

22 The Convent of Santa Catalina in Arequipa

23   Native hut overlooking Lake Titicaca

24   An oil tanker in the desert near Talara

25 Port at Salaverry, built by British civil engineers George Wimpey
    & Co. Ltd.

26 Early conditions in a Lima *barriada*

27   Llamas grazing in the *puna*

28   Native House at Junín

29   A market scene on the Southern Railway

30   Indian dancers (near Cuzco)

The historian Jorge Basadre, usually very fair-minded, no doubt reflects what would be the retrospective opinion of the majority of his fellow-countrymen when he condemns Leguía's foreign policy as one of 'subservience'. His pro-Americanism does seem to have been carried to ridiculous lengths. Portraits of President Monroe were hung in the principal reception room of the Peruvian Foreign Ministry as well as in the dictator's own private office. In 1920, the Fourth of July (American Independence Day) was declared a public holiday in Peru. During the banquet given for President Herbert Hoover, when he visited Peru in December 1928, Leguía eulogized the Monroe Doctrine and Pan-Americanism, describing them as 'the religion of the future'. In the same speech he condemned those who disputed 'the directing role of the Colossus of the North'. And his words were backed by deeds. For example, when the U.S.A. pulled out of President Wilson's own creation, the League of Nations, Peru followed suit, although she had been a signatory of the Treaty of Versailles and one of the founder members of the League.[1] Or again, during the Pan-American conferences in Havana (1928) and in Washington (1929), during a time when the U.S.A. was under heavy fire from most of the Latin American republics because of her intervention in Nicaragua (a move was being made by the Latin American delegations to persuade the Pan-American Union to endorse a policy of 'non-intervention'), the Peruvian delegation, by advancing all sorts of ingenious legal formulae to complicate the issue, did everything in their power to support the American position. The U.S. delegate to the conference in Havana, James Brown Scott, was so pleased with this performance that he sent a telegram afterwards to Leguía praising the work of the Peruvian delegation.[2] In the following year, on 17 June 1929, the American Ambassador in Peru, Alexander Moore, during a banquet which he gave for Leguía, was so carried away by enthusiasm for his guest-of-honour as to exclaim 'May God give you long life. For the greatness of Peru you should live for ever. I ask you, gentlemen, to drink to one of the greatest men in the world – the Giant of the Pacific, Augusto Leguía'.[3]

But this eleven-year-old honeymoon between Peru and the U.S.A. was brought to an abrupt end by the economic depression which hit the world in 1929–30. In his grandiose schemes for developing Peru, Leguía had overreached himself. He had borrowed too heavily. He had prided himself on the annual increase in his budget; but

[1] Peru rejoined the League of Nations in August 1929. According to his enemies, this was because Leguía was seeking to obtain a Nobel Peace Prize.
[2] Basadre, op. cit., Vol. 9, pp. 4083–7.
[3] Ibid., Vol. 9, pp. 4223–4.

reserves now declined disastrously. In all Peru's principal exports – petroleum, cotton, sugar, coffee, and silver – there was a slump. Frenzied appeals to U.S. financiers for further assistance met with no response. Nor were forced loans from local foreign companies of any use in averting the financial disaster with which the country was faced. The value of the Peruvian sol began to decline; there was increasing unemployment and misery and a smouldering discontent. All that was needed was a spark for this to burst into flames.

On 22 August 1930 the garrison of Arequipa revolted. There were simultaneous uprisings in other parts of the country. The leader of the movement was a junior-ranking soldier, Lieutenant-Colonel Luis Sánchez Cerro.[1] He telegraphed to the President demanding his resignation. After his cabinet had resigned and after an unsuccessful attempt to form a new government, Leguía and his son, Juan, bowed to the storm and took refuge in a warship in Callao harbour. A *junta*, headed by Sánchez Cerro, took over the government.

In his first manifesto to the nation, issued in Arequipa, Sánchez Cerro condemned in strong terms Leguía's economic policy, and accused him of having put the country at the mercy of foreign capitalists whose vast monopolies had acquired a stranglehold. This anti-foreign tirade was heady wine for the mob which, since the dictator's downfall, had got thoroughly out of hand, looting the houses of former members of Leguía's government and tearing his name from streets and monuments. For a few days there was heavy street-fighting in Lima between the mob and the police; members of the diplomatic corps, who were on their way to see the President of the *junta* to demand assurances about the lives and property of foreigners, had to pick their way into the palace through pools of blood.

Having vented its spleen against Leguía, the mob then directed its wrath against foreigners in an unprecedented wave of xenophobia. Shops and business premises owned by foreigners were raided and looted. In the Cerro de Pasco mines the Indian workmen got so much out of hand that all foreign employees, including many British subjects, had to be temporarily withdrawn; and similar disturbances were threatened in the oilfields.

It was thus in an atmosphere of hatred and violence that the golden age for U.S. capital which President Leguía had inaugurated and maintained for eleven prosperous years came to an end. Almost overnight the foundations of his dictatorship, seemingly so solid, crumbled away and collapsed. Most of his former supporters, the men who in Congress had sung his praises with such fervour, were

[1] Sánchez Cerro had taken a leading part in the *coup d'état* which unseated Billinghurst, and had also once before risen against Leguía.

quick to desert him. All that was left of the body of 'new men' who in 1919 had set out with such enthusiasm to modernize Peru was a handful of rich, badly frightened politicians whose outlook on political and social questions was now little different from that of the rest of the conservative oligarchy. As for Leguía himself, he was cast by Sánchez Cerro into that same island prison of San Lorenzo to which so many of the dictator's own enemies had been despatched. There he languished for two years until, old and fatally ill, he was allowed to go to hospital. He died on 6 February 1932.

Chapter 12

The Emergence of APRA

I F ONE HAD TO PICK OUT a single man as the founder or at least
the inspiration of the revolutionary movement in Peru, there can be
little doubt that the title should go to González Prada (1840–1918),
a teacher and writer who had lived through the depressing aftermath of the War of the Pacific and had much influence among the
university students and intelligentsia of his day. A free-thinker, he
startled his young admirers by daring to attack the Roman Catholic
Church for its conservatism, clericalism, and its control of education.
But in his later years his main interest was the plight of the downtrodden Indian. He ascribed Peru's lack of a sense of nationality,
and the decadence into which she had fallen since the War of the
Pacific, to the division of the country between white men and
Indians, living side by side in mutual hostility and incomprehension,
the one ruthlessly exploiting the other. He saw little to be hoped for
from the benevolent theories of the positivists, since he did not believe that the white landowners would ever willingly divest themselves of their feudal power. So he preached what was in effect a
doctrine of revolution. Feudalism must be destroyed, and the Indians
exhorted to rise against their masters 'in pride and rebellion'.[1]
    If González Prada was the prophet of the new movement, it was
left to a disciple, José Carlos Mariátegui (1895–1930), to translate
his ideas into the more concrete form of a political philosophy. Of
middle-class background, Mariátegui was too poor to go to the university and was further handicapped by a crippled leg. He worked
his way up in life the hard way, becoming the copy-boy in a Peruvian newspaper office at the age of twelve, a working journalist at
sixteen, and ending up as the owner and editor of his own avant-
garde magazine, Amauta, which made intellectual history in Peru.
Mariátegui accepted an offer by Leguía, who wanted to keep him
out of trouble, to go to Europe on a fellowship; but, to Leguía's
chagrin, he returned to Peru a convinced Marxist. He then provided
for the edification of his fellow-countrymen a Marxist diagnosis of
the problems of Peru, first published in a series of articles in Amauta

    [1] Stephen Clissold, Latin America: A Cultural Outline (London, 1965),
pp. 42–5.

148

and subsequently put together in a book which has become something of a Peruvian classic.[1]

Mariátegui's analysis of Peru's economic history – as a good Marxist he saw economics as the basis of history – was roughly as follows: Inca society was a golden age in which the Indians, practising a primitive form of agrarian communism, provided everything that was needed for their own good life as well as a sufficient surplus to support the superstructure of the Inca state. But the Spanish conquest had destroyed this harmonious state of affairs. An agricultural economy which had been nicely geared to meet the needs of the Indians was now supplanted by an alien feudal system from which only the Spanish and creole landowners benefited; the old communal system of agriculture survived only in the more remote and poor regions of the Andes. To make matters worse thousands of Indians were taken away from their villages to work the gold- and silver-mines, or to become house-servants of Spanish masters in the cities. Spain, according to Mariátegui, contributed nothing to Peru except viceroys, courtiers, adventurers, priests, doctors, and soldiers: it did not colonize the country. Instead of putting available Indian manpower to productive use, the Spaniards almost succeeded in exterminating the Indians, so much so that negro slaves had to be imported to work on the coastal *haciendas*.

Nor did independence from Spain do anything to remedy the desperate situation of the Indian population – the feudal landowning system was merely transferred from the hands of the Spaniards to their creole descendants, while the liberal measures designed by the architects of independence to give the Indians the status of free men in a free society weakened the position of the Indian communities, which hitherto had enjoyed, in theory at any rate, the protection of the Spanish Crown. But Independence did have one important result for the Peruvian economy. Freed from the restrictions of Spanish commercial policy, Peru was now opened up to trade with the capitalist countries of Europe and North America. In the export of guano and nitrate she found in the nineteenth century a new and rich source of wealth. But its exploitation meant that foreign imperialism (to use the Marxist description of the process by which Peru's development was assisted by foreign loans) obtained its grip over the country; and, working in close association with the foreign bankers, a new class of local capitalists (but one with close family links with the landowners) came into being, providing the economic foundations of the *civilista* oligarchy.

Finally, in the twentieth century, according to Mariátegui,

[1] José Carlos Mariátegui, *Siete ensayos de interpretación de la realidad peruana* (Lima, 1928).

American economic imperialism very largely took over from the British and European banks who had financed the guano boom, with major investments in mining and oil; and there also took place at this time a considerable amount of local industrialization in and around the coastal cities. But although these developments produced the beginnings of an industrial proletariat and urban middle class – the essential ingredients for any social revolution on Marxist lines – the transformation of Peru into a truly capitalistic and industrial society was retarded by the continued existence, in parallel with modern industry, of feudal conditions in the countryside.

As González Prada had pointed out, there were two Perus and it was this lack of integration that was holding the country back. It meant that half the people of the country lived outside the modern economy at a bare subsistence level, a fatal bar incidentally to the growth of local industry. It also meant that the feudal mentality of the landowners pervaded the outlook of the business oligarchy, with the result that capitalism in Peru tended to be much too conservative in its ideas and to lack enterprise. In short, said Mariátegui, feudalism was the number one enemy in Peru. It had to be swept away before there could be any real social progress.

Mariátegui did not, however, preach bloody revolution as an immediate programme. He envisaged a gradual regeneration of the Indians by building upon the old communal system of co-operative labour which had survived in many parts of the country. This process, according to his plan, would be assisted by the central government, by education adapted to the needs of a rural population, and by the introduction of modern methods of farming. Mariátegui does not say much about his plans for the industrial worker. But one can take it that as an avowed and passionate socialist his views would have followed the orthodox Marxist line – once feudalism had been destroyed capitalism would thrive; but capitalism would in due course produce its antithesis in the shape of an industrial proletariat which, along with the peasants, would be the spearhead of the revolution to come.

Mariátegui's ideas about the Indian problem were closely similar to those of Víctor Raúl Haya de la Torre, the other important disciple of González Prada, and for a time the two men worked closely together. The son of rich parents in Trujillo, Haya became interested in student politics in the university and was elected President of the San Marcos Federation of Students when he was twenty-four years old. At a congress of students which met in Cuzco in 1920 he launched the idea of founding night-schools for workers, later to be known as the Popular Universities, which were named after González Prada. Both Mariátegui and Haya de la Torre took an active interest in this venture in adult education, lecturing to the workers and contributing articles on political and social questions to *Amauta* and other left-wing journals. This close collaboration between the two was brought to an end, however, when in 1923 Haya got himself into trouble with Leguía by bringing out the students and workers in a mass demonstration in protest against the dictator's pious plan to dedicate Peru to the Sacred Heart. As a result of this incident Haya was thrown into prison. Having staged a hunger strike as a protest against his arrest, he was deported on 9 October 1923. Mariátegui, who had not been involved in this event, remained in Peru to carry on the revolutionary struggle.

But Peru had not heard the last of Haya de la Torre. In Mexico City, on 7 May 1924, he founded his Popular Revolutionary Alliance for America, more usually known by its initials APRA. This new alliance was conceived as a revolutionary organization for the whole of Latin America, which would have local parties in each country. Its Peruvian founders in exile kept themselves busy for the next few years travelling all over the world in search of ideas and inspiration and in doing propaganda for the new movement. In fact, however, although small *Aprista* cells were created in a number of Latin American countries, *Aprismo* only really caught on in the country of its founder – Peru. As the man on the spot, Mariátegui did a lot at first to foment the new movement in Peru, but as time went on he found that he did not see eye to eye with Haya de la Torre on points of doctrine. The correspondence between the two men became increasingly acrimonious. In 1928 they parted company; and Mariátegui founded his own Socialist Party of Peru in opposition to APRA. In 1930 there emerged from the womb of the Socialist Party the Communist Party of Peru. Thus, from this time onwards, the revolutionary movement was split between the various communist and extremist groups stemming from Mariátegui's original creation and Haya de la Torre's APRA which, despite persecution by Leguía's police, continued to make good headway in Peru.

Mariátegui, who had always had to battle with ill health, died in 1930 while still quite a young man. He seems to have been both honest and sincere, and his name is still revered in left-wing intellectual circles in Peru. While he was certainly a convinced Marxist, it seems a little doubtful whether he was ever actually recruited as a member of the Communist Party. But whether he was or not – and many good men were duped by communism in the 1920s – his writings give one a feeling of the passionate sincerity of a man who for a long time was torn between the philosophical certainties of Christianity and Marxism.

Haya de la Torre, to whom the torch of the Peruvian revolutionary movement now passed, was a man of very different character.
Mariátegui was an intellectual through and through and, one suspects, not very good at politics. Haya de la Torre, in contrast, was
always the political activist, preferring people to books, and liking
stimulating conversation more than anything else. (He was always
bubbling over with the latest ideas, whether these came from Einstein, Toynbee, or Karl Marx.) But while fond of intellectual theory,
his approach to politics was essentially pragmatic. Would this or
that idea, however successful abroad, be likely to work in Peru?
This was the question he asked himself on his travels during his
exile, as he picked up ideas from every quarter – from the communists, the fascists, the British Labour Party, the Social Democrats
in Germany, and, most important of all, from the Mexican Revolution.[1]

The original APRA programme, as promulgated in Mexico in
1924, had five planks:

   (1) Action against Yankee imperialism
   (2) The political unity of Latin America
   (3) The nationalization of land and industry
   (4) The internationalization of the Panama Canal
   (5) The solidarity of all peoples and all oppressed classes.

This was, and still is in theory, the 'maximum' programme of the
alliance – the ideal towards which it is supposed to work. Within this
general framework each national party was expected to work out
its own 'minimum' programme. Faced with the realities of Peruvian
conditions, *Aprista* doctrines have in practice undergone a great
many changes since these general aspirations were first proclaimed.

For example, it was not very long before the adjective 'Yankee'
was dropped from the anti-imperialist line and the latter considerably watered down. In the Mexico of 1924, when APRA was
created, there was a strong feeling against the United States of
America – and in Latin America generally. On the other hand,
Haya de la Torre was always sufficiently a realist to know that
Peru must depend on foreign, and mainly United States, capital for
its development. Thus the *Apristas* were quite soon making a distinction in their pronouncements between foreign capital and foreign
imperialism. Foreign capital, they agreed, was both needed and acceptable in Peru, provided that it could be kept under control and
made to obey the local laws. Foreign capital only became foreign
imperialism when it interfered in internal politics or looked to its

---

[1] He may even have picked up an idea or two from the author's father,
Dr R. R. Marett, Rector of Exeter College, under whom he studied social
anthropology at Oxford.

own country for diplomatic support if it should come into conflict with Peruvian interests.

A similar toning-down has taken place in the application of the third plank of the programme, which called for the nationalization of land and industry. This part reflected the socialistic thinking of the founders of the movement. The *Aprista* founding fathers, observing what had been happening in Peru under Leguía, saw the danger of foreign capital obtaining control over more and more of Latin American sources of wealth unless people took positive steps to acquire full possession of their own resources. But it was never made at all clear in the *Aprista* literature how nationalization was to be brought about – this was something which each local party would have to decide in its own country in the light of the prevailing conditions.

To justify his relatively soft line on foreign imperialism and socialism, Haya de la Torre developed an ingenious 'space–time' theory of history which gave him a conveniently free hand to apply the Marxist dialectic to Latin America, without having to accept the conclusions about the evolution of society which Marx, sitting in the reading room of the British Museum and thinking in terms of European conditions in the early twentieth century, had laid down as a dogma for the entire world. Haya's argument ran as follows: there is no absolute time nor any absolute space, as was thought until Einstein's scientific revolution. In history, the concept of a single universal scheme is no longer valid. Marx's ideas were the product of his epoch and his European environment; they are not eternal truths. They do not necessarily apply to Latin America, or Indo-America, as Haya preferred to describe the area. Indo-America must work out her own destiny in accordance with the realities of her own space–time. It might, for example, be true, as Marx had argued, that in Europe imperialism was the last stage of capitalism, but this only applied to the developed countries. The weak nations of Indo-America, however paradoxical this might seem, must encourage the imperialist process since only this would generate the powerful proletariat, which in turn would lead to the socialist revolution. Thus, this convenient theory allowed the *Apristas* to be all things to all men, and left them free to play their hand pragmatically as circumstances dictated.[1]

It would be wrong to conclude, however, that APRA in its early

[1] *Pensamiento político de Haya de la Torre* (Lima, 1961). Compiled by the leading *Apristas* Luis F. Rodríguez Vildosa, Carlos Manuel Cox, and Andrés Townsend Ezcurra, the five volumes of this work contain an excellent summary of Haya de la Torre's political thoughts. Vol. III describes his 'space–time' theory of history.

PERU

days was lacking in revolutionary fervour. Unlike the communists, who slavishly followed the party line, the *Apristas* made a genuine attempt to devise a revolutionary programme of reform which would be suited to Peruvian conditions; and let there be no doubt that the minimum programme, which they advocated for Peru when the party came to life after the fall of Leguía, was quite revolutionary enough to frighten the ruling class and to provoke the deadly enmity of the triple-tiered Establishment of oligarchy, army, and Roman Catholic Church, whose vested interests the *Apristas* were attacking. Indeed, if one wanted to criticize the APRA programme it could be charged that it was unduly provocative, and hence almost bound to be counter-productive.[1]

For example, this is how Manuel Seoane described the domestic programme of APRA:

'Basically we aspire to the liberation of our human capital, the worker...from the economic slavery that weighs on him. Since the Indian constitutes the majority of the population we must win his economic freedom as a first step.... Our true capital is not only the Peruvian citizen but also the riches of our soil which is also enslaved. The principal Peruvian products, our copper, petroleum, cotton and sugar, are monopolized by imperialistic enterprises or by creole minorities who exploit and tax the country without giving it any benefit, but rather leaving a sorry trail of arbitrariness, theft and abuse. This constructive work cannot be completed within the archaic mould of the present Peruvian institutions nor with the men who by their acts or their refusal to permit others to act have led Peru to ruin. This constructive work must be completed by breaking the selfish centralism of Lima with a system of scientific, administrative decentralization by the young and honourable forces of the country.'[2]

There was not much here to comfort the foreign capitalists and the local business oligarchy. Nor was the rest of the Establishment spared. For example, the minimum programme called for the separation of Church from state, a political aim which had been favoured by the liberals in the nineteenth century, and was now once again, to conservative consternation, revived by the *Apristas*. The issue here was basically one of education; the *Apristas* were not against religion as such. Born in the movement for university reform, APRA

---

[1] For a critical study of APRA see Frederick B. Pike, 'The Old and the New Apra in Peru: Myth and Reality' (*Inter-American Economic Affairs*, Vol. 18, 1964).

[2] Quoted Harry Kantor, *The Ideology and Program of the Peruvian Aprista Movement* (Stanford, Calif., 1953). This American author is sympathetic towards the aims of the movement.

was intensely interested in education, seeing in it the key to the social transformation of the country. The *Apristas* argued that education must be a monopoly of the state, so that it could be freed from both reactionary clerical control and the restrictive influence of the landowners, who opposed education because of their fear that it would weaken their hold over their Indian serfs. Thus, separation of Church and state, combined with APRA's ambitious plans for an all-embracing scheme for national education (including rural education for the Indians) was bound to arouse the hostility of those two pillars of society the Church and the landowners. Nor was that other most important pillar of all, the army, neglected; for the APRA minimum programme proposed to remove the armed forces from politics – a proposal which could only be regarded by the military as an intention to destroy the army and create an APRA-controlled military machine in its place.

More generally the *Aprista* minimum programme for Peru envisaged a far-reaching scheme of social reform covering every aspect of the national life. Very much in the forefront of the plan but regarded as a long-term rather than an immediate aim was agrarian reform and rural education, designed to redeem the Indian masses along the lines advocated by Mariátegui. A more immediate priority was the economic development of the country, as a first step towards which the *Apristas* proposed to set up a statistical agency and convene a national economic congress – but after that the economic plan was left rather vague. The immediate socialization of industry was not apparently envisaged; but there would be increased state intervention in the economic life of the country to plan, stimulate, and finance production, and this would be accompanied by state ownership of certain important economic sectors and the creation of co-operatively owned enterprises. As befitted a popular party there were, of course, as well a wide range of projects designed to improve the lot of the workers and the middle class – new social services of every kind, housing, sanitation, and a complete overhaul of the educational system. All this, of course, would cost a vast amount of money which presumably could only come out of the pockets of the rich, insofar as the larger schemes for development were not financed by foreign capital.

Finally, mention must be made of the APRA plan to overhaul the public administration, eliminating graft and nepotism; and an even more ambitious plan to create in Peru a new type of *Aprista* state, in which there would be social justice and full democratic rights for all citizens. What was envisaged was a functional democracy – a political system in which the citizen would have rights and duties as a citizen but also rights and duties flowing from his participation in the country's economic life. There is a fascist ring about this proposal. The new state, the *Apristas* claimed, would be based on the three oppressed and exploited groups in Peru: the workers, the farmers, and the middle class. It would have two enemies: the present feudal rulers of Peru and the foreign imperialists. This kind of talk, vague though it was, seemed to be almost deliberately designed to alarm and alienate the Peruvian upper class.

Nor was it only the ambitious extent of APRA policies which alarmed the Establishment. As soon as it was allowed to come out into the open, it became apparent that APRA was much better organized than any other political party in Peru. The party rank and file were subjected to the strictest discipline under the supreme leader, Haya de la Torre;[1] the party's tentacles were spread widely in the student organizations in the universities, in the trade union movement, and in the junior ranks of the civil service and the armed forces. The party had its well-organized Youth Movement, to say nothing of its thugs, known popularly as the *búfalos*. While professing to be democratic in its constitution, APRA was in fact run on more or less totalitarian lines; it was capable of embarrassing any government in power by organizing strikes, mass demonstrations, and, on occasions, engaging in acts of terrorism. Apart from all this, it was undoubtedly immensely popular among the manual workers, artisans, white-collar workers, students, and intellectuals, and even in certain segments of the middle class. In short, Peru had never before seen such a formidable political machine.

[1] Pike, op. cit., p. 28 writes: 'Membership cards were awarded only after a close scrutiny of the applicant and after party chiefs were satisfied that the prospective member would follow party discipline and ideological pronouncements with the same blind loyalty of a Communist Party card-holder.'

Chapter 13

APRA versus the Establishment

AFTER LEGUÍA'S FALL FROM POWER in August 1930, it was not until the summer of the following year that the country had settled down enough to hold a presidential election. The two main contenders in this struggle were Haya de la Torre and Colonel Sánchez Cerro. The latter, finding the spot too hot for him and unable to obtain nationwide support, had gone into voluntary exile abroad after a few months as President of the first *junta* which had taken over the government. He had now returned to Peru to try his luck for a second time. Haya de la Torre had likewise just returned from eight years of exile to lead his party in an all-out bid for power. Meanwhile a series of weak and unstable *juntas* had been holding the fort in the presidential palace, while the people prepared themselves for what was probably the first really free election in Peruvian history.

Haya de la Torre was the dark horse in the race. Outside his own circle of friends and supporters the country had seen too little of him in recent years to be able to take his measure. But very soon he was making his mark. His fiery doctrine of social revolution was exactly what a lot of the people – in particular the students, the labour-leaders, and the intellectuals – wanted to hear. The Depression had caused great suffering for the urban working and lower-middle classes; there was hunger, misery, and unemployment in the slums and poorer quarters of the cities. The people were in a revolutionary mood. Moreover, Haya de la Torre was a superb showman, an expert in the art of staging mass demonstrations. The well-organized APRA shock brigades emerged from hiding and paraded in the streets holding aloft revolutionary banners and singing their song to the tune of the *Marseillaise*.

But Sánchez Cerro, the revolutionary colonel who had dared to challenge the mighty Leguía, was also not lacking in popular appeal. A dark complexion betrayed his Indian blood; for unlike Haya de la Torre he was a man of the people. His fellow *cholos*[1] took him to their heart and it was not long before he had organized his own

[1] A word used by Peruvians to describe 'the man in the street'. It has no specific racial connotation.

dusky following – in some ways more proletarian in spirit and composition than the ranks of APRA – in a party which he called *Unión Revolucionaria*. From this time onwards groups of young men from the two rival parties fought in the streets in a manner reminiscent of the battles between Nazis and communists in contemporary Germany. Peru had never seen anything like it before.

Whereas Haya de la Torre preached a near-Marxist doctrine of war to the death against the Establishment (he was equally hostile, however, towards the communists), Sánchez Cerro appealed for national unity; all the social classes, he urged, should work together for the salvation of Peru. While strongly anti-communist – and for electoral purposes the *Apristas* were equated with the communists in his propaganda – his own programme was not lacking in both nationalistic and revolutionary fervour. The wicked men of the Leguía régime must be brought to justice; the great foreign monopolies must be broken; positive steps must be taken to better the lot of the workers and peasants. With his own partly Indian background, Sánchez Cerro was perhaps more genuinely concerned than the *Apristas* about the lot of the Indian peasants. An important plank of his platform was a programme of Indian educational and agrarian reform.

Caught between the two fires of these popular parties were the members of the Establishment – landowners and business and professional men – some of whom had been former supporters of Leguía, others recently returned from exile abroad, but all bewildered and alarmed by the disaster which had overtaken Peru. For the most part they heartily disliked both candidates – Haya as a renegade intellectual who had betrayed his own class; Sánchez Cerro as a crude, uneducated, and unpredictable soldier, who did not seem to possess either the experience or the judgement to make a good President. It was a choice between two evils; but in most oligarchical minds there could be no doubt which was the lesser evil. In the absence of a candidate of their own who had a chance of winning Sánchez Cerro was obviously their best hope.

On 11 October 1931 the elections took place in an atmosphere of calm. Thanks to the efficient vote-getting organization of the *Unión Revolucionaria*, coupled with the wealth, influence, and brains of the oligarchy, Sánchez Cerro was returned to power, but only after a close race with APRA. The voting was as follows:

Sánchez Cerro	155,378
Haya de la Torre	106,551
Other candidates	41,673
Total votes	303,602

Cheated of victory the *Apristas* shouted 'fraud'. But in the opinion of most impartial observers the elections were fair. Supporters of Sánchez Cerro were able to point to the fact that the provisional *junta* of Samánez Ocampo, who were responsible for supervising the elections, had no desire to perpetuate themselves in office, nor were they sponsoring any 'official' candidate of their own.[1]

Be that as it may, this election had far-reaching consequences for the future of Peru. Haya de la Torre had demonstrated his great popularity with an important and politically conscious segment of the population. He had sufficiently scared the members of the Establishment to make them determined to prevent him from ever entering the presidential palace. The *Apristas* for their part drew the not perhaps unjustified conclusion that they were unlikely ever to obtain power by constitutional means. Thus they became hardened in an attitude of militancy. It might possibly have been better for Peru if Haya de la Torre had won this election and thus been made to justify in responsible action his claim that 'only APRA could save Peru'. But he did not win. For the next twenty-five years the political life of Peru was polarized between the Establishment, stubbornly defending its position against what it regarded as subversion, and APRA, fighting tenaciously what it deemed to be the battle of the common man. The ups and downs of this struggle, which are the theme of this and the succeeding chapter, can best be summarized by considering them in relation to the efforts of successive Presidents to cope with this intractable problem.

The situation of APRA during the brief but unhappy presidency of Sánchez Cerro can be summed up in four words – 'War to the death'. An autocrat by temperament, for all his popularity with the masses, Sánchez Cerro had no intention of suffering any nonsense from the powerful APRA minority in Congress. Nor was APRA, a movement developed underground and organized upon totalitarian lines, of the stuff of which 'loyal oppositions' of the English type are made.

In February 1932, receiving reports of revolutionary plots, the President reacted violently by closing all the opposition newspapers, and arresting Colonel Gustavo Jiménez, Minister of War in the late *junta*, together with twelve *Aprista* congressmen and journalists. APRA retaliated by organizing hostile street demonstrations in Lima and Callao, which resulted in considerable bloodshed. The surviving members of the opposition protested against the violation of the immunity of Congress by the arrest of deputies within its precincts,

[1] For the first time, at this election the use of the secret ballot was provided. But there was still the danger that officials in charge of the polling-booths might be tempted to cheat.

and the President of Congress, Dr Luis Eguiguren, retired for two weeks in protest against this breach of the constitution. Nevertheless, further deportations followed, including that of Manuel Seoane, a prominent *Aprista*, and nearly all the remaining APRA deputies in Congress. Haya de la Torre went into hiding.

In the following month an attempt was made in church on the life of the President, who was wounded in the shoulder. The perpetrators were two young men of good families who were said to be *Apristas*. Despite the protests of their friends, they were condemned to death by court martial; but under popular pressure the President was induced to commute this sentence to lifelong imprisonment. Meanwhile some 200 arrests were made.

On 7 May the crews of two cruisers in Callao harbour mutinied and overpowered their officers. However, the next day, after a show of force by aeroplanes and submarines which had remained loyal, the crews surrendered. Once more APRA was believed to be implicated and eight sailors, who were considered to be the ringleaders, were shot.

As a result of all these troubles Haya de la Torre, who had been hiding for some time next door to the Mexican Legation, was arrested. The Mexican minister was accused of having secret interviews with him and was declared *persona non grata*. Thereupon the Mexican government gave the Peruvian minister in Mexico his passports and broke off diplomatic relations.

In July, after an abortive military revolt in Las Palmas (in which APRA do not seem to have been involved), a far more serious and exceedingly bloody revolution broke out in Trujillo, the *Aprista* stronghold. The garrison and police were overpowered, the prison doors opened, and the prisoners released to make room for the government authorities who were imprisoned in their place. The President ordered sea, land, and air forces to concentrate upon Trujillo which, after a fierce fight, was captured. The revolutionary movement was then suppressed with much cruelty and bloodshed. Casualties amounted to between 1,000 and 2,000 and forty-four people were sentenced to death by court martial.

Haya de la Torre was accused, though never tried, of having planned the Trujillo outbreak. A motion was brought up in Congress for his deportation, but rejected. Many feared that he would be shot. George Lansbury, the English Labour leader, was reported in the Peruvian Congress as having telegraphed direct to Sánchez Cerro: 'Your republic would be covered with shame if Haya de la Torre's life were taken'. This called forth an angry outburst in the press against Lansbury for attempting to interfere in Peru's internal affairs.

Meanwhile, as though these internal troubles were not enough, Peru in September 1932 became involved in a serious dispute with Colombia which brought the two countries to the verge of war. Leguía's agreement with Colombia, which involved the handing over of the Amazon river port of Leticia to the Colombians, had been extremely unpopular.[1] On 1 September a group of armed Peruvians from Iquitos decided to take the law into their own hands and seized the port. At first Sánchez Cerro disclaimed all responsibility for this act. Later, under the pressure of *Aprista* propaganda calling for strong action, his attitude towards Colombia became increasingly aggressive until war seemed to be imminent.

On 30 April 1933 the unhappy régime of Sánchez Cerro was brought to an abrupt end. The President had just reviewed on the racecourse a parade of some 25,000 youths who had been mobilized for the expected war with Colombia. As the car in which he was seated emerged from the gates of the Jockey Club a youth of seventeen jumped on the running-board and shot him; he died in hospital a few hours later. Marshal Oscar Benavides, the Chief of National Defence, was a witness of the scene. A man of action, who in 1914 had staged the successful *coup d'état* in favour of the *civilistas*,[2] he drove straight from the racecourse to the palace and assumed command there. Thus, when the Congress met that same evening to elect a new President in accordance with the constitution, they had merely to ratify an accomplished fact. Marshal Benavides was elected President for the remainder of Sánchez Cerro's presidential term.

The sudden removal of Sánchez Cerro was like the lifting of the fog-bank which hangs over Lima for seven months of the year. Now suddenly the sun appeared again in the sky. Under the firm hand of Benavides Peru quickly returned to normal and the economic development of the country, interrupted by the Great Depression, was resumed. In a short soldierly speech addressed to Congress President Benavides announced his programme. He did not, he said, belong to any political party and he had no hatreds. He would strive for unity and harmony amongst the whole Peruvian family. True to his word, the tyranny quickly came to an end. The prison doors were opened and thousands of political prisoners released. Large numbers of political deportees, too, were allowed to return to their own country.

In foreign affairs, also, the new President strove for peace. Benavides could see no point in fighting an expensive war over Leticia and must have realized that the Peruvian case was extremely weak, since

[1] See above, p. 144.
[2] See above, pp. 132–3.

there was no doubt about the legality of the Peruvian-Colombian Treaty of 1922 (ratified by Peru in 1928) which had resulted in Leticia becoming Colombian territory. Accordingly, after unofficial talks with the President-elect of Colombia, Alfonso López, who happened to be a personal friend of Benavides and was invited to visit him in Lima, Peru agreed to accept a cease-fire formula prepared by the League of Nations, to which Colombia had appealed, and to enter into negotiations in Rio de Janeiro with a view to a permanent settlement. The talks in Rio were successful: in 1934 Peru agreed to abide by the terms of the treaty of 1922 and the Peruvian troops were withdrawn from the area. There has been no further trouble between Peru and Colombia on this frontier.[1]

More generally in the international field Benavides was successful in restoring Peru's badly shattered credit, especially in the U.S.A. The wave of xenophobia induced by the Great Depression subsided, and Peru's normally friendly relations with the U.S.A. were resumed. The Peruvian sol, which had been devalued in 1930 and again more severely in 1931, was stabilized at a value of between 23 and 25 U.S. cents. Meanwhile Peru's international trade began to recover. As a result of the Depression the total value of Peruvian exports had dropped from $134 million in 1929 to 38 million in 1932, a loss of 72 per cent in income. During the same period imports decreased from $76 million to only 16 million, while fiscal expenditure in Peru dropped from 257 million soles in 1928 to 98·6 million in 1932. Under Benavides (1933–39) the Peruvian economy went through a period of healthy readjustment. The drop in foreign trade forced the nation to adapt itself to a reduced level of real income, manifested by a scarcity of imported manufactured goods. Economic growth, which Leguía had financed by foreign loans, became more dependent upon the potentialities of the domestic sector – Benavides, unlike Leguía, was content to limit his plans for development to the means of the country. Meanwhile, with their accustomed buoyancy, exports steadily increased in value between 1933 and 1937, thanks to a recovery in world markets, although they did not during this period reach the boom levels in pre-Depression years.[2]

As regards internal politics, the advent of Benavides, a man with good social connections, meant a return to power, under the protection of the army, of the old *civilista* oligarchy, represented in this generation by such political figures as the two sons of Mariano Prado, Jorge and Manuel, which the middle-class Leguía had done his best to destroy in 1919. As a political entity the *Civilista* Party

[1] Pike, *The Modern History of Peru*, p. 269.
[2] Robinson, op. cit., pp. 398–400.

had ceased to exist, and this once closely-knit political group was now divided into a number of factions. Nevertheless, being temporarily united by a common loyalty to Benavides, the Establishment, with its wealth, brains, and well-entrenched social position, represented a formidable combination of political power. Bitterly opposed to the new régime and the political and social interests which it represented were the rump of Sánchez Cerro's former supporters in the now fascist-orientated *Unión Revolucionaria* on the one hand and the left-wing APRA Party on the other. It is difficult to say which of these two political movements, both of which were led by competent demagogues, presented the greater danger to the government.

At first Benavides tried to co-operate with the *Unión Revolucionaria*, and Dr Luis Flores, its chief, and other leading members of this party were given posts in the cabinet. But he found it impossible to work with them. Their one thought was vengeance for the murder of Sánchez Cerro; their insistent demand a reign of terror designed to destroy APRA, which they considered to be responsible for this crime. Benavides, for his part, was determined to carry out his policy of forgetting the hatreds of the past and restoring peace and harmony. At length, after five months in office, when it became clear that both the people and the army were prepared to support him in this endeavour, the President reorganized his cabinet, leaving out the black-shirted Luis Flores and his friends.

From now onwards there was an open and bitter enmity between Flores and Benavides – an enmity reflected in the rump Congress which, already purged by Sánchez Cerro of APRA members, was now split between those who supported the President and those who remained faithful to *Unión Revolucionaria* and the memory of Sánchez Cerro. But the power and influence of this party were no longer what they had been in its heyday. The product of the despair, misery, and xenophobia caused by the Great Depression, this pseudo-fascist movement had lost most of its *raison d'être*; it had degenerated into a political machine, still capable of snatching the votes of the more unthinking sections of the population, but no longer possessing any real ideology or programme to offer to the people.

With APRA, too, President Benavides at first attempted a policy of appeasement. Members of this party who had been imprisoned by Sánchez Cerro were allowed to go free. On 9 August 1933 the government-sponsored Amnesty Bill was passed unanimously by Congress and on the same evening the Prime Minister, Jorge Prado, who had been dining at the British Legation, drove straight to the prison where Haya de la Torre had been confined for fifteen months.

He released the APRA leader unconditionally and conducted him personally to a car which conveyed him to a friend's residence. Haya de la Torre, for his part, offered his support to the government in carrying out their policy of peace and goodwill.

But the honeymoon did not last long. Once more allowed to parade in the streets, APRA soon both annoyed and alarmed the government by the evident popularity it enjoyed among the masses. At the big public demonstration staged by the mayor of Lima to celebrate the signing of the agreement with Colombia, the *Apristas* spoiled the effect by putting a large contingent into the procession under their banner and a streamer bearing the legend 'Reopen the University'. As this marched by, APRA sympathizers in the crowd of some 40,000 persons frantically waved white handkerchiefs, thus indicating that well over half the people present were supporters of the party. Again, on the occasion of the festival of San Juan at Amancaes, just outside Lima, the *Apristas* took a further opportunity of showing their strength. This they did first by painting huge signs, such as 'Viva el APRA' and their symbol, a star, on the surrounding hills, and secondly by occupying in force a small hill just behind the stands where the officials and the public were seated, from which they interrupted the proceedings by singing songs and shouting slogans.

At the end of 1933 the government forestalled an alleged *Aprista* plot against the President by having all troops and police mobilized. Many arrests were made. Throughout 1934 there were frequent APRA-fomented strikes and the year ended with another abortive plot to overthrow the government in which, on this occasion, APRA appear to have joined forces with the small remnant of the *Leguístas*. However, the enterprise was premature and ill-conceived, and was easily put down. Haya de la Torre's brother, Agustín, was arrested along with Oscar Leguía, the late President's nephew.

In the face of this determined opposition the government could only fall back upon the time-honoured method of suppression; the usual arrests and deportations followed. APRA retaliated by a campaign of terror, during which a bomb was thrown into the Congress building and another bomb went into the offices of *El Comercio*. But April 1935 produced an event which, by its horror, overshadowed all previous attempts to intimidate the government. This was the assassination of Antonio Miró Quesada – the doyen of the family which owns *El Comercio* – and his wife in the street at midday. The assassin was alleged to be a member of the *Aprista* youth organization.

There are no doubt two sides to this story of the quarrel between APRA and Benavides, and it is difficult to know where the truth lies. It is the old problem of the hen and the egg. Apologists for Benavides claim that the *Apristas* made such an intolerable nuisance of themselves that they had to be kept in check. In *Aprista* literature Benavides is depicted as a tyrant only a little less oppressive than Sánchez Cerro. The abortive plots and occasional acts of violence of the APRA rank and file were, it was claimed, the inevitable result of the persecution to which the party was subjected. Since most of the officials of the APRA high command were either in jail or hiding, they could not, it was further argued, be held responsible for the isolated acts of the party's supporters driven to desperation by the repressive actions of Benavides' ever-vigilant police. Be that as it may, the murder of the Miró Quesadas was a blessing in disguise for the government. Benavides could now, with a clear conscience, take the sternest measures against APRA. This he did with such vigour that by the end of 1935 the forces of opposition had apparently been reduced to impotence.

But no amount of persecution could destroy the popularity of APRA with the mass of the people. This was brought home painfully to Benavides when in 1936, his term of office having come to an end, he tried to stage-manage an election to put his oligarchical friend and supporter Jorge Prado into the presidency as his successor. But Prado lacked popular appeal. Not only was the fascist Flores campaigning actively against him, but APRA, too, being unable under the ban to put forward a candidate of their own, had found a 'front' man, in the person of Dr Luis Eguiguren, who stood as the candidate of a more or less mythical Social Democratic Party. It soon became clear that Eguiguren, with APRA support, would head the list, with Flores running not very far behind. Benavides had to act quickly. He persuaded Congress to pass a law declaring illegal all votes given for the Social Democratic candidate, since the participation of *Apristas* in the election was banned under the constitution. The National Election Committee then declared the whole election null and void. Finally, Congress extended Benavides' term of office for another three years, and then dissolved itself. Thus, Benavides was handed on a platter almost complete dictatorial powers. The *Apristas,* who took their defeat remarkably quietly, returned once more into the shadows. Apart from one or two minor incidents no serious attempts were made by APRA to disturb the public order during the next three years.

Marshal Benavides ruled the country for six years. There can be no doubt that, by strong-man standards, he was a good President. He brought peace to the country when it badly needed it after the almost total breakdown of law and order during the unhappy reign of Sánchez Cerro. The economic and social advances made during his time in power were truly formidable: thousands of miles of roads; extensive irrigation works; the completion of the new port and dry dock at Callao; great numbers of workmen's dwellings; popular restaurants serving a good meal at a cost of 30 centavos; greatly increased expenditure in education and the social services; modern barracks constructed and the army rearmed; a new naval hospital; the army, police, and civil servants paid promptly and regularly; all contracts made since 1933 met punctually and in full. Moreover, the budget had shown a rising surplus year by year, and internal inflation was kept well under control. These were some of the impressive material achievements of a President who, whatever one might think about his political methods, had given the nation a much-needed breathing-space. He was what the Peruvians call *dinámico* – a man who got things done.

But the basic political problem of Peru remained without a solution. So long as APRA remained underground, enjoying the loyalty of a large segment of the working population, but an object of fear and suspicion to the Establishment, there could be none of that peace and harmony in the Peruvian family which Benavides had set out so hopefully to achieve.

Chapter 14

The Taming of APRA

WHILE IT MAY BE SUSPECTED that the late President Manuel Prado would prefer to be remembered for his role upon the international stage, in which he always liked to shine, it seems more probable that the verdict of history will be that his most important contribution towards the well-being of his countrymen was his success in taming the wild men of the APRA Party and bringing them to heel. Not that Manuel Prado should take all the credit for what happened; there are two sides to every process of reconciliation. The fact remains, however, that it was Prado who during his first term of office (1939–45), initiated the movement towards a better understanding between APRA and the Establishment; and it was Prado again who, after a long period of renewed strife, brought the reconciliation to its consummation when the *Apristas* decided to support his candidature for a second presidential term in 1956.

Manuel Prado, who succeeded Marshal Benavides in 1939, was more successful in stage-managing his election than had been his brother Jorge in 1936. Although a member of a leading oligarchical family, and fundamentally a conservative, the new President was sensitive to the winds of political change. He fully realized the need for any presidential candidate in modern Peru to cultivate the urban working and middle classes. Thus, during his campaign he went out of his way to woo the labour unions. Whether at this time he put out peace feelers to the outlawed *Apristas* is a matter of conjecture. Certainly, as soon as he was in office, he made it abundantly clear that he wished to coexist peacefully with *Aprismo* and forget the bitterness of the past.

In this policy of appeasement he was greatly helped by the change in APRA's own outlook caused by the outbreak of the Second World War. Haya de la Torre had always taken a stand on the side of the democratic powers in their struggle against the fascists, the Nazis, and Franco's Spain, and now that war had broken out he and his party were firmly on the side of the Allies. It was no doubt partly because of this wartime alignment that the APRA leaders began at this time to soften their line on the subject of United States economic imperialism. They now preached the doctrine that the co-operation of foreign capital was needed in order to create in Peru the conditions necessary for the development of true democracy. In 1944 the name APRA was officially dropped in favour of the more innocent title *Partido del Pueblo* (People's Party), and a resolution was approved at a general meeting of the party advocating a just settlement of the Peruvian foreign debt and an equitable agreement with foreign bond-holders with a view to re-establishing the country's credit. As a sop for Roman Catholic opinion, the party also agreed to drop from its programme the separation of Church and state, a cause for which in the nineteenth century the liberals had fought with such passion. This change of attitude of a party which in the past had preached the blood and thunder of Marxist doctrine could hardly fail to make some impression on public opinion both at home and abroad. Among liberals in the U.S.A. the conviction grew that APRA represented the true forces of democracy in a country which for too long had groaned under the heel of a rich oligarchy. It also encouraged President Prado to persevere with his policy of appeasement, in the hope, no doubt, of concerting some sort of an understanding with *Aprismo*, which would give him a larger following in the labour unions.

Unlike President José Pardo, who had been neutral in his personal attitude towards the issues of the First World War, President Manuel Prado, when faced with the problems of the Second World War, was from the beginning a firm and, with his love of France, a passionate supporter of the Allied cause. Such an outlook, however, was unusual in the Peruvian oligarchy. Many Peruvian conservatives, believing in strong dictatorial government in their own country, had been adherents of Franco in the Spanish Civil War and were now in consequence in sympathy with the Axis. Not that fascism, either in its crude form as practised in Peru by the blackshirted Luis Flores of *Unión Revolucionaria*,[1] or in the more refined version preached by José de la Riva Agüero,[2] ever really caught on in Peru. For the majority of the members of the oligarchy the war was simply a question of 'business as usual'. As for the average man in the street, this titanic struggle between foreigners was regarded as though it were a football match – the crowd was ready to cheer whichever side put up the bravest show. In these circumstances, and with the assurance of wholehearted *Aprista* support (and with the support also of the local Communist Party once Soviet Russia had

---

[1] See above, p. 163.

[2] A leading intellectual of 'the generation of 1900', Riva Agüero saw democracy as a slippery slope leading to communism. His remedy for Peru was to return to the medieval, Roman Catholic, Hispanic tradition which he considered was embodied in fascism (see Pike, op. cit., p. 258).

become a belligerent), Prado had no difficulty in steering his country along its now traditional pro-American path. Early in 1942, after the Japanese attack on Pearl Harbour, Peru broke off relations with the Axis powers and thereafter co-operated closely with the U.S.A., permitting the American air force to build an airfield at Talara. In co-operation with the U.S. intelligence agencies, suspected Axis agents were interned. In 1945 Peru declared war on Germany and Japan.

Before this, in 1941, Peru became engaged in a little war of her own against Ecuador – again the old trouble about the boundaries in the Amazon basin in the regions of Jaen and Maynas.[1] Castilla's invasion of Ecuador in 1859 had settled nothing.[2] In 1887 Ecuador agreed to put the case to arbitration, but on two occasions between 1903 and 1910 and between 1936 and 1938 the negotiations broke down. Border clashes in 1940–41 led to a state of war in which the Ecuadorian army was decisively beaten at Zarumilla by a Peruvian force commanded by Marshal Eloy G. Ureta. In the subsequent peace negotiations held in Rio de Janeiro at the beginning of 1942, under the auspices of the Organization of American States, a Pact of Peace, Amity, and Limits (known as the Rio Protocol) was signed by the two countries and guaranteed by Argentina, Brazil, Chile, and the United States. The agreement recognized Peru's *de facto* control of the upper Amazon basin, based on victory in war and on a strong colonial title. Ecuador has since disputed the juridical base of the protocol, but the Peruvians insist that it is valid, was freely ratified, and is unalterable.

These military and diplomatic victories were hailed with great joy in Peru, and for a time both Prado and Marshal Ureta basked in the sun of popular approval. But as its term of office approached its end there was a growing discontent with the Prado régime. As the result of wartime inflation and shortages prices sky-rocketed. Between 1940 and 1945 the money supply increased by 260 per cent and there was a corresponding rise of 86 per cent in the cost of living.[3] By 1944 the food situation had become serious, with shortages of rice, meat, potatoes, and flour. In the same year a series of labour troubles culminated in a general strike.

Thus, by 1945, with new elections approaching, it was clear to Prado that the majority of the people wanted a change. With Allied victory on the horizon the democratic tide was flowing strongly throughout the world, making its influence felt even in far-away Peru. President Prado was a man of good political judgement, as also in his own way was Marshal Benavides, who had recently

[1] See above, p. 82.   [2] See above, p. 111.
[3] Robinson, op. cit., p. 401.

returned to Peru from Buenos Aires where he had been serving as Peruvian Ambassador. Both men realized that the people were in no mood to accept another 'controlled' election such as Benavides and Prado had staged so successfully in 1939. They were both, too, well aware of the popularity of APRA, and no doubt encouraged by the new moderation in the policies of this party to believe that there was now a real chance of the Establishment being able to come to terms with it. After some negotiations behind the scenes between the political leaders, it was agreed finally that the ban on APRA's participation in the election should be lifted, provided that Haya himself did not run for the presidency. APRA agreed to give its support to a neutral candidate, Dr José Luis Bustamante y Rivero, a high-minded lawyer from Arequipa, of good family and of moderately progressive views.

In the memorandum in which he conveyed his acceptance of the candidacy, Bustamante stated that he would only take office on condition that the country returned to constitutional government. He promised, moreover, that if he was elected his presidential term would be one of 'reconstructive transition', during which there would be no extreme 'rightist' or 'leftist' measures. The announcement of Bustamante's candidature created a great sensation. Adherents poured in from all over the country, including many who hastened to forsake Marshal Ureta, the hero of the recent war with Ecuador, who was the only other serious candidate in the field, and whom originally Prado had supported.

The rehabilitation of APRA was an important step in the political history of Peru. To celebrate the event a mass meeting was held which was attended by a record number of over 80,000 persons. The meeting was addressed by Haya de la Torre, who thus made his first public appearance since APRA was outlawed. His words were moderate and conciliatory, including friendly references to Britain and the United States and a disclaimer of all desire to redistribute the wealth in Peru. This was made in the following reassuring terms: 'In Peru it is not a question of taking from those who have but rather of creating riches for those who have not'.

The election took place on 10 June 1945 and was conducted in a more orderly fashion than had been expected. Before the result could be announced, Marshal Benavides died of a heart attack on 2 July. His sudden death in the middle of these profound political changes deprived the country of one of its most able statesmen at a time when his presence was most needed. The result of the election was announced on 21 July, Bustamante winning by 305,590 to 150,720 votes for Marshal Ureta. Furthermore, his supporters won a substantial majority in the Senate and the Chamber of Deputies.

APRA, as the largest party within the winning alliance, obtained 18 out of 29 seats in the Senate and 53 out of 84 seats in the Chamber of Deputies. They had now truly come into their own.

Transmission of the mandate took place on 28 July, Peru's National Day. Bustamante's first cabinet was composed entirely of non-party men, chosen for their technical knowledge, who were to support the President in his task of restoring democratic rule and establishing the country's finances on a sound basis, whilst striving to improve social and economic conditions. Censorship was immediately removed and complete freedom of the press granted. APRA announced that it did not seek any public appointments, but promised that it would support Bustamante's government.

José Gálvez, an APRA sympathizer, who held the office of First Vice-President (under the Peruvian constitution there are two Vice-Presidents) was elected President of the Senate; the first act of this body was to pass, unanimously, a motion expressing satisfaction at the Labour victory in the British elections. In the Chamber of Deputies (whose President, León de Vivero, was a prominent *Aprista*) the first steps were to repeal the unpopular emergency laws, which had so radically curtailed freedom in Peru, and to grant an amnesty to all political prisoners.[1] Thus 1945 was a time of great hope in Peru. The story of the subsequent three years of Bustamante's government is essentially that of the failure of this hope to materialize.

In his book,[2] written in exile, Bustamante places the blame for the failure squarely on the shoulders of APRA, who now held the dominating position in Congress. He complains that the *Aprista* senators, instead of supporting the constitutional President for whom they had voted, took their orders from Haya de la Torre, who thus ruled behind the scenes as a shadow President. In addition, so Bustamante claimed, APRA used its position of influence in the labour movement, not to help the government, but to harass it by causing strikes and other disturbances. For example, a strike of the APRA-controlled Lima Regional Federation of workers in August 1947 seriously disrupted the life of the capital, and was only broken after a number of arrests and the temporary suspension of constitutional guarantees. In these circumstances it is not surprising that all the old Establishment fears and suspicions of APRA were revived among Bustamante's right-wing supporters. For example, it was noted with alarm how much *Apristas* had infiltrated into the

---

[1] The Peruvian constitution guarantees to the citizen every kind of democratic right such as freedom of speech and assembly, etc. But Benavides and Prado suspended many of these rights under emergency legislation in order to keep APRA under control.

[2] *Tres años de lucha por la democracia en el Peru* (Buenos Aires, 1949).

teaching profession; it had become a common experience in the
provinces to see processions of schoolchildren, enrolled in the APRA
Youth Movement taking part in political rallies. Or again, the
right-wing press was full of stories of acts of terrorism, allegedly
committed by *Aprista* thugs, the *búfalos*.

Without a party of his own to back up his actions, Bustamante
found himself situated between two irreconcilable forces and vigorously opposed by both – APRA intent on the total capture of power;
the extreme right highly dissatisfied because he would not order the
repression of the APRA Party. The *Apristas* for their part claim
that they found it impossible to work with a President who seemed
unable to make up his mind on any course of action; and in his
weakness allowed himself increasingly to become a prisoner of his
right-wing supporters, who blocked systematically all the measures
of social reform that APRA was anxious to introduce.[1]

Meanwhile, to add to his troubles, Bustamante had inherited from
his predecessor the economic problems of inflation and shortages
which had been caused by the Second World War. No sooner did
the war come to an end than the U.S.A. cut back its purchases of
Peruvian commodities, this at a time when the suppressed demand
arising out of wartime shortages was encouraging the demand for
increased imports. Thus between 1945 and 1949 imports were consistently greater than exports, placing a heavy burden on the Peruvian exchange. In any case, by 1945 internal inflation had reached
such intensity that it had become essential to do something to curb
the drain on Peru's dwindling reserves of foreign exchange. Bustamante was faced with the choice of a major devaluation – i.e. allowing the sol to seek its true value according to supply and demand –
or an attempt to sustain the artificial rate of 6·50 soles to the dollar
by means of exchange and other controls. The latter policy was
adopted. But it did not halt the inflation. During the decade 1940–
49 the cost of living in Peru rose by no less than 262 per cent.[2]

In an effort to improve the economic situation, Bustamante in
1946 signed a contract with the unpopular International Petroleum
Co., allowing it to explore for oil in the Sechura desert in northern
Peru, on land which Benavides during his presidency had set aside
as a national reserve. In accordance with their now pro-American
policy, the *Apristas* in Congress gave this measure their enthusiastic
backing. For this very reason, no doubt, it came under heavy fire in
business circles, to the extent that the two leading right-wing Lima
dailies, *El Comercio* and *La Prensa*, joined together – exceptionally,
for on most issues they differ – in a violent attack upon the contract,

[1] This explanation was given to the author privately by a leading *Aprista*.
[2] Robinson, op. cit., pp. 400–1.

taking the nationalistic line that the Peruvian patrimony was being sold to foreigners. It is significant, however, that the brunt of the attack was directed against the hated *Apristas*; Bustamante himself was let off quite lightly for his part in this affair.[1]

The final rupture between the Establishment and APRA came with the murder on 8 January 1947 of Francisco Graña, the editor of *La Prensa*, who had taken a leading part in the campaign. This crime, which its enemies were quick to lay at the door of APRA, served as a catalyst. The politically conscious part of the population was divided into two clearly defined and strongly opposed factions – on the one hand, APRA, with its large following in the ranks of organized labour and among the white-collar workers; on the other hand, the newly formed National Alliance, consisting of elements of the right and centre together with a smattering of socialists, who found themselves temporarily united in a common determination to break what they saw as the design of APRA to create a one-party state. For tactical reasons, the small and not very influential Communist Party, which had been the object of bitter attacks by the APRA leaders, sided temporarily with the predominantly right-wing National Alliance, although it did not form a part of it.

President Bustamante found himself left with practically no organized political support upon which he could lean. While he still genuinely hoped to lead his people along democratic lines he regretfully came to the conclusion that there was no hope of democratic government for the time being, and that there must therefore be stronger government. The three APRA cabinet Ministers having resigned at the time of the Graña murder, he strengthened his administration on 12 January 1947 by appointing officers of the armed forces to five cabinet posts. General Manuel A. Odría, who had the reputation of being a strong-man, occupied the key position as Minister of the Interior.

In August 1947 the Congress ceased to function. The so-called 'independent' or anti-APRA senators absented themselves from the Senate and a quorum could not therefore be obtained for the election of a President of the Senate. By a provision of the Peruvian constitution one house cannot sit unless the other is functioning, so this action of the independent senators put an end also to the activities of the APRA-dominated House of Representatives. For the rest of his time in office Bustamante strove manfully to bring the party leaders together in order to resolve the deadlock that had arisen in Congress and, having failed in this endeavour, announced his government's decision to call a Constituent Assembly. However, before this could take place Bustamante had fallen from power.

[1] Pike, op. cit., pp. 285–6.

Forced to govern by decree, he came to rely more and more on the loyalty of the armed forces. On 31 October 1947 the cabinet was once more reorganized, Admiral Roque A. Saldías, who had a good record as a cabinet Minister in President Benavides' administration, becoming Prime Minister and with eight service officers occupying cabinet posts as compared with only three civilians. On 28 February 1948, after an abortive allegedly APRA-inspired revolt, in which junior and non-commissioned officers in the air force and the army were involved, an all-military cabinet was appointed, Admiral Saldías remaining as Prime Minister and General Odría, who had been largely instrumental in putting down the revolt, as Minister of the Interior.

These two officers, gravely disturbed by the extent to which APRA had managed to insinuate itself into the lower ranks of the armed forces, demanded that the President should outlaw the party. But Bustamante, true to his democratic faith and perhaps calculating that APRA was less of a danger when it worked in the open than it would be if forced once again to go underground, refused to act. On 17 June 1948 Saldías and Odría resigned on this issue and the cabinet was reorganized once again with civilians occupying most of the key posts.

Having quarrelled with a powerful section of the military and with APRA in open enmity against his régime, Bustamante could expect trouble from either quarter; and it was an even bet whether this would first come from the right or from the left. It came from the right. On 5 July 1948 the garrisons in Puno and Juliaca, led by Lieutenant-Colonel Alfonso Llosa, revolted. The armed forces as a whole, however, remained loyal and under the supreme command of General Hurtado the revolt was crushed.

The right having failed, it was now the turn of the left to strike. Early on Sunday morning, 3 October 1948, naval ratings, assisted by armed civilians, revolted in Callao and took control of most of the units of the Peruvian navy lying at anchor in Callao harbour. A fierce battle ensued with the air force attacking the mutinous ships, while loyal infantry and tanks dislodged the insurgents from the buildings in Callao which they had occupied. Finally, after considerable bloodshed, this new revolt was quelled. A state of siege was declared throughout the republic and on the next day Bustamante, who placed the blame for the revolt squarely upon the shoulders of APRA, signed a decree outlawing that party.

But this came too late to appease General Odría and those other officers who for more than a year had been demanding that the President should take strong action against APRA. Had they not warned the President time and time again that such a revolt was impending – yet nothing had been done to forestall it? It was only because of the loyalty and fighting spirit of the armed forces that the country had been saved from disaster. With these arguments to justify his action Odría, on 27 October 1948, raised the standard of revolt in Arequipa. This time there was no fumbling. On 29 October in Lima a deputation of military officers of high rank, led by General Hurtado, Inspector-General of the Army, and General Zenón Noriega, went to the President to demand his resignation. The latter, stubborn to the last, is reputed to have replied that he would only leave the palace as a prisoner or as a corpse. The garrison in Lima then declared for Odría; and Bustamante, still protesting that he had not resigned, was packed off to Buenos Aires on an aeroplane. On 30 October Odría arrived in Lima and took over as President of a new military *junta*.

Bustamante's experiment in constitutional government had failed. Once more the country had a strong-man in the presidential palace who had seized power by force and now proceeded to govern by decree with an all-military cabinet. APRA, whether for good or bad reasons, had failed to play a constructive part in what had promised to be a genuinely democratic and progressive régime. Its leaders once again went into hiding, prison, or exile abroad. Haya de la Torre sought asylum in the Colombian Embassy, where he remained a heavily guarded prisoner for several years. Thus, to all appearances, the clock had been put back to approximately where it had been in the time of Marshal Benavides. Indeed, the familiar cycle was to be repeated for a second time – anarchy followed by military government; the military dictator made respectable by an election; his constitutional term completed and then another election; his successor a civilian President drawn from the ranks of the oligarchy in the person of that same Manuel Prado who had followed Benavides. But, as we shall see, history never quite repeats itself, not even in Peru.

A forceful and intelligent soldier, born of middle-class parents in Tarma in the high Andes, President Odría (1948–56) was a typical example of the better type of military leader who so often in Peru has taken charge of the government in a time of turmoil. The stability of his régime, since it was a military dictatorship, depended in the last resort upon the loyalty to the President of the armed forces. In a less direct way it depended upon the support of the oligarchy. But being a man of the people himself, and with his Ministers also mostly men of *mestizo* blood, Odría was well aware of the need also to court the popularity of the people. In this he was largely successful, achieving what seems to have been a fair balance between the repressive measures required to keep APRA under control and his need to provide bread and houses, and other benefits, for the underprivileged.

His harsh law of internal security, which gave the military government complete power to deal with its enemies as it liked, was not unlike similar measures which Sánchez Cerro and Benavides had found it necessary to impose. During his eight years in power he had no serious trouble with the *Apristas*. Nor was there anything new about his attempts to help the working class – Leguía, Sánchez Cerro, Benavides, and Manuel Prado all realized that concessions must be made to labour. The new President, like his predecessors, embarked upon an ambitious and comprehensive social programme.[1] As visible evidence of this, around Lima and in the provinces new schools, new hospitals, and new housing estates sprouted like mushrooms. His wife was an assiduous social worker in the poor quarters of Lima.

In his economic policy Odría returned to the time-honoured principle of *laissez-faire* (Bustamante having introduced a system of exchange, import, and price controls which never worked very well). Like most of Peru's strong-men in the past, the President was very conscious of the latent resources of the country and the need for foreign capital to develop them – hence his desire to improve the credit of Peru in the eyes of the world. His economic policies paid off well, giving rise to an accelerated rate of industrial growth.

In 1950 Odría, like Benavides before him, decided that the time had come to make his military government respectable, and elections were held. He was returned unopposed. His two opponents, the socialist Dr Luciano Castilla and General Ernesto Montagne, representing a conglomeration of more or less left-wing groups, had their candidatures ruled out of order by the National Elections Committee.

Now constitutional President, Odría ruled Peru for his full remaining term of six years. There were some labour troubles (a general strike in 1953 was organized but broken in a matter of days). There was also a mounting trade deficit caused by his large programme of public works. But these were minor difficulties for a President who was undisputed master in his own house. Such opposition to his régime as existed was largely underground. Congress, without APRA membership, was subservient towards the executive and gave no trouble apart from a quixotic attempt by Luciano Castilla to organize a small opposition group of socialists in the Senate. It was not until 1954, when Odría announced that he would

---

[1] Odría, like Benavides, was anti-union but not anti-worker. While he gave employers what amounted to complete liberty to destroy the unions, he would give startling wage and social benefits to the workers (Payne, op. cit., p. 51).

not stand for another term, that the politicians began to raise their heads and manoeuvre for position. During this and the following year there were one or two abortive military plots, which were nipped in the bud, and a growing discontent with the régime. By and large Peru had had a good President in Odría, but at the cost of a loss of political liberty.[1] The people now wanted a change.

It is at this point that we shall see a radical departure from the normal pattern in which traditionally the departing military dictator should have handed over, by means of a carefully controlled election, to a civilian President of his own choosing. This is the way Odría wanted it to be, but he was defeated by the strength of the new popular forces which had been germinating during the long and politically sterile years of his dictatorship. He tried to form a group of 'National Unity', but found that no politicians of any weight wanted to be contaminated by any form of pact with a régime which had become unpopular and was obviously on its way out. In the end Odría did succeed in finding a civilian leader for his somewhat motley group of supporters in the highly respected lawyer Hernando de Lavalle. But the majority of the oligarchy supported the candidature of Manuel Prado who, hurrying back from Paris, had decided to make a bid for a second term.

But what really rocked the boat in this election was the sudden appearance in the lists of the youthful Fernando Belaúnde, heading a new party called the National Youth Front – later renamed *Acción Popular*. Belaúnde, an architect by profession who had entered politics during the time of Bustamante,[2] stood on a radical reform ticket, with particular emphasis on the need to do something about the plight of the downtrodden Indian peasants. It soon became apparent that he had strong support in the south (the Belaúndes come from Arequipa), and more generally among the younger generation, many of whom had become disillusioned with APRA.

Faced with this new danger from the left, both Odría and Prado turned their eyes anxiously towards the *Apristas* who, although like the communists not allowed to take any official part in the elections, had emerged from hiding and were once again playing a leading role in the trade unions, and also backing their own 'independent' candidates for Congress. If the 'independents' had supported Belaúnde he would undoubtedly have been swept into power with overwhelming popular backing. But the old-guard *Aprista* leaders were not prepared to be eclipsed by this bright comet from the south.

[1] This is the author's own assessment. He lived in Peru during the first three years of Odría's government.
[2] His father, Rafael Belaúnde, was Prime Minister in Bustamante's first government.

The orders went out that the APRA rank and file should support Manuel Prado, who was duly elected, with APRA support, but only after a very close race with Belaúnde.

At long last, and largely thanks to Manuel Prado, the *Aprista* lion and the Establishment lamb lay down together. Prado had understood that the Establishment could not win an election without some support from the *Aprista*-dominated trade unions and the urban working and middle classes. Haya de la Torre had presumably come round to the view that APRA would never get anywhere without some measure of Establishment support. Thus this marriage of convenience, or *convivencia* as it is known in Peru, had the promise of fruitful results for all concerned. Of course, to the militant left wing of the party this was a frightful betrayal, and some of the extremists deserted either to Belaúnde or to the communist camp. But the party rank and file, and its old-guard leaders, accepted a new situation philosophically. Many of them were now well on in middle age and their political views had mellowed with the passing of the years. Moreover, the political atmosphere of 1956 was very different from what it had been in 1931. Then the urban working and middle classes had been hungry. The people were in a mood for revolution. But in 1956, thanks to the combination of *Aprista* agitation and the intelligently benevolent social policies of Benavides, Prado, and Odría which this had stimulated, the working class in the cities was now relatively prosperous. It was the voteless Indians in the countryside who were the forgotten men of Peru. Most of the people in the cities were content to live within a capitalistic system provided that their standard of living would continue to improve. Thus the change in APRA's line towards a policy of moderation reflected quite accurately a corresponding change in the mood of the party's most important supporters.

With Prado back in the presidency all might seem to have returned to normal. But the political map of Peru had been turned upside down.

Chapter 15

The Rise and Fall of
Fernando Belaúnde

I   The Presidential Candidate

IT MAY BE DOUBTED whether the average observer – businessman, journalist, or diplomat – living in Peru in 1956 would have seen that any very fundamental change had occurred in the political situation as a result of that year's election. On the contrary, with the conservative Manuel Prado back in the presidency, an ever-watchful army in the background as a further insurance policy, Haya de la Torre apparently a reformed character, and the young Fernando Belaúnde stopped in his tracks, the immediate prospects for the Establishment had seldom looked so good.

Moreover, most of the business indicators were pointing upwards. Having quickly recovered from the ill-effects of Bustamante's weak period of government, the economy had made remarkable progress in the last eight years under Odría. A few random statistics will suffice to show the extent of the changes which were taking place. In the decade 1950–60 electrical power production increased 1·50 times; mining 2·28 times; and manufacturing industries 1·69 times.[1] Indeed, hardly a month went by without some new factory coming into production. Towards the end of Odría's time this accelerated rate of growth had created stresses and strains in the economy, causing headaches for the government and a good deal of industrial unrest. But these troubles were no more than the result of the too rapid economic expansion; there was no reason why, with good management, the economy could not quickly be brought back under control.

Of course, if one wanted to delve beneath the surface, there were also some disquieting statistics to be found, which Fernando Belaúnde kept digging up during his travels in the hinterland – awkward facts such as that the population (now some 12 million) was growing so fast that there was not enough food in the country to maintain an adequate diet for the Indians, nor enough land or jobs to give them employment. But the comfortably situated people in the

[1] Robinson, op. cit., p. 327.

coastal cities, most of whom had never visited the *sierra*, had lived for so long with the 'Indian problem' in their backyard that it hardly entered their consciousness. Even foreign diplomats, tied to the social round in Lima, were apt, after a few years of service in Peru, to take the Indian situation for granted; if they were prudent they would end their general political despatches with the warning note that one day there must be trouble in the *sierra*, but without suggesting that there was any particular imminence about the danger.

It was thus under a more or less cloudless political sky, but with some urgent economic problems to be tackled, that Manuel Prado took office again. As a change from the previous military régime, his government consisted of civilians, except for the Ministers of the three armed services. Unlike Odría's mostly dark-complexioned *mestizo* Ministers, the cabinet was recruited almost exclusively from the creole upper class – if they had been Englishmen they would have been wearing Old Etonian ties.[1] Prado's aim in choosing this gentlemanly team was to satisfy the public demand for a government of high calibre which would improve administrative standards, restore individual liberties, and pursue a non-contentious programme. But he had to walk very delicately, with his support coming from two such diverse sources as the oligarchy and the *Apristas*. He had somehow to pursue a social policy which would not offend the business community, but at the same time be progressive enough to enable the APRA leaders to show their rank and file that co-operation with the government had its rewards. Significantly, the first acts of the new Congress were to legalize APRA, repeal the internal security law, and grant amnesty to all political prisoners. Only the Communist Party remained illegal in accordance with Article 53 of the constitution, barring all parties directed from abroad.

Rather surprisingly, in view of Haya de la Torre's failure to find common ground with men like Benavides and Bustamante, the new relationship between the *Pradistas* and APRA worked very smoothly. There is, of course, nothing like a common enemy to make the most unlikely partners work together; for now Belaúnde's *Acción Popular* constituted the spearhead of the left-wing opposition in Congress, with the tacit support of the communists who lay outside the law. Once one gets over the initial shock, remembering the past history of APRA, it is possible to see that in many ways this *convivencia* between APRA and Prado was a sensible arrangement. The labour movement stood to benefit in a practical way, since the government

[1] For example, Prado's first Minister of Finance was the aristocratic Juan Pardo, son of President José Pardo and grandson of President Manuel Pardo, the founder of the *Civilista* Party.

now had to lend an attentive ear to its demands. The APRA labour leaders, for their part, would not normally wish to push their demands to the extent of bringing the government into discredit. A considerable degree of harmony in labour relations therefore seemed likely. Against this advantage, however, the enforced mildness of APRA labour leaders in their disputes with employers would inevitably provide an opening for more militant leaders drawn from the ranks of communism or *Acción Popular*.

Prado himself seems to have been more interested in foreign affairs than in domestic politics. He liked to cut a figure on the international stage. He had always had a great admiration for both France and Britain, and was anxious, partly as a means of reducing Peru's dependence on the U.S.A., to draw closer to these and other European countries. In 1956 he promulgated what came to be known as the Prado Doctrine[1] – a somewhat vague scheme which envisaged a drawing-together of the Latin American republics and the countries of Europe in order to make common cause against totalitarianism. Later on during his term of office, in 1960, he paid an official visit to London and in return the Duchess of Kent and Princess Alexandra visited Peru.

But troubles at home soon diverted the President's thoughts from the more congenial problems of international diplomacy. Prado always had bad luck when it came to economics. His first government had been plagued by the shortages caused by the Second World War. Now, in 1958, he was to be plagued once again by a continuing bout of internal inflation, which caused domestic prices to rise and resulted in serious discontent. There were over 200 strikes in that year and a series of violent incidents and riots which shook the government and the credit of the country.

All this was grist to the mill of the *Belaúndistas* in Congress and the communists outside who, between them, increasingly began to challenge the position of APRA as the party of the people among the students and in the trade union movement. In April 1958 the city of Cuzco, in the heart of the southern Andes, was taken over by what were probably communist-inspired rebels, their cause being supported by Belaúnde's *Acción Popular*, as also by the normally right-wing *El Comercio*. Here was another striking example of *convivencia* on the opposition side. In the following year constitutional rights had to be suspended during a two-month long strike of bank employees and Belaúnde was imprisoned for a time.

However, the year 1959 saw a turn in the economic tide. Prado in desperation had called in as doctor one of his most persistent

[1] So-named by the French Foreign Minister, Christian Pineau, who enthusiastically supported Prado's initiative.

critics, Pedro Beltrán.[1] He was appointed Prime Minister in July in place of Gallo Porras who resigned.

Under Beltrán's able, if conservative, management the always resilient economy staged an impressive recovery: public expenditure was kept under control; the budget balanced; exports increased; and both the cost of living and the exchange rate were stabilized. But while he had excelled as an economic manager, Beltrán came under increasing criticism for his failure to make much progress in housing or push through Congress the Land Reform Bill for which all the popular parties were clamouring.[2] Beltrán resigned on 3 November 1961, being succeeded by Moreyra y Paz Soldán as Prime Minister of a caretaker government before the new presidential election. The strength of the new political forces which had emerged so dramatically in the last decade – and created a completely new political pattern – would now be put to the acid test of the popular vote.

The three principal candidates in this election were Fernando Belaúnde, representing *Acción Popular*; Haya de la Torre, the leader of APRA; and General Manuel Odría, who had returned from abroad to make a second bid for the presidency. Also putting up candidates, who had no chance of winning but were nevertheless of some importance politically, were the Christian Democrats and various splinter groups of the extreme left.

Since his defeat in 1956, Belaúnde had been campaigning continuously, visiting every corner of the country by aeroplane, motorcar, on mule-back, and even on occasions shooting the rapids of the jungle rivers in a canoe. No previous presidential candidate had taken so much trouble to get to know his own country and see for himself the problems of the people in its most remote corners. While in opposition Belaúnde had created an impression of being something of a radical, but if one examines his books and speeches it is apparent that he was never really very far to the left.[3] Indeed, there

---

[1] Beltrán received his economic training in the London School of Economics. As a disciple of Adam Smith, he was a strong upholder of old-fashioned principles of sound finance.
[2] The problems of agrarian reform in Peru are discussed in Chapters 18 and 19. Beltrán's ideas on this subject were conservative. Under his 'Peruvia' plan of March 1960 the settlement of landless peasants in the *selva* was to be encouraged. Under a law submitted to Congress in the same year (but never enacted) the size of landed estates was to be limited to 250 hectares on the coast and 1,000 hectares in the *selva* (R. J. Owens, *Peru*, London, 1963, p. 59).
[3] Belaúnde's political doctrine is to be found in his two books, *La conquista del Perú por los peruanos* (Lima, 1959) and *Pueblo por pueblo* (Lima, 1960).

was very little of ideological substance which separated the thinking
of the principal parties – they were all agreed that the basic problems of Peru were hunger, land-shortage, education, and housing,
for which the obvious remedies were agrarian reform, economic
development, schools, houses, and communications. If they differed
it was largely in relation to method and personalities.

Although perhaps a radical by Peruvian standards, Belaúnde had
shown in his campaign no interest in any form of doctrinaire socialism. In the south he had the backing of the local communists, but
he always made it clear in his speeches that he was opposed to international communism and intended to have no truck with it. He
aspired neither to overturn nor to replace the existing order, but
rather to put the established institutions to work and not leave them
inactive, as he claimed had happened while Prado was in power.
What was needed, he argued, was an overall plan for the economy
and to establish priorities for the country's development. He was
particularly keen on the idea of building roads to open up and
colonize the vast untapped region of jungle (the *selva*) to the east of
the Andes. He saw clearly that credit must be obtained if this plan
was to become feasible and he promised, if elected, to mobilize both
internal and international financial resources. But perhaps the most
attractive and distinctive feature of Belaúnde's political philosophy
was his belief that Peru should look back to her Incaic past for
inspiration. Each remote village in the Andes must work as a community to improve its conditions, building its own school or access
road, or whatever else might be needed. The central government
would provide technical assistance under his scheme of *cooperación
popular*, but the initiative and the hard work must come from the
people themselves. The title of his book in which these ideas were
put forward, *The Conquest of Peru by the Peruvians*, sums up his
political philosophy.

The Christian Democrats gave the impression of being somewhat
more extreme and doctrinaire than *Acción Popular*, but they had
no leader with Belaúnde's popular appeal. This party had been
founded by former supporters of the ill-fated President Bustamante
– men like Dr Correa Elías, a career diplomat who had been Bustamante's Foreign Minister; Dr Luis Bedoya Reyes, a future mayor of
Lima who had run Bustamante's propaganda; and Hector Cornejo
Chávez, now the leader of the party, who had been Bustamante's
personal secretary. While there were in fact considerable differences
of view within the party – Cornejo Chávez represented its left wing
– the official party line was one of equal hostility to both the oligarchy and communism.[1] The Christian Democrats stood for social

[1] For the political theory of the Christian Democrats see Hector Cornejo.

justice, planning, agrarian and tax reform (including a more highly graduated income tax). The party was not against private enterprise as such, but held that it must be guided by the state so as to fulfil a social function; foreign investment would be welcome, but it must not expect too many privileges. In short, the Christian Democrats appeared to favour a mixed economy. In certain special cases they were not averse to state-owned enterprises – for example, they supported the nationalization of the unpopular International Petroleum Corporation.

From the foregoing brief description of the political programmes and philosophies of *Acción Popular* and the Christian Democrats, it will be obvious that both parties between them had stolen a good deal of the thunder from the *Apristas* who had suffered persecution, imprisonment, and exile for preaching very similar doctrines over the last thirty years. That is no doubt why Haya de la Torre and the APRA leadership resented these upstart interlopers so much: they were trespassing on APRA preserves; worse still, they sought to snatch the prize of office from the one man, Haya de la Torre, whose sacrifices in the cause of social justice and reform surely now at long last deserved to be rewarded.

Haya de la Torre is an intriguing and controversial figure – in public a rabble-rouser, in private a man of great personal charm and intelligence. For thirty years, mostly behind the scenes, he has played a leading part in the political life of Peru and, at the same time, more than any other Peruvian, has achieved an international reputation in social democratic circles abroad. He still holds in a remarkable way the loyalty of his many supporters in Peru. But during his long and turbulent career he has made many powerful enemies. The Peruvian army has never forgiven him for his alleged complicity in various incidents affecting the discipline and loyalty of the armed services. This prejudice proved once again to be a fatal handicap to the cause of APRA in the election. For otherwise, in spite of the new competition from the left, APRA, especially in the north of the country, was still extremely strong, because of its control over most of the trade unions. Belaúnde's strength, in contrast, lay mainly in the south and among the younger generation. However, of the two parties APRA had the best organization, with its cadres of disciplined party members who had been hardened by so many bitter struggles in the past.

Odría's soldierly political philosophy was embodied in the slogan 'Deeds not Words'. He promised order and an undying hostility to all forms of communism, two things which would appeal to the

Chávez, *Nuevos principios para un nuevo Perú* (Lima, 1960) and *Que se propone la democracia cristiana* (Lima, 1962).

business oligarchy; but at the same time he offered enough social progress to please the workers. Indeed, as regards social reform, his promises were just as generous as those of his competitors. Although a military man, he was not the choice of the army. The younger generation of army officers – and this was perhaps a sign of the times – favoured Belaúnde more than any other candidate. That amorphous body the oligarchy was split asunder in this election. There was no oligarchical candidate as such. Some businessmen supported Odría; others, having seen the practical advantages of *convivencia*, favoured APRA; and a few adventurous members of the business community were prepared to take a risk on Belaúnde and *Acción Popular*. There was, however, little business support for the Christian Democrats, whose doctrines were not of the sort to appeal to believers in the virtues of untrammelled private enterprise.

Finally, out in the wilderness on the extreme left were the communists and various other exotic splinter groups. These extremist elements were of some importance marginally, being able to command perhaps about 100,000 votes throughout the country, and with the ability as well to cause a good deal of trouble to any government in power by stimulating peasant land invasions and small-scale guerrilla activities in the mountains.[1] There were strong communist cells among the students in many of the universities.

The election was held in June 1962, and those with the right to vote – 2 million who had passed the literacy test out of a population of 12 million – trooped to the polling-booths which were heavily guarded by watchful soldiers. On 30 June the following results were announced by the National Electoral Jury:

Haya de la Torre	33·0% of the votes
Belaúnde	32·0% of the votes
Odría	28·5% of the votes
Other candidates	6·5% of the votes

These results showed that each of the three principal candidates had a more or less equal following, but in different parts of the country – Haya de la Torre mainly in the north (the traditional *Aprista* stronghold) and around Lima; Odría in Lima, where he and his wife had made themselves very popular with the working class, and in certain provinces which had benefited most from his programme of public works; Belaúnde mainly in the south with his strength centred upon Arequipa and Cuzco. Haya de la Torre had a slight edge over his two competitors, but just lacked the one-third of the votes necessary to obtain the presidency. According to the constitution, it was now up to the new Congress to elect the President.

In the congressional elections APRA had come out the leading

[1] See below, Chapter 18.

party with 114 seats, *Acción Popular* in second place with 78 seats, the *Odriistas* with 42 seats, and the various other small parties of the left with 7 seats. Since the supporters of Odría were unlikely to side with Belaúnde, it looked like a foregone conclusion that Haya de la Torre would be elected President if the members of Congress were allowed freely to exercise their choice. But the army chiefs were determined to keep out Haya de la Torre at all costs. Immediately upon hearing the results they published charges that there had been electoral frauds in the APRA northern stronghold and requested that the National Electoral Jury should re-examine the matter. Belaúnde joined in this demand for a re-check of the results. But the National Electoral Jury refused to budge, claiming that they were satisfied that the elections had been fair. President Prado, too, refused to take any action in support of the army's request.

In this situation of deadlock there followed a series of private conversations between the candidates and the chiefs of the armed forces in order to seek a compromise solution. Haya de la Torre, realizing that the army was against him, appears to have been the most conciliatory of the three candidates. Belaúnde, apparently confident of ultimate victory, retired to Arequipa where, in a dramatic gesture, he had trenches dug in the streets and erected barricades around his party's headquarters. Haya de la Torre then entered into conversations with Odría, and at the last moment it looked as though, after some hard bargaining, agreement would be reached for APRA to support their old enemy, the general, for a second term in the presidency. But it was now too late. Opinion in the army had hardened in favour of military intervention. On 18 July 1962 tanks pushed open the gates of the palace and President Prado was arrested in front of his whole cabinet. He was then taken to Callao and interned comfortably on a ship in the harbour where he spent the last ten days of his presidency as a prisoner. He was released on 29 July and left by air for Paris on 1 August. Meanwhile, the Joint Command of the Armed Forces, headed by General Pérez Godoy, took over the government of the country. The elections were annulled.

In Washington, where APRA was held in high esteem and still regarded by American liberals as 'the wave of the future', the news of this military *coup d'état* was received with consternation. President Kennedy denounced it as a setback to the Alliance for Progress and forthwith suspended diplomatic relations and military and economic aid. Venezuela, whose democratic government lay under a similar threat of military intervention, supported by the Dominican Republic, Honduras, and Costa Rica, proposed a meeting of American Foreign Ministers to discuss policy towards régimes established by *coups d'état*. But the principle of non-intervention is engrained in the Latin American philosophy and the proposal was rejected by the Organization of American States after a debate on 10 August. Meanwhile, the military takeover was received quite calmly in Peru. Belaúnde and his supporters were content to bide their time. A general strike organized by *Apristas* quickly collapsed and there were no reprisals; the trade unions were not molested in any way. The military *junta* not only respected the freedom of the press and other civil liberties, but promised that new elections would be held in 1963, with no obstacles put in the way of the successful candidate. On the strength of these assurances, the United States government resumed diplomatic relations and economic aid on 17 August, although military aid was not restored to Peru until 12 October. Great Britain, in accordance with her normal diplomatic practice,[1] had already recognized the new government, without waiting for a lead from the U.S.A.

For the next year Peru was ruled by a triumvirate of theoretically co-equal officers. The leading spirit was Pérez Godoy, a soldier of progressive views who was convinced that the army could do a better job than the politicians in tackling the problems with which the country was faced. Such a 'Nasserite' attitude towards politics is common enough among the military in Latin America today. The new *junta* entered upon its self-appointed task with vigour. A new agency, *Instituto de Planificación*, was established to draw up a National Development Plan. One of the first fruits of the *junta*'s development programme (a scheme first proposed by the Prado government) was a major hydro-electric project on the Mantaro river, for the construction of which a preliminary contract was awarded to an Anglo-German consortium.[2] Agriculture, too, was given high priority, with the emphasis on colonization schemes and technical training, and credit facilities for small farmers. When challenged by an outburst of illegal peasant invasions of *haciendas* in the valley of La Convención, near Cuzco,[3] the *junta* acted with admirable restraint, realizing that the invasions could not be halted by force, but that the problems of the peasants needed urgently to be tackled. Many of the measures which the *junta* put forward to deal with this situation were later incorporated into Belaúnde's agrarian reform law of 1964.[4] Nor were urban problems neglected. A new

---

[1] In the British concept, diplomatic recognition does not imply moral approval of a foreign government. It merely recognizes the fact that a government (however chosen) is in effective control of the country concerned.

[2] But, alas, after many vicissitudes, Belaúnde's government gave the final contract to an Italian group.

[3] See below, pp., 222–4.

[4] See below, Chapter 19.

agency, *Junta Nacional de la Vivienda*, together with a housing
bank, was established in order to deal with slum clearance, workers'
housing, and the problems of the squatter settlements.[1]

So far so good. But in early 1963 – with the new election already
in view – political storm-clouds began to gather. In January there
was a communist witch-hunt, and a large number of suspects were
arrested. In March, Pérez Godoy was replaced on the *junta* by
General D. Nicolás Lindley, a hard-headed descendant of Yorkshire
ancestors. According to his enemies Godoy had begun to display
dictatorial tendencies. (It must indeed have been frustrating for an
ambitious man to have only a year in which to complete his task of
national renovation.) With Godoy's departure – and he went peacefully – the reforming zeal of the *junta* (there were rumours that
Godoy had wanted to expropriate the oil industry) noticeably declined.[2] However, to its credit, these internal troubles did not prevent
it from carrying out its promise to hold new elections in June 1963.

The three principal candidates were the same as in the previous
year, but there was an important difference in the line-up of the
parties. Belaúnde, realizing that he was too weak to go it alone, had
entered into an alliance with the Christian Democrats, while most
of the extremists, instead of supporting their own candidates, decided
to back Belaúnde. This additional support from the extreme left was
sufficient to give Belaúnde an edge and secure for him more than
the one-third of the votes required for victory. The results were as
follows:

Belaúnde	39·0% of the votes
Haya de la Torre	34·0% of the votes
Odría	25·5% of the votes
Others	1·5% of the votes

Thus, Belaúnde, on his third attempt, just scraped into the presidency, and this time the army were content to accept the verdict of
the people. But it was a narrowly won victory which promised
trouble for the future, since Belaúnde's supporters, even including
his unreliable left-wing allies, did not command a majority in the
new Congress. The results of the congressional elections had been as
follows:

	Senate	Deputies
APRA	18	58
Acción Popular/Christian Democrats	20	50
Unión Odriista (UNO)	7	27
Independents	—	5
	45	140

[1] See below, Chapter 20.　　[2] Pike, op. cit., p. 302.

Thus Belaúnde's 'Alliance' could be outvoted at any time by a combination of *Apristas* and *Odriistas*, who formed a 'coalition' to consolidate the predominance of the opposition.

The new pattern of politics which emerged in 1963 consisted of an uneasy balance between two political blocs of roughly equal strength, the one in control of the executive and enjoying the support of the army, the other in opposition and with the predominant voice in Congress. The old unhappy polarization between left and right had for the time being disappeared. APRA had now assumed a mantle of bourgeois respectability; indeed it was very difficult to detect any significant difference between its ideology and that of Belaúnde's *Acción Popular*. Both parties were based on middle- and working-class support and, in Peruvian terms, represented some advance towards the left, but not to an extent seriously to threaten or frighten the oligarchy. If they differed it was mainly in their popular images. APRA, with its long history of strife and compromise, had begun to look somewhat tarnished. Haya de la Torre, a heroic figure from the past, had become the Grand Old Man of Peruvian politics. Thus, in 1963 a considerable proportion of the younger voters, who in the past would probably have supported APRA, rallied to the cause of Belaúnde. In early middle-age, handsome, and with his Messianic belief in the future of Peru, coupled with his deep concern for the well-being of the under-privileged, he seemed to offer to his fellow countrymen the prospect of a break from the familiar cycle of alternate military and oligarchical rule – perhaps even a move at long last in the direction of a more broadly-based, democratic, and socially progressive society. But this hope (like that which was felt for a moment in 1945 when Bustamante was elected President) has not been realized.

II   Belaúnde in Office

AT FIRST ALL WENT QUITE WELL for Belaúnde, in spite of his lack of political support in Congress. His popularity was demonstrated in December 1963 when he carried out his electoral promise of holding municipal elections throughout the country – the first to be held for many years. His supporters in *Acción Popular* and among the Christian Democrats won a stunning victory even in the north, where the position of the *Apristas* was supposed to be impregnable. In the capital the opposition put up as their candidate for mayor of Lima the popular María Delgado de Odría, renowned when First Lady for her charitable work. But she, too, was roundly defeated by Belaúnde's supporter, the Christian Democrat Luis Bedoya Reyes, who resigned as Minister of Justice to take part in the contest.[1]

[1] See above, p. 183.

Soon after he had assumed office, Belaúnde discarded the various extremist left-wing groups who had supported his candidature. Adopting a middle-of-the-road policy, he sought to obtain the agreement of the *Aprista/Odriista* opposition to a minimum programme of action. In 1964 Congress, with *Aprista* support, approved a somewhat watered-down but nevertheless important Agrarian Reform Law,[1] but there was little or no co-operation on most other matters. Throughout his term of office the opposition parties in Congress did everything possible to make life difficult for Belaúnde, blocking his measures, refusing to pass his budgets, and using the congressional power of interpellation to dismiss his Ministers. (It became something of a record if any of Belaúnde's Ministers held their jobs for more than six months.[2]) Belaúnde, a man of sincere democratic convictions, showed exemplary patience under great provocation. In spite of his undoubted popularity in the country at large he made no attempt to challenge the power of Congress or restrict its activities, as so many Presidents in the past had done. Nor did he call upon the army for help. He steadfastly resisted any suggestion that he should appoint an all-military cabinet which Congress would not have dared to molest and persevered fruitlessly in his attempts to come to terms with the opposition.

Fitting almost exactly the specification of the democratic and socially progressive political leader who was expected to carry the torch of the Alliance for Progress in Latin America,[3] Belaúnde was more fortunate in his international relations. The developed countries of the world – the U.S.A., Britain, Germany, France, Japan, Canada, and even smaller countries like Israel, Denmark, and Finland, actively competed to be associated with his ambitious plans for developing Peru by means of roads, irrigation, hydro-electric projects, and so on.[4] When it comes to bilateral national aid from one country to another there is usually a commercial motive behind the offers, since such government-to-government grants or long-term loans are normally tied to the purchase of goods by the recipient from the country providing the finance. By this means the donor

[1] See below, Chapter 19.
[2] The Peruvian Congress has the right to interpellate Ministers who must resign if they are censured.
[3] See below, p. 267.
[4] See below, pp. 233–4. 'Competition' may seem an odd word to use in the context of foreign aid; for, in theory, the motive behind international and national aid programmes is charitable – the rich nations holding out a helping hand to the poor. International aid, provided through such channels as the World Bank, is indeed designed with no other object than to assist the recipient country in areas of development where such assistance is most needed.

countries assist their own export trade.[1] In Peru, during the time of Belaúnde's government, the many major engineering works projected under the development programme created a potentially lucrative market for foreign capital goods of every kind. International competition to obtain a share of this business became intense.

This enhanced international interest in Peru as a profitable field for investment and trade was marked by such unprecedented events as the visits to Lima by President Lübke of West Germany in January 1964; President de Gaulle in September of the same year; and the British Foreign Secretary, Michael Stewart, in January 1966 – the first time in history that a British Foreign Secretary had set foot in South America. The visit of President de Gaulle – a tremendous *tour de force* and a great compliment to Peru – especially thrilled the Peruvians. Even so, Belaúnde kept his head. In one of his speeches of welcome to de Gaulle he remarked that Peru had two loves – a love for France because of her culture; love for the U.S.A. because of her economic power. The Peruvian attitude towards the realities of power in the world could not have been more succinctly put.[2] In fact, during Belaúnde's time, Peruvian relations with the U.S.A. were somewhat clouded by a dispute with the International Petroleum Company.[3] American aid flowed into Peru in considerable quantities, but not perhaps to the extent that it would have done without this cloud on the horizon.[4] Not that relations between the two countries were ever really strained. The United States Ambassador, J. Wesley Jones, was held in high esteem in Peru. If in private Belaúnde was sometimes heard to complain about American aid – he made the same complaint about the international lending agencies – it was not because the amount of money offered was too small, but because of the red tape involved in such transactions. Belaúnde was a man in a hurry when it came to his much-cherished development plans.

Although foreign capital was pouring into Peru at a satisfactory rate, there remained the difficult problem of how to finance such an ambitious programme of development and social betterment without causing internal inflation, especially since the opposition in Congress refused consistently to sanction any tax increases. In 1965 the first signs of serious inflation – an increase in the cost of living of 15 per cent – began to cause concern in financial circles. As had happened frequently enough in the past, this latest bout of inflation was

[1] In 1966 the British government made a tied loan to Peru of £500,000 for the purchase of bridging equipment.
[2] The author has quoted this remark from memory.
[3] See below, pp. 194–6.
[4] According to Pike, op. cit., pp. 318–19.

caused by an increase in public expenditure, resulting in heavy budget deficits. It was the familiar phenomenon, which Pedro Beltrán in his newspaper *La Prensa* had nicknamed the *maquinita*,[1] of the government, unable to finance its expenditure by taxation, subsisting by means of loans from the central bank; in other words, by an expansion of the money supply, which in its turn brought about a secondary expansion of credit. Internal inflationary pressures inevitably had repercussions on the balance of payments, by creating a greater demand for imports on top of the demand already created by the process of industrialization and the heavy programme of public works.

Adding still further to the pressure on the balance of payments was the heavy outflow of official exchange in order to service the rapidly mounting foreign debt. Leguía during the eleven years of his dictatorship is estimated to have increased the Peruvian foreign debt by about $100 million in order to finance his development programme. Belaúnde, for the same worthy object, increased it by more than five times that amount, from a figure of $187·4 million in 1962 to an estimated 742·2 million in 1968. As a result, the annual payments to cover amortization and interest on these loans increased from $39·4 million to 140·8 million. Much of this money was loaned to Peru by international agencies such as the World Bank, the International Development Bank, etc., on suitably long and easy terms of credit. But more than $200 million represented advances by private suppliers, often on relatively unfavourable terms. Just before Belaúnde's downfall, his Minister of Finance, Manuel Ulloa, was busy visiting the major financial capitals of the world (including London) in an effort to negotiate the refinancing of Peru's foreign loans on more favourable terms.

On 1 September 1967 the exchange rate of 26·82 soles to the U.S. dollar, which Belaúnde in the previous April had promised to sustain, could no longer be maintained and the Central Bank withdrew its support from the exchange market. In early October a dual exchange market was established with a system of exchange certificates for exports and imports and a free market for other transactions. The rate for certificates was fixed at 38·70, i.e. a devaluation of 30 per cent. Meanwhile the free rate floated steadily downwards. In the autumn of 1968 it had reached a low point of 47 per U.S. dollar – a depreciation of about 57 per cent.

In a desperate effort to mend his political fences – his relations with Congress were now at their worst – Belaúnde appointed as Prime Minister the First Vice-President, Edgardo Seoane, a man of rather left-wing views who was Secretary-General of *Acción Popu-*

[1] The little machine pouring out unbacked paper money.

lar and was already being tipped off – presidential elections were due in 1969 – as Belaúnde's probable successor. To balance this appointment and appease the oligarchy, two leading lights from the business community, Tulio de Andrea and Pablo Carriquiry, were appointed to the key Ministries of Finance and Development. It looked like a good combination; but it did not work. Seoane's plans for remedying the economic situation, which included such unpopular features as a real-estate tax, a tax on the capital of limited liability companies, a revised income tax structure, and a total ban on the import of luxury goods, were much too radical for the opposition's taste and were rejected. Tempers became heated. A violent attack on the government's financial policy was launched in the newspaper *Correo*, owned by the fish-meal king, Luis Banchero Rossi. Belaúnde's favourite project of the *carretera marginal*[1] was criticized in Congress and he retorted by calling his critics 'defeatists' and 'deserters'; speculators against the sol were described as 'delinquents'.

Towards the end of 1967 the political crisis came to a head with the resignation of Seoane as Prime Minister and his replacement by the more moderate Dr Raúl Ferrero. Seoane was annoyed because Belaúnde, in November, had held two 'summit' meetings with the opposition in an effort to secure support for the government's economic measures. Not only did Seoane resign from the government, but he and his left-wing followers in *Acción Popular* withdrew their support from Belaúnde, the Christian Democrats having taken a similar step in November. Thus Belaúnde's 'Alliance' ceased to be. The one-time popular President had become almost entirely dependent upon the goodwill of the *Apristas* in Congress.

In March 1968 the new government introduced, in conjunction with the budget, a series of fiscal and related measures – higher profits tax and reduced exemptions from customs duties; restrictions on commercial bank credit; new hire-purchase regulations; new conditions for public-sector borrowing abroad; a prohibition on the soliciting of Peruvian investments in mutual funds or deposits abroad; and a 90-day suspension of non-essential imports. In the following month a new list of prohibited imports was decreed, together with a 15 per cent surcharge on non-essential imports and a consumption tax on imported goods and those with a high import content. This decree (No. 173) and the accompanying proposals for new taxation on real estate and companies' net worth were received with such hostility by commerce, industry, and the opposition parties as to cause Raúl Ferrero to resign together with his entire cabinet.

[1] See below, pp. 230–2.

A new cabinet was formed under Dr Osvaldo Hercelles and with a prominent businessman and financier, Manuel Ulloa, as Minister of Finance. At the end of June the unpopular decree No. 173 was cancelled and replaced by new emergency legislation providing for increased taxation, both direct and indirect, but with some substantial concessions made to meet the complaints of business: import restrictions were to be maintained until March 1969; a 10 per cent surcharge on non-essential imports would be reduced by stages during 1968; the 10 per cent export tax would be replaced by a bond issue subscribed by exporters; a freer use of exchange certificates would be allowed to ease pressure on the free market. Meanwhile, as a sop to nationalistic sentiment, the legislation affecting the position of foreign banks in Peru was tightened. These proposals met with the approval of the *Aprista* opposition in Congress, but were unpopular in left-wing political circles. Anyhow, they came too late to save Belaúnde.

In the early morning of 3 October 1968 – a little more than five years after the Peruvian people had freely chosen Fernando Belaúnde as their President and eight months before the end of his legal term – tanks of the Peruvian army broke through the wrought-iron gates of the palace. The President was hustled off to the airport by a posse of colonels (without even being given time to put his reading-glasses in his pocket) and thrust, protesting, into a plane bound for Buenos Aires. Later on the same day, General Juan Velasco Alvarado, Chairman of the Joint Armed Forces Command, took over as President and appointed an all-military cabinet. The new military government justified its action by claiming that Belaúnde in office had proved himself incompetent to govern and had allowed the country to fall into economic and administrative chaos. Nationalism, morality, and authority were to be the watchwords of the new régime.

According to one persistent rumour the underlying cause of this military takeover was fear that, with Belaúnde discredited and his supporters in disarray, the army's bugbear, Haya de la Torre, with his strongly entrenched APRA still intact, would emerge victorious at the next elections. A simpler explanation is that, having witnessed the decline in Belaúnde's economic and political fortunes, the soldiers quite genuinely came to the conclusion that the discipline and patriotism of a military government were needed to clean up the mess. In any case a pretext for military intervention was provided by the storm of protest at Belaúnde's unpopular agreement, concerted in August 1968 with the International Petroleum Co., concerning the La Brea and Pariñas oilfields.

The ownership of the surface and sub-surface rights in this extensive oil property in northern Peru was acquired in 1924 by the American-owned (but Canadian registered) I.P.C. by purchase from the British London and Pacific Petroleum Co. Between 1911 and 1915 the Peruvian government issued three Supreme Decrees which sought to bring the property in regard to taxation and other matters under the terms of the mining laws, but the British company disputed the legality of these measures. In 1921 the British and Peruvian governments agreed to submit the dispute to international arbitration, and in the following year, in Paris, a decision was handed down by the arbitrators which was favourable to the company. President Leguía agreed reluctantly to accept the terms of the arbitration on behalf of the Peruvian government, but they were never ratified by the Peruvian Congress.

Nationalist opinion in Peru has never accepted 'the *laudo* of Paris' and various arguments have been put forward by Peruvian lawyers and politicians to support the view that it is not legally binding on Peru, and that therefore since 1924 the I.P.C. has been enjoying tax exemptions and other privileges to which it was not entitled under Peruvian law. On these grounds, it has been calculated that I.P.C. owes the Peruvian government the astronomical sum of 690 million dollars in back taxes. So intense is the feeling on this subject that in Peruvian politics the I.P.C. has become like a red rag to a bull, and the wildest accusations have been made against the company. Whatever may be the rights and wrongs of the case in both law and equity, passions run too high for this to be a subject which can any longer be discussed or dealt with objectively in Peru.

In the course of the elections of 1963 Belaúnde promised that he would 'vindicate Peru's rights over the La Brea and Pariñas oilfields', and it was his attempt to keep this promise which five years later led to his downfall. He was faced with the choice either of expropriating the properties, which would have been the popular thing to do, or negotiating a new agreement with I.P.C. on more favourable terms. To expropriate would have meant for Belaúnde to risk a first-class row with the U.S.A., upon whom he depended very greatly for development finance. So, after a good deal of backing and filling, he chose the path of negotiation. The agreement reached with I.P.C. in 1968, after five years of bargaining, was that Peru would acquire the ownership of the La Brea and Pariñas property – hence vindicating her rights as Belaúnde promised – but at the same time a contract was signed for the sale of 80 per cent of its crude oil to I.P.C.'s Talara refinery. The government also cancelled its claim for tax arrears from I.P.C. on the understanding that the American company would expand its Talara refinery.

When the terms of this agreement became known there was a tremendous outcry from both leftist and right-wing groups in Congress. It was set off by the resignation of Loret de Mola, the president of the government-owned oil company (E.P.F.), who complained that the agreement was over-generous to I.P.C. Later an element of scandal was introduced into the controversy when Loret de Mola accused the government of deleting the final page of the crude-oil contract which had contained important safeguards for E.P.F. Belaúnde, who five years before had been such a popular figure, found himself with scarcely a friend in Peru. On 2 October, in a vain attempt to retrieve his now desperate political position, he appointed a new cabinet, with the somewhat unlikely figure of Manuel Mujica Gallo (famous for his collection of Inca gold objects and hunting trophies) as Prime Minister, but with Manuel Ulloa still at the Ministry of Finance. But this last of Belaúnde's administrations survived for less than twelve hours. On 3 October 1968 President Velasco Alvarado took office; the next day the much criticized agreement of the former government with the I.P.C. was cancelled; on 9 October, designated as 'A Day of National Dignity', the military government expropriated the oilfields in dispute together with the I.C.P.'s refinery at Talara.[1]

[1] The international repercussions of this event are discussed in Chapter 22. The chapters which follow describe in more detail the many problems – economic, social, political, and international – which led to Belaúnde's downfall and now face the new government.

Part Four

PROBLEMS AND PROSPECTS

Chapter 16

Problems of Economic Development

THE STRIKING CONTRAST between the strength of the Peruvian economy in most of its normal outward manifestations and its fundamental inner weakness is a natural and perhaps inevitable result of the peculiar geographical configuration of the country. In its three constituent zones – the irrigated valleys of the Pacific coastal desert, such fertile country as can be found in the high mountains of the *sierra*, and in isolated clearings of the jungles of the *selva* – are to be found every kind of soil, climate, and altitude, producing a wide variety of crops such as sugar, cotton, rice, coffee, maize, barley, etc., as well as an abundance of tropical fruits. In the highlands there are vast areas of grassland suitable for cattle. Both the desert and the mountains are rich in minerals – silver, lead, zinc, copper, iron ore, petroleum, etc. From the cold waters of the Humboldt current comes the raw material of a very large fish-meal industry. Yet, in spite of this abundance of riches, Peru is a poor country even by Latin American standards.[1]

Although she is the fourth largest of the Latin American republics (after Brazil, Argentina, and Mexico), with an area of 1·3 million square kilometres, less than 2 per cent of her land (just over 2 million hectares) is cultivated. This narrow base has to support 12 million people. Moreover, both the population and the wealth are very unevenly distributed between the three geographical zones. Eighty per cent of Peru's industry is concentrated on the Pacific coast, but this region supports only a favoured 33 per cent of the population, whose income per head is double the national average of about £100. In the *sierra*, where 53 per cent of the population are concentrated – the majority illiterate peasants – the average income is estimated to be no more than £30 or £40 a year, a figure so pathetically small as to be virtually meaningless in European or North American terms.[2] Perhaps a better way of putting it is to say that something like one-third of the 12 million inhabitants of Peru live virtually outside the market economy.

[1] The Peruvian environment was described in Chapter 1.
[2] C. T. Smith, Article on Peru in *The Times* Special Survey, 13 September 1967.

Despite this fundamental inner weakness, the Peruvian economy in the twentieth century has shown an inherent strength and buoyancy which augurs well for the future, provided that sound economic policies are followed. During the period 1950–65 the gross national product increased by 128 per cent; in recent years the growth rate has averaged about 6 per cent – one of the highest in Latin America. This compares with an average growth in the population of 3 per cent.[1] In short, although it may be low and very unevenly distributed, the average income per head of the people is steadily improving. It must be noted, however, that this very satisfactory progress has been the result almost entirely of private enterprise – of private investment both national and foreign. Until the financial crisis of 1967–68 successive Peruvian governments in the twentieth century, with one short lapse under Bustamante, adhered religiously to the principle of economic liberalism, avoiding the imposition of controls on foreign trade and payments, and indeed with a minimum of interference in the economy. This policy of *laissez-faire*, although unfashionable in the modern world, has certainly produced good results for Peru in the past, and has become accordingly an article of faith for all but a small minority of the Peruvian business community. It has also been popular abroad and largely accounts for the good international credit which Peru has enjoyed in recent years.

Essentially the strength of the Peruvian economy lies in the diversity of its export products – minerals, cotton, sugar, and, since 1950, fish-meal – all of them the fruits of private enterprise, both foreign and national, and depending for their sale on international credit and world markets. The figures are truly amazing – a 250 per cent increase in exports between 1950 and 1965. However, although there is no reason to be gloomy about the future, it may be doubted whether such a high rate of expansion can be maintained in future years. A well-informed forecast in 1967 suggested that exports will show a 6 per cent annual rise over the next four years as against 9 per cent over a similar period in the immediate past.[2]

The most astounding increase, which in part explains the recent high rate of growth, has been in the fish-meal industry. Starting more or less from scratch in 1950, fish-meal accounted for no less than 44 per cent of Peruvian exports in 1965, a bonanza reminiscent of the guano boom in the nineteenth century. Some quick fortunes have been made in this industry, and there have also been quite a few bankruptcies caused by inadequate and too optimistic local

[1] Rómulo A. Ferrero, 'Peru's Economic and Financial Situation', *Bank of London and South America (B.O.L.S.A.) Review*, Vol. 1, No. 6.
[2] *B.O.L.S.A. Review*, Vol. 1, No. 11, pp. 601–8.

financing. The fish-meal industry is no longer expanding rapidly; indeed it is likely to shrink as the multiplicity of small plants go out of business. But there is no reason to expect in the foreseeable future a decline in export revenue from this source. When plans for the manufacture of fish protein and the creation of modern fishing ports and refrigeration plants have been completed, it may well be that an important domestic demand for fish products will develop to supplement the export trade. At present only rich men in the cities eat fresh fish; and, if they want to keep their appetite, they are wise not to inquire too closely into the primitive way in which the fish is handled both on the trawlers and in the ports before reaching the customer's plate.

Agricultural exports accounted for 28 per cent of the total in 1965. The backbone of the agricultural export sector of the economy is the traditional, well-run cotton and sugar estates on the coast, many of them owned and managed today by companies rather than individuals. Any substantial increase in the output of coastal agriculture depends upon the success or otherwise of the various irrigation schemes now in hand and the unpredictable future of international price-levels for these crops. Where there is probably more room for expansion of agricultural exports is in such tropical and semi-tropical products as coffee, rice, palm-oil, and so on, whose cultivation in Peru may be expected to increase if and when plans for developing the resources of the *selva* come to fruition. Here again, however, prices depend on highly volatile world markets, and there is a great deal of competition from other exporting countries.

The third important source of export revenue is mining, which in 1965 accounted for 27 per cent of the total, i.e. a figure more or less equal to that of agriculture. It is mining, however, which would seem to have the most exciting possibilities for expansion in the 1970s. Many Peruvian fortunes have been made and lost in mining ventures large and small. However, when it comes to large-scale mining operations, which require a great deal of capital in a country of Peru's ruggedness, the field is dominated by a handful of big U.S.-owned and managed corporations. The oldest, founded in the early part of the twentieth century, is the Cerro de Pasco Corporation, a major producer in the central Peruvian highlands of copper, lead, and zinc. For a long time this corporation was the giant of the Peruvian mining industry, but in recent years a number of other major companies have begun to compete for the title. For example, at Toquepala, 60 miles west of the port of Ilo, at an altitude of 11,000 feet, the Southern Peru Copper Corporation has opened up one of the largest low-grade copper deposits in the world at a cost of $237 million. With perhaps even richer deposits available for exploitation at another site, Cuajune, it is estimated that Peru's copper production could increase threefold by 1974. A third major mining enterprise in Peru is the Marcona Mining Company, which exploits the extensive iron-ore deposits on the coast near Nazca, about 250 miles south of Lima. It has been estimated that these deposits may contain over one billion tons of ore. Finally, there are ambitious plans afoot to exploit the phosphate deposits in the Sechura desert in northern Peru. The Kaiser Group, who are undertaking this task, envisage an annual output of 2–3 million tons, with full production being reached in 1971. The investment may amount to $100 million, and the annual value of exports could reach $25 million.

Obviously, foreign investment on this scale depends not only on the state of world markets for metals (which in the last decade have been very favourable to Peru), but also on Peruvian mining legislation, which until now has been reasonably liberal in its treatment of foreign corporations. For this reason, the international financial community will no doubt be pondering very carefully the implications of the military *junta*'s action in expropriating the oil properties of the I.P.C. Although it is too early to reach any firm conclusion, it is to be hoped that this isolated act of xenophobia does not presage any fundamental change in Peru's traditional benevolent attitude towards foreign capital. I.P.C. has always been regarded in Peru as a special case. Moreover, it must be remembered that the oil industry in Peru is today more a domestic than an export industry, since the fields in the region of Talara are getting old, while the domestic consumption of petroleum products has steadily risen. Not that it would be wise for Peru to ignore the possibility of important new oil deposits being discovered both on the coast (experiments are being made with off-shore drilling) and in the jungles to the east of the Andes, where in the past a number of wild-cat wells have been brought into production. It will be interesting to see how energetically, and by what means, exploration for oil will be carried out under the new conditions.[1]

While exports are the traditional source of wealth of the Peruvian oligarchy – they account for some 15 to 20 per cent of the gross national product – there are nevertheless many wealthy Peruvians, and a number of foreign firms, who have found it profitable to invest in local industry. Compared with the Big Three of Latin America (Brazil, Argentina, and Mexico), Peru has been a late starter in industrial development. But impressive progress, almost amounting to an industrial revolution, has been made since the end of the Second World War. In 1965 industry accounted for 17 per

1 See below, pp. 269–70.

cent of the g.n.p., a figure which at that time was only 3 per cent less than that of agriculture; truly the factory has come into its own in modern Peru. Already most of the obvious possibilities for import substitution have been exploited, covering such fields as food, beverages, tobacco, textiles, footwear, clothing, leather and rubber goods, cement, glass, ceramics, and so on. Now the tendency is to move into more sophisticated industries such as chemicals, ship-building, engineering, steel, and petroleum. The phosphate deposits in the Sechura desert and petroleum provide the basis for what ought to become a flourishing chemical industry. Fish-meal has created the demand for locally built trawlers and their equipment; indeed, Peru, with the help of British shipwrights, is now building her own oil tankers. On the side of engineering, most of the leading motor manufacturers now have their local assembly plants; and there is even – perhaps rashly since it has never paid its way – a state-owned steel corporation with a rolling-mill at Chimbote. The most recent and most ambitious venture is the takeover by the Peruvian state oil company of responsibility for managing the greater part of the national petroleum industry through all its successive stages of exploration, production, refining, and marketing.

Industry, as it has grown up so far, is heavily and unhealthily concentrated in the Lima-Callao area, which is responsible for some two-thirds of the gross value of industrial output. Ringed by something like 3,000 factories, Lima now has a population of 2 million. Efforts are being made to remedy this situation by the setting-up of tax-free industrial estates in provincial cities such as Arequipa and Tacna. The estate in Arequipa – the second largest city of Peru and the most important industrial centre in the south – was already fully booked in 1967 with sixty-two factories, and there is no reason why similar results could not be obtained elsewhere. For example, the city of Piura in the north would seem to have excellent prospects for industrialization, being situated close to the phosphate deposits in Sechura and the oilfields of Talara, and with road communications across the Andes with the rich tropical valleys of Marañón.

In its development, Peruvian industry has enjoyed the advantages of abundant labour and ample sources of relatively cheap power. With so many torrential rivers, the Andes have a tremendous potential for hydro-electric development, with the added advantage that in many cases schemes for producing electrical power can be combined with irrigation. There are also important, but still largely untapped, reserves of natural gas and coal. In spite of these assets, Peruvian industry, as in most developing countries, is still something of a luxury – 'status-symbol' is perhaps a better description. It could only have come into being on its existing scale behind the protective wall of high tariffs and with the encouragement of tax concessions. Protected from foreign competition, Peruvian manufactured products are expensive and not always of high quality. With one-third of the population virtually outside the money economy, the market for manufactured goods in Peru is limited to the towns and in most lines provides much too narrow a base for anything like mass production.

There are probably not many responsible Peruvians today in business and banking circles who would disagree, at any rate in theory, with the eminent Peruvian economist Rómulo Ferrero,[1] when he asserts that the first problem of the country, social as well as economic, is to integrate the *costa* with the *sierra*, and develop the *selva*. Fifty-one per cent of the population are engaged in agriculture, but it contributes less than 20 per cent to the g.n.p. According to modern 'structuralist' economic theory, it is axiomatic that the existence side by side in a country of an archaic and inefficient peasantry and an emergent modern industrial society is bound to cause distortions in the economy. It leads to such undesirable phenomena as an increasing shortage of home-grown food (which therefore has to be imported, to the detriment of the balance of trade), the mass migration of uprooted peasants to the towns at a rate far beyond the capacity of industry to absorb them, industrial output limited by the smallness of the market, and, as a final and fatal result, inflation.

A British economist, C. T. Smith,[2] sums up the problem of Peru in the following terms: 'the land and its productivity are the keys to economic betterment of this predominantly peasant society. . . . In the long run, the rehabilitation of the sierra population and the modest participation of the highland farmer in a cash economy will do most to raise the levels of internal demand within Peru and thus to stimulate further urban and industrial growth as well as the profitable and stable colonization of the empty east.'

This view is supported by Ferrero when he says that what is required is 'concerted action in road-building, education, efficient agrarian reform to increase the low farm productivity, and aid for modernization of the primitive Indian communities'. It is, however, when the practical ways and means of bringing about these desirable results are discussed that the economists, the bankers, the businessmen, and the politicians find themselves in disarray. How far? How fast? By what methods? These are the fundamental questions of policy which have to be answered in Peru, and underlie most of her current political troubles.

[1] Ferrero, op. cit.
[2] Smith, op. cit.

Belaúnde is not the first President of Peru to come to grief by trying to do, perhaps with rather too much enthusiasm, what both Smith and Ferrero have diagnosed must be done. In the nineteenth century President Balta over-extended the country's economy with his too rapid building of the railways. President Leguía, also, tried to do too much in the way of development on the shaky foundation of onerous foreign banking loans, and his financial edifice came crashing down in 1930 when hit by the World Depression. And on a less dramatic scale other Presidents have found themselves up against similar economic problems. José Pardo was faced with the shortages and rising prices of the First World War; Manuel Prado and Bustamante had to cope with the inflationary conditions caused by the Second World War; as recently as 1960 Manuel Prado, during his second term, had to call in Pedro Beltrán. The latter deflated drastically, to the detriment of the social improvements, in housing, agrarian reform, and so on, for which at that time the politicians were agitating. The luckiest Peruvian Presidents in recent times have been Benavides and Odría. Both dictators ruled their country during periods when the international terms of trade for Peru were exceptionally favourable, and so were able to carry out major development programmes without causing excessive inflation. The dilemma remains, however, that Peru can never have a really healthy economy until the infrastructure has been modernized and greatly expanded; but no way has so far been discovered of bringing about a sufficiently rapid rate of expansion while maintaining conditions of monetary stability.

The financial crisis which resulted in Belaúnde's downfall was the result of a downturn in export earnings (copper and fish-meal) combined with excessive governmental expenditure on the development programme. The President's financial advisers believed until the end that the exchange rate of the sol could have been saved in 1967 if Congress had been prepared to pass the necessary legislation to increase customs duties and export and other taxes, as the government had requested. In all countries taxation is a sore subject. Ask almost any businessman in Peru, foreign or Peruvian, and he will tell you without a blush that the burden of taxation is already much too heavy in a country whose future depends so much on private enterprise. Writing in 1967 before the devaluation, Rómulo Ferrero[1] noted gloomily – and he was in favour of a national development programme – that although between 1950 and 1965 taxes in Peru had increased from 11 to 15 per cent of the g.n.p., this had been inadequate to meet the 'excessively' rapid growth of public expenditure. By contrast, the report of Milton C. Taylor, Director

[1] Ferrero, op. cit.

of a Fiscal Mission to Peru of the Joint Tax Program of the Organization of American States and the Inter-American Development Bank, is instructive.[1] He complains that 'in Peru elaborate development plans have been made without serious thought given to the problem of financing them'. Noting that a mere 10 per cent of the population receive 60 per cent of the country's income, and a tiny minority of wealthy men (0·25 per cent) put 35 per cent of the total income into their pockets, he comes down in favour of a more equitable distribution of income and wealth by such means as taxes on real property and net wealth, death and gift taxes, increased income tax, corporation tax, etc., instead of relying, as had increasingly become the practice in Peru, mainly on indirect taxes which in 1963 accounted for 65 per cent of the revenue collected. 'All this', he writes, 'is a tall order to ask of any country. It is obvious that none of these reforms can be easily introduced either technically or politically. But something else should be equally obvious – unless fiscal reform of this magnitude is undertaken, Peru cannot have an open, viable and non exploitive society. . . .'

The indications (in early 1969) are that the new military government will seek to re-establish Peru's reputation for monetary stability and sound but unspectacular economic growth within the framework of a free economy. Its immediate concern is to refinance the foreign debt and balance the budget, thus assuring monetary stability. The programme of economic recovery presented by the new government to the I.M.F. is said to be substantially similar to the one presented by Manuel Ulloa, and none of the taxes imposed by the former government towards the end of its term have been repealed. Meanwhile it has been emphasized that foreign capital will be welcomed in Peru – the oil expropriation being a case apart and the result of special historical circumstances.

On the other hand, while a policy of sound finance is to be the watchword, the soldiers have made it clear that they are well aware of the political and social side of the equation – in particular the urgent need to improve the standard of agriculture and the lot of the peasants. The new Minister of Agriculture, General José Benavides (a son of the Marshal), has said that his aim is to make Peru agriculturally self-sufficient and thus avoid the heavy drain on foreign exchange reserves (estimated at about $150 million in 1969) caused by the import of food. As short-term measures imports of lamb and dairy products will be restricted and the sale of beef is prohibited on two days a week. The longer-term plans of the government envisage the establishment of food-processing and refrigera-

[1] Milton C. Taylor, 'Taxation and Economic Development – A Case Study of Peru' (*Inter-American Economic Affairs*, Vol. 21, No. 3, 1967).

tion plants, a continuation and intensification of agrarian reform, the development of the agricultural potential of the *selva*, and an increase in the supply of fish for human consumption. The agricultural landholdings of the Cerro de Pasco Corporation (valued by the corporation at $12 million) are to be expropriated and distributed, together with its herds of sheep and cattle, among the local communities of the region.[1]

In short, the new government evidently intends to embark on fundamental structural reforms in society, with economic recovery as the necessary preliminary.[2] What remains to be seen, however, is whether it will be possible to achieve a fast enough rate of social progress to satisfy the demands of the people and politics, while maintaining the economy on an even keel. In order to study the social and political aspects of the problem of development it is necessary now to leave the economists, the bankers, and the businessmen, as they pore over figures and charts in their comfortable skyscraper offices in Lima, and take a journey into the high Andes. If only in spirit, the unbelievable ruggedness of this mountainous region has to be experienced in order to appreciate the depth of poverty and hopelessness in which the Indians are sunk, and the formidable problem of their emancipation.

[1] *B.O.L.S.A. Review*, Vol. 2, No. 24, pp. 675–8.

[2] Since the above was written the Peruvian government has introduced a radical agrarian reform programme (see page 237 footnote). Also, according to recent newspaper reports, plans are afoot to nationalize the communications network (telephones, etc.) and possibly also the supply of energy. A commission has been appointed to draw up a national fisheries policy. In short, there is every sign that the new military leaders of Peru intend to live up to their claim to be a 'revolutionary' government (see also Appendix).

Chapter 17

The Indian Peasantry

Belaúnde has described in moving terms how, when he was campaigning for the presidency in 1956, pitiful delegations of Indians awaited him in every township of the *sierra*, having travelled long distances over mountain-trails in order to seek his aid. His petitioners, it must be emphasized, were not militant agitators waving banners and shouting slogans. As of old the Indians might have prostrated themselves in supplication before the all-powerful Inca, the provider of all good things, so these groups of humble villagers, the elders carrying their silver-mounted staffs of office and dressed in their traditional garb, greeted the presidential candidate with all the honours due to a great chief before laying their troubles at his feet. Their needs were simple – enough land to support their families; a roof over their heads; protection against the depredations of the local landowner; or perhaps help over some cherished scheme for a village school, a road to the nearest market-town, a bridge over the neighbouring gorge, a dam across the river.

Belaúnde, while still on tour, made a rough and ready calculation of the cost of these requirements, multiplying the average figure for each region he had visited by the 1,400 district capitals of the country, and came to the agonizing conclusion that to satisfy all these demands, however modest they might seem to be in their local context, would be far beyond the financial capacity of any Peruvian government.[1]

From this experience was born his plan for a two-tiered approach to the problems of the Indian peasants. Because of the limitations of finance the central government should attempt no more than to provide the essential elements of the rural infrastructure, building the highways so badly needed to open up the country and under-taking major works of irrigation and colonization. It must also, of course, concern itself with such national problems as education, health, and agrarian reform. But below this level of essential govern-mental action, proposed Belaúnde, the Indians themselves must be mobilized to play the major part in the tremendous task of their

[1] Fernando Belaúnde, *La conquista del Perú por los peruanos* (Lima, 1959).

208

own emancipation. If a village wanted a school, then the people must get out their tools and build it themselves – at the most the government would supply a teacher and some books. The same principle would be applied in the case of such things as access roads, local irrigation works, terracing, sanitation, and so on. The hard labour must come from the people through voluntary effort. The government would supply no more than the essential equipment, plus such technical assistance and advice as might be needed. For the success of this imaginative plan for self-help in the villages (*cooperación popular*) Belaúnde relied very largely on the tradition of mutual assistance and co-operation, which had been the basis of Inca society, and still survives in the Indian communities in the practice known as *aine*.[1] A people whose ancestors had created the remarkable communal structure of the Inca state, Belaúnde argued, must surely be capable of a similar achievement today, given competent leadership and all the advantages of modern technology.

Such was Belaúnde's dream when he took office in 1963. The fact that only a small part of the dream had been realized when he fell from power five years later does not necessarily mean that his vision was at fault. It does, however, underline the tremendous difficulties of a problem compounded of so many deep-seated and interrelated evils – low agricultural productivity, extreme poverty, inadequate standards of nutrition and health, illiteracy, ignorance, superstition, and perhaps worst of all, a stubborn refusal by many Indians to try to come to terms with the modern world.

Even the term 'Indian', as it is commonly used today in Peru, is an obstacle to progress. In spite of the glory of the Inca past, it has come to be the label of a second-class citizen. Although constituting some 40 per cent of the population, the Indians do not feel themselves to be a part of Peru, and indeed many of them do not appear to want to have any part in what they regard as an alien whiteman's world. This attitude of mind – resentful, suspicious, defensive, and resistant to modern ideas – is not, however, fundamentally the result of racial prejudice as such; the division in Peru is more social and economic than of blood and skin-colour. A so-called and self-styled Indian may quite likely have some white blood in his veins – he is an Indian because he lives like one. On the other hand, a *mestizo* may be a pure-blooded Indian. He enjoys what he considers to be the superior status of *mestizo* because he has broken with the Indian past and adopted the modern way of life, perhaps by recruitment into the army, or by going to work in a mine or on a coastal farm, or by migrating to the city. Many sociologists see in this process of 'mestization' the eventual solution of the country's social and

[1] See below, p. 218.

racial problem. But 'eventual' is the operative word. Mestization is
in large measure the product of industrialization, and there is a
limit to the extent and speed with which an underdeveloped and
fundamentally agricultural country like Peru can be transformed
into a modern industrial state.

Thus the Indian peasantry survives and will continue, and it
remains faithful to a primordial way of life which is the despair of
social reformers, but over thousands of years has shown a remarkable capacity to survive. Even in his agriculture, the very basis of
his livelihood, the Indian is intensely conservative. For example,
although four centuries have elapsed since the Spanish conquest,
he has never taken to the European plough, but prefers to use the
native digging-stick and clod-breaker which have come down to him
from pre-Inca times. True, his crops, depending on altitude, now
include such European plants as wheat and barley in addition to
the indigenous potato, maize, quinoa, etc., but he has never adopted
the European, money-making, attitude towards his farming activities. If left to his own devices he will produce no more than is
needed to support his family. Nor will he readily modernize his
agricultural technique. In the Indian villages there is a way and
time for doing everything as fixed as the stars in their courses.
Mishkin,[1] for example, gives some fascinating glimpses of the super-
stitious ritual which accompanies every activity of the Indian
farmer. Offerings of coca and liquor are made periodically to the
earth. Dates of planting are determined by the phases of the moon,
the full moon being regarded as particularly inauspicious. When
there has been no rain the children are sent out into the fields as
good Christians to recite the *Misericordia*. However, to make
doubly sure that the gods will get the message, they are also expected to weep copiously, in the belief that, by sympathetic magic,
the heavens will be induced to do likewise. The communal digging
of the land is a ritual in which those who take part work to a regular
rhythm, wielding their digging-sticks in unison like guardsmen on
parade. As they work the men keep time by singing a chant. At
prescribed intervals there is a break when the owner hands out a
ration of coca to his helpers. Similar rituals are observed at the time
of sowing and harvest.

The herding of domestic animals forms a more or less important
part of the activities of most Indian farmers, depending upon altitude. In high altitudes, especially in southern Peru, herding is the
principal activity of the community; the land is for the most part
left uncultivated. The coarse *ichu* grass of the high *punas* is edible

[1] Bernard Mishkin, 'The Contemporary Quechua' (*Handbook of the South
American Indians*, Washington, 1946), Vol. 2, p. 425.

only for the llama and the alpaca.[1] In the vast empty spaces of the *puna*, under the cold gaze of the snow-clad mountains, lonely herdsmen, wrapped up to their eyes in their *ponchos*, guard their small flocks of these supercilious-looking creatures. It is a bleak existence, but the Peruvian Indian is never defeated by nature. The wool from the back of his animals keeps him warm; the coarse tufted grass of the *puna* is used to thatch the roof of his house. The dried dung of his llamas is burnt as fuel.

At lower altitudes, where crops such as alfalfa can be grown, horses, mules, donkeys, sheep, goats, and cattle are raised. However, large-scale ranching is only possible on the *haciendas*, some of which cover hundreds of miles of country. The average Indian is not likely to own more than a few scrawny animals. A common sight in the Andes is the convoys of heavily laden mules and donkeys (the llama is not much use as a pack-animal[2]) picking their way delicately along precipitous mountain paths. In prehistoric times the Indians never invented the wheel, and even today wheeled vehicles are a rare sight once the main highways have been left behind. Indeed, many of the poorer Indians still act as their own beasts of burden. As in Inca times, they trot along on bare feet almost doubled up under the incredible loads they manage to carry on their backs.

With inadequate land to make a decent living, and exploited either by the landowners or the *mestizo* middlemen in the towns, the standard of life of the Indian peasants, whether owning their own land in a community or working in an *hacienda*, is extremely low. The houses usually have only one room and lack windows and furniture. At night the whole family, including the smaller domestic animals such as dogs and guinea-pigs, huddle together in the cold with the skins of llama laid out on the pounded earth floor to serve as beds. The two frugal meals a day, eaten at sunrise and sunset – luncheon is provided only on special occasions – consist mainly of potatoes, usually taken in the dehydrated form of *chuñu*, and various kinds of grain preserved in the same way. Fresh meat is virtually never eaten; occasionally some dried meat, *charqui*, may be thrown into the family cooking-pot, from which every morning and evening there emerges a thick stew heavily seasoned with chilli. This diet, which is almost entirely lacking in fresh vegetables, citrus fruit, butter, and fats, is deficient in protein and its calorific content is a long way below normally acceptable standards. Thus, as a result of under-nourishment, combined with poor hygiene, the conditions of health in the Indian villages are deplorable. Even so, by some

[1] The vicuña, with its valuable fur, also runs wild in the *puna* – it has never been domesticated.
[2] A llama can only carry a load of 65 lbs. and soon tires.

miracle, the birth-rate greatly exceeds the death-rate, so that the Indian population is increasing on Malthusian lines on a much too rapid scale.

To keep themselves going, the Indians regularly chew coca, a plant cultivated on the eastern slopes of the *cordillera*. The cocaine content of the leaves produces indifference to hunger, pain, cold, and weariness; indeed, the drug has become a necessity of life in the Andes.[1] The Indians also occasionally drown their sorrows by drinking *chicha*, a potent liquor distilled from maize. It is not uncommon to enter a village and find almost all the men drunk. However, as in all his activities, there is a traditional time for drinking; it is considered perfectly proper and indeed right that a man should get drunk on a market-day or when celebrating a fiesta. But an Indian peasant on his own land will seldom be drunk on a working-day.

Illiteracy, especially among the adults, is still widespread in the Andes. In 1940, in six departments of the *sierra*, 72 to 88 per cent of persons fifteen years or over were illiterate. Eighty to 88 per cent of the children between six and fourteen had never attended a school. Today the figures for adult illiteracy are probably somewhat better, and certainly a lot more of the children now have the chance to go to a primary school. In his mid-term message to the nation on 28 July 1966, President Belaúnde claimed that out of a school population of 2,329,920 children only 123,020 or 5·3 per cent lacked the opportunity to attend a school. But he was speaking, of course, about the country as a whole. The left-wing writer Víctor Villanueva[2] claimed that only 25 per cent of the children attended school in the province of La Convención, near Cuzco, and 79·6 per cent of the population over seventeen years of age were illiterate.

The problems of establishing schools in the remote regions of the *sierra* are formidable. The *haciendas* are bound by law to provide them, but this obligation is often evaded; it is not in the interests of the landowner that his Indians should be educated. And although the Indians are increasingly clamouring for schools in their villages, many parents are reluctant to allow their children to attend them – especially the girls – because they are wanted to work at home. Nor does the existence of a school in a rural area ensure that the children will derive much benefit from their education. They often have to travel on foot many weary hours each day in order to reach the nearest school. The teaching is usually of poor quality, without ade-

---

[1] In 1946 7 million kilograms of coca were consumed, syphoning off an important part of the Indian income which might otherwise have been spent on food.

[2] Victor Villanueva, *Hugo Blanco y la rebelión campesina* (Lima, 1967).

quate books or equipment. Most Indians are brought up to speak Quechua or some other native Indian language, but the lessons are in Spanish. In all these circumstances many Indian boys and girls, who may just manage to learn to read and write in Spanish in a halting way, soon lose the art when they return to the grinding toil of their normal lives. In short, rural education is caught up in a vicious circle. The economic conditions of the people are too bad to allow the schools to flourish; but the economic conditions cannot be improved until the Indians receive some education.

Having examined some of the grim facts of the economic and social infrastructure, it is a relief to turn for a moment to the more pleasing aspects of the Indians' life. For if one's social conscience can be held in check nothing can be more pleasurable than to wander in the homeland of the Indians. The superb grandeur of the scenery; the colourful markets and fiestas; the rich harvest of ancient lore to be garnered; the pleasure of 'getting away from it all' and tasting the flavour, without experiencing too much of the discomforts, of an older primordial world – there is something to please almost every traveller's taste.

The most important Indian markets, in towns such as Huancayo or in the vicinity of Cuzco, can be reached without difficulty by tourists, but a horse or a jeep is needed to visit the more typical markets which are held periodically in every village. Often combined with religious fiestas, these markets and fairs are the principal social event of the countryside, providing a break from the weary toil of the fields. On these festive occasions the Indians can be seen enjoying themselves in the finery of their traditional costumes. Behind a picturesque façade the squalor of Indian life recedes temporarily into the background.

The Indians travel long distances to the market, driving their laden mules or donkeys, or carrying the produce on their backs. Once there, the men enjoy themselves drinking, while the women do the trading. Each woman sits impassively before her wares – which may consist of no more than a little pile of potatoes, or a few ears of corn – spread out on a *poncho* on the ground. The transactions are usually petty, and much of the business is done by means of silent barter. However, there are certain goods, such as coca, aniline dyes, hats, and textiles, which today are usually sold for cash.

In the more important markets the visitor can admire the wide range of arts and crafts to which the Indians, both men and women, devote any time which can be spared from the fields. One stall may be displaying beautifully hand-woven *ponchos* and blankets. Another will contain a rich assortment of pottery – bowls, jugs, and dishes and decorative pieces, large and small, representing almost anything from bulls, horses, and llamas to replicas of churches. There is practically nothing required by an Indian that is not home-made – cloth and baize, straw mats and baskets, wooden spoons, footwear, halters, skins, straw hats, decorated gourds, and ornaments of every kind. Nor should the visitor fail to inspect the stalls which cater for the needs of the village *brujo* with their strange assortment of reme-dies – dried-up parts of animals and foetuses, herbs, minerals, coca, sea-shells, and coloured earths – which all have their place in the Indian's medicine chest. Of course, in the larger markets in the towns there will also be on display factory goods and other products from the coast, brought in by *mestizo* traders, who buy the produce of the countryside such as eggs, poultry, grain, skins, etc. In return they sell to the Indians city-produced goods such as kerosene, aniline dyes (which are largely ousting the native vegetable dyes), matches, coca cola, blue jeans, and so on. Thus it is not quite true to say that the Indians live outside and contribute nothing to the national economy. What is true is that they do not contribute nearly enough or get enough in return for their labours.

Sooner or later, if he is lucky, the traveller in the *sierra* will come upon a village which is celebrating its Saint's Day. The programme begins at dawn with solemn Mass in the church, after which an effigy of saint or Virgin is walked in pious procession around the streets. Having paid this tribute to Christian religion, the fun begins. To the music of percussion and woodwind instruments of Inca vintage, masked Indians dance to a pagan rhythm until nightfall. The masks may depict the anthropomorphic jaguar of Chavín times or be imaginative caricatures of Inca high officials, Spanish conquistadores, landowners, judges, priests; indeed of anybody who figures either as a hero or a villain in the Indian folklore. In these dances, as the Indians become more and more drunk, there is a good deal of horseplay. But the underlying theme is serious. In the combination of Christian and pagan ritual the Indian expresses his deepest feelings. In his religion – which is described as 'a loose jumble of beliefs, ideas and practices, disconnected and unsystem-ized'[1] – doctrine is rudimentary and mysticism notably absent. For example, the Christian ceremony of baptism is valued for the practical reason that it is believed that the child who dies unbaptized will haunt the community and keep away the rain. Marriage is regarded as lucky; after several years of cohabitation most couples get married in church as soon as they have saved enough to pay for the ceremony. Ritual, whether Christian or pagan, is performed for the strictly practical purpose of ensuring that the results of toil will

[1] Mishkin, op. cit., p. 462.

be blessed and defended from evil powers. As for ethics, the Indian equates morality with traditional custom. To be wicked is to break the custom; the good man follows it slavishly.

A British writer[1] who has travelled widely in the Andes sums up the Indian character in the following terms. The children, he notes, are intelligent and alert; but the adults, especially the men, tend to look blank and stupid. In part this appearance of apathy is the cumulative effect of undernourishment and overwork, combined with the dull hopelessness of a life which offers no consolation and no prospects of improvement. But it is also, Osborne believes, to a considerable extent an unconscious protective measure against the encroachment of an alien influence. The Indian has no interest in the white man's world and no desire to understand it. If it is thrust upon him he shuts his mind against it, assuming a mask of blank stupidity.

However, in his own natural habitat – among his own people – the Indian is very far from being stupid. In natural and agricultural lore he has the slow but sure practical intelligence of the typical countryman. In his arts and crafts he combines manual dexterity with artistic taste. He may not be much interested in money or profit, but he has a deep attachment to the land. In his dealings with his own people he is dignified, ceremonious, and considerate. He has a strong feeling of loyalty both to his family and to his own community, and a tradition of mutual aid and co-operation in the working of the land and in other matters of communal concern. But his loyalties are essentially local. Neither Osborne nor Mishkin could detect any feeling of national consciousness among the Indians.

Here then are some solid qualities of character on which to build. The major problem of any reform programme for the Indians is to break through the psychological barrier which shuts them off from the white man's world, and to devise measures adapted to their skills and aptitudes which do not destroy, but can be grafted on to, the body of traditional custom to which the Indians cling. There are, however, signs that the isolationist shell in which the Indians hide themselves is beginning to soften. Osborne and Mishkin were describing conditions in the 1940s. The shower of petitions which descended upon Belaúnde when he was electioneering in 1956 suggests that the apathy and suspicion of the Indians, which have been noted by so many observers in the past, are gradually being replaced by 'rising expectations' and a desire for some of the amenities of modern life. Indeed, it could hardly be otherwise. As the new highways pierce their way up the Andean valleys, as more Indian children go to school, with transistor radios blaring the message of the

[1] Harold Osborne, *Indians of the Andes* (London, 1952), pp. 201–36.

twentieth century in almost every village store, with city-made goods invading the rural markets, and above all with the tales taken back to their families by Indians who have migrated to the towns, isolation from the modern world is becoming impossible even in the most remote corners of the mountains. But of more immediate importance politically – its implications will be examined in the next chapter – is the rising clamour of an increasingly landless peasantry for land. The humble Indian petitioners, who so meekly put their troubles to Belaúnde in 1956, have been replaced in some parts of the Andes by well-organized syndicates of militant peasants who have shown themselves ready to take the law into their own hands if their hunger for land cannot be satisfied in any other way. It may be premature to say that 'a wind of change' is blowing in the Andes. But the barometer is certainly pointing to changeable weather ahead.

Chapter 18

'Land or Death'

IF, AS SO MANY WRITERS have depicted it, the Inca empire was an Indian paradise, this was only because every peasant in the realm was allotted enough land to make a bare living. The Indian may have been as poor then as now, but as a landowner he was a contented man. Today in the *sierra* only a lucky minority of the Indians possess their own land and live in their own free communities. Virtually all the best land has long since been absorbed by the great estates (*haciendas*), on which the majority of the Indians, without possessing any land of their own, are forced to work under conditions of feudal serfdom.

Those fortunate Indian communities which have managed to survive with their land intact are usually descended from pre-Inca *ayllus*, or at least date from colonial times. The classical system of land tenure has disappeared, however, as a result of the republican legislation which made each head of family the outright owner of his own plot. Instead of the communal land being reassigned periodically for the use of individuals on the basis of family size, as was the practice in Inca times, it now passes through inheritance to offspring. Thus today, some members of the community have relatively large holdings, while others have become virtually landless as the result of successive sub-divisions among children. There is, however, still some control maintained in the community over the pattern of landholding. To ensure crop-rotation, the land is divided into separate lots, or *suertes*, and the council of village elders decides when they should be cultivated or lie fallow. Ideally each family should have a smallholding in several *suertes*, the most valuable land being that close to the water on the valley bottoms, the least productive the non-irrigated plots on the hillsides. In addition, for grazing purposes, the Indians usually own lots in the *puna*, probably thousands of feet above the level at which their village is located.

In some communities there are still lots of land set aside for the upkeep of the municipality and the local saint, recalling the Inca's tripartite division of the land between peasant, Church, and state. In others, although the land is no longer redistributed periodically

among the families, the ritual of land assignment has been retained.
Each year the governor of the district (a *mestizo* representative of
the central government) visits the community in order to reaffirm
the existing land boundaries and settle any disputes. It is a solemn
occasion – bands play; the great man is treated to a feast; offerings
of coca are made to the local saint, whose effigy is paraded through
the village; the governor is accompanied everywhere by a guard of
village officials, wearing shoes for the occasion and blowing conch-
shells. But the most important survival from ancient times – and it
is on this that Belaúnde mainly pinned his hopes – is the practice of
mutual aid known as *aine*. At the times of sowing, ploughing, and
harvesting the neighbours rally round and help each other; each
peasant is bound by tradition to give this service to his neighbours.
For more ambitious projects, perhaps the repair of the irrigation
system or the church, or the building of a school or access road, a
large contingent of the community may be mobilized under the
system known as *minga*.

Thus, although the land of the community is now individually
owned, there is still a strong sense of social cohesion based on close
ties of kinship and shared interests. While not illegal, it is considered
a crime for anyone in the community to sell his land to an outsider.
Members are quick to rally to the defence of the common interest
in such matters as water and grazing rights, or to forestall any
attempt by the local *hacienda* to encroach upon the community
land. Sometimes, indeed, if the community becomes desperately
short of land, the members may band together in order to seize
some of the unused land of a neighbouring estate.

The system of government in the communities has its roots both
in the Inca and Spanish systems. The hereditary *curacas* of Inca
and colonial times have disappeared. The senior officer in the village
is the *alcalde* (mayor) who is supported by *regidores* and other
Spanish-style subordinate officials. The *alcalde* is normally chosen
by an informal meeting of village elders (the Indians respect old
age), although his nomination has to be approved by the district
governor. During his term of office, the *alcalde* carries the much-
prized *vara*, a wooden staff of office richly adorned with silver
ornaments and religious symbols, which is handed down from generation to generation. Some *alcaldes* are effective bosses in their communities. Others are merely stooges of either the district governor,
or, more remotely, of the owner of the nearest *hacienda* who often
has the governor in his pocket.

Ever since the time of Mariátegui social reformers in Peru have
pinned their hopes for the redemption of the Indians upon the concept of model 'Indian Communities' which would retain the virtues

of the old system but employ modern methods of agriculture. In 1920, alarmed by the symptoms of peasant unrest in the Andes, Leguía wrote into his constitution of that year a clause according legal recognition to the Indian communities, and in the following year a Bureau of Indian Affairs was created. The existing constitution of Peru, which was introduced by Sánchez Cerro in 1933, goes even further towards the recognition of the Indians' right to their own land. Article 47 calls for the encouragement of moderate and small rural ownership, and gives the government power to expropriate lands in private ownership, especially those not being exploited. Article 211 specifically justifies the expropriation of private lands for apportionment to the Indian communities.

In 1952 an American team of anthropologists from Cornell University, working in co-operation with the Peruvian government, established a 'model' community at Vicos in the department of Ancash. They took over an *hacienda*, taught the Indians modern methods of farming, supplied them with the necessary equipment, and, after a suitable period of training, handed over the management of the estate to a communal council. The experiment seems to have had quite encouraging results. From the profits of their labour the Indians have been able to construct schools and communal buildings. Their standard of agriculture is greatly improved. The modernization of the Indian communities was also an important feature of Belaúnde's programme and a new section of the Ministry of Labour was established by his government for this purpose. By the end of 1965 well over 2,000 of the estimated 5,000 surviving Indian communities in Peru had been surveyed and in many instances persuaded by agents of the government to undertake, largely on their own efforts, the building of roads, clinics, and schools.[1]

But there is still a great deal to be done. Most of the communities possess too little land to produce any surplus; their methods of agriculture are primitive; the council of village elders is hopelessly conservative and unenterprising in its ideas, if not actively resentful of interference from outside. In such backward communities the individual Indian farmers, unorganized and defenceless, are exploited, not only by neighbouring landlords, but by shopkeepers, merchants, petty officials, moneylenders, and even in a small way by the priests. For in the *sierra* the townsfolk have always made their living out of the peasants by selling them bad liquor and extravagant paraphernalia for fiestas, collecting tithes and first fruits, charging interest, and exploiting voluntary labour services for church and town.[2] Even

[1] Pike, op. cit., p. 318.
[2] Andrew Pearse, 'The Indians of the Andes' (Claudio Véliz, ed., *Latin America and the Caribbean – a Handbook*, London, 1968).

so, the Indian living on his own land, however inadequate, and in his own free community, however inefficient, can consider himself to be a very lucky man compared with the majority of peasants, who have no land of their own and are forced to work as *colonos* in the *haciendas*.

In the highlands (but not on the coast) there still survives the old-fashioned feudal system of land-ownership known in Peru as *gamonalismo*. The forms of contract vary, but the essence of the system is that the Indian *colonos* are paid by being given the use of a plot of land, with only a minimal wage paid in the form of cash. In return for the use of the land and its product the Indians are bound under contract to give services to the landowner, working his land for a prescribed number of days, and with many other often highly onerous obligations. By these means the peasant ties himself hand and foot to the *hacienda* in return for the barest possible living.

Gamonalismo stems from the Spanish conquistadores' concept of land-ownership as a symbol of prestige – a qualification to be a member of the aristocracy.[1] The *gamonal* regards his estate not primarily as a business enterprise, but as a source of prestige and power. By the possession of land he becomes the boss of his region, with local politicians, officials, magistrates, and even sometimes the parish priest, in his pocket. A masterful figure in his broad-brimmed hat and with a pistol at his belt, he is lord of all he surveys; or he may be a professional man in the city, seldom visiting his estate, but pulling the strings of local politics from a distance. Economically, his estate is likely to be inefficiently run, since power rather than profit is his main concern. In many highland *haciendas* large tracts of land are left uncultivated for want of capital, and the methods of cultivation are normally no better than in the Indian communities.

Gamonalismo is, of course, an anachronism in this modern age, and it is so recognized by the vast majority of thinking Peruvians of all political parties, apart from those with a vested interest in its perpetuation. We saw how González Prada, the Grand Old Man of Peru's revolutionary left wing, led the way at the turn of the century with his rhetorical call to the Indians to rise up in rebellion against their feudal masters; how his disciple, José Mariátegui, in his famous essays, pin-pointed feudalism as the number one enemy of Peru; and how Haya de la Torre's concept of Indo-America recognized the importance of integrating the Indian peasants into modern society and doing away with the feudal estates.[2] By the

[1] David Lehmann, 'The Agrarian Working Class' (*Latin America and the Caribbean – a Handbook*, London, 1968).
[2] See above, pp. 148–51.

1920s *indigenismo* had become a popular intellectual cult. Its leading exponent, Luis E. Valcárcel, preached that the only true Peru
was Indian Peru. Like González Prada, he looked forward to the
day of the massive Indian uprising which he felt sure must soon take
place.

On a more practical level Bustamante's ill-fated government
passed a law designed to regulate work on the *haciendas* and remove
the worst of the abuses of the feudal system. General Odría issued a
decree ordering the expropriation of all unused lands (*terrenos
eriazos*) whose owners failed to comply with government specifica-
tions for improvement. But all these measures remained a dead
letter. The landowners, strongly entrenched in local politics and
the Congress, and as members of the Establishment, were not prepared to tolerate any interference by government in their affairs. It
was only on the coast that there was some improvement in the lot
of the peasants during the first half of the twentieth century. In this
region most of the *haciendas* were efficiently run estates, growing
crops for export such as sugar and cotton. The owners regarded
their farms as commercial enterprises rather than as feudal estates.
The Indian workers, too, through contact with the towns, had
begun to acquire the *mestizo* outlook towards money and work, and
on the whole preferred to receive cash wages rather than perform
feudal services. In this modern attitude they were encouraged by
Aprista and socialist trade union officials, who made a start in
organizing the peasants along industrial lines. It only needed a few
strikes for the owners to see the light, and, whether unionized or not,
the conditions of service of the peasants on the coast began greatly
to improve.

But in the *sierra* the feudal system remained inviolate until, in 1952,
it was unexpectedly threatened from a distance when the National
Revolutionary Movement (M.N.R.) seized power in Bolivia. This
revolution, the aftermath of the Chaco War, was spearheaded by
the radical intelligentsia and militant miners in the towns, but its
weight was provided by the Indian peasants who, organized in rural
syndicates, invaded the land of the *haciendas*. For the first time in
Andean history the peasants emerged as a decisive political force on
a national scale. In the following year the revolutionary Bolivian
government enacted a far-reaching agrarian reform law which, to a
large extent, has put an end to feudalism in Bolivia. These events,
just across the waters of Lake Titicaca, could hardly fail to have
repercussions in Peru, particularly in the neighbourhood of Puno
and Cuzco where *gamonalismo* flourished and the conditions of the
peasants were still in every way as bad as had been those of their
neighbours in Bolivia before the revolution.

In 1958 a young *mestizo* from Cuzco, Hugo Blanco,[1] began organizing rural syndicates on the Bolivian model in the valley of La
Convención, near Cuzco. Blanco's mother was the daughter of a
peasant; his father was a lawyer who specialized in Indian litigation.
At the University of Cuzco, where he studied agronomy, the young
Blanco came into contact with the communists, whose influence has
always been very strong in the former capital of the Inca, surrounded as it is by the dire poverty of their descendants. In Argentina, where Blanco went to complete his studies, he was favourably
impressed by Perónism and joined a Trotskyist organization. (The
official Communist Party in the Argentine was opposed to Perón.)
Upon returning to Peru he became a member of the Peruvian
branch of the Trotskyist faction known as the P.O.R. (*Partido
Obrero Revolucionario*). Bitterly opposed by the orthodox Communist Party of Peru, P.O.R. later amalgamated with other extremist splinter-groups to form the *Frente de Izquierda Revolucionaria*
(F.I.R.).

Starting more or less from scratch in 1958, Blanco in three years
succeeded in forming no less than 148 rural syndicates in the valley
of La Convención alone. These were linked together in a regional
federation, which in its turn formed part of a departmental federation of rural syndicates with its headquarters in Cuzco. In this
central organization Blanco occupied the key post of secretary of
agrarian reform, while at the same time keeping in close touch with
the local syndicates. The secret of Blanco's success as a peasant
organizer was that he identified himself with the Indians, speaking
fluent Quechua and working himself as a *colono* on a plot of land
on the *hacienda* of a certain Don Alfredo Romainville. In this way
he was able to overcome the suspicions which even the most well-
meaning 'white men' arouse when they try to concern themselves
with Indian affairs. He was accepted by the Indians as one of their
own kind.

At first the rural syndicates confined themselves to organizing
strikes of *colonos*. This action was immediately successful in bringing the landowners to their knees, for a *gamonal* is nothing without
a body of submissive serfs to attend to his needs. The striking
colonos continued to till the plots of land which had been allotted
to them for their own use, but refused to perform any service for
the *hacienda*. Deprived of labour, the landowners were forced either
to go out of business or bribe their peasants to work with offers of
cash wages. *Gamonalismo* had been struck a deadly blow.

Later, no doubt taking a leaf from the Bolivian book, the rural

---

[1] The details of Hugo Blanco's career which follow are based on Villanueva, op. cit.

syndicates started 'invading' the *haciendas*. Each *colono* seized for himself and claimed the outright ownership of the land he had been working as a feudal tenant. Unused land in the *hacienda* was like-wise appropriated and divided among landless Indians. With the peasants acting in unison, to the battle-cry of 'Land or Death', there were few landowners who dared to stand up to these invasions, and the authorities were powerless to prevent them without running the risk of provoking a civil war. Some of the peasants were armed, but there was very little shooting and no burning and looting of *haciendas*, such as had occurred in Mexico forty years before when Zapata's peasant army went on the rampage. If he did not resist, the landowner, with his wife and family, were allowed to drive away unmolested to Cuzco. In most cases the owner was left in possession of that part of the *hacienda* which had always been worked for his account. But if he wanted labour to work this land he would now have to pay for it. However, if the landowner was deemed by his former serfs to be guilty of crimes against the peasants, then, in reprisal, the whole *hacienda* might be seized. Thus there were now two authorities in the countryside: the rural syndicates administering their own rough and ready justice, and the agents of the legal government who were impotent to deal with such an unprecedented situation.

The land invasions reached their apogee in the middle of 1963 when Quillabamba, the chief town of the valley of La Convención, was occupied by armed peasants. They were only halted when Belaúnde intervened personally and met the peasant leaders in Junín, promising a programme of radical agrarian reform. But Hugo Blanco was not in Junín to celebrate this victory. In 1962 he was imprudent enough to attack a police post and during the scuffle a policeman was killed. Blanco went into hiding, but was captured in May 1963. Tried by a military court in Tacna, he was condemned to twenty-five years' imprisonment. He still languishes in gaol.

It remains to be seen what will be the verdict of history on Hugo Blanco: in oligarchical and military circles in Peru he is understandably considered to be a 'communist' agitator of the reddest hue. It must be admitted, however, that, illegal though it may have been, his peasants' revolt was brilliantly successful not only in attaining its immediate objective – land for the peasants – but in its long-term political results as well. Without much doubt the peasant syndicate has come to stay in the *sierra* as an instrument for protecting and asserting Indian rights. The importance of this development is recognized by the leading political parties – *Acción Popular*, APRA, and the Christian Democrats – who are competing with each other to form their own rural syndicates in the *sierra*. The Christian

Democrats in particular have been very active in this field. Membership in syndicates is likely to have a profound effect upon the outlook of the Indian peasants by inducing them to work together with intelligent and sympathetic 'white' politicians from the city on matters which are very close to their hearts. Meanwhile, although by no means finished, *gamonalismo* is almost certainly on its way out in Peru. The landowners in the *sierra* are faced with the choice of abandoning their land to the peasants or greatly improving their methods of agriculture, so that they can afford to attract labour by paying reasonable cash wages. Meanwhile, *gamonalismo* is losing its political attractions. The local political boss is becoming an anachronism in an age when well-organized political parties are competing for the support of the peasants, and with the countryside increasingly invaded by officials and experts of every kind.

These are only long-term tendencies, of course, and the demise of feudalism is very far from being an accomplished fact in most parts of the *sierra*. However, the peasant revolt in the valley of La Convención did have an immediate political result. It forced the Peruvian government to take agrarian reform seriously as a matter of urgent concern. The members of the military *junta* of 1962–63, instead of reacting repressively, were intelligent enough to see that it was useless to try to put the clock back. Energetic measures were taken to round up the leaders of the revolt, but no serious attempt was made to dispossess the Indians of the land they had seized. Instead, measures for agrarian reform, hastily concocted, went a long way towards legalizing the *fait accompli*. Many of the *junta*'s ideas were subsequently incorporated in the bill for agrarian reform which Belaúnde put before Congress in 1963, only two months after taking office. In the following year a comprehensive plan for agrarian reform, which represented a compromise between the views of Belaúnde's *Acción Popular* and APRA, became the law of the land.

Hated by the oligarchy, Hugo Blanco, ironically enough, was never very popular either in left-wing circles in Peru. The orthodox Communist Party, jealous of his achievements, denigrated him by calling him a lackey of Yankee imperialism, on what grounds it is difficult to imagine. Even in his own Trotskyist circle he was criticized for confining his energies too narrowly to the organization of rural syndicates. Encouraged by the success of Fidel Castro in Cuba, his associates in the F.I.R. were dreaming grandiose dreams of guerrilla bands in the *sierra* which would be the spearhead of a revolutionary movement on a national scale.

Thus, in 1961, while Blanco stubbornly stuck to his peasants, his companions in the F.I.R., under the leadership of an Argentine revolutionary, Hugo Bressano, set about the task of organizing cadres of guerrilla fighters in Peru. The fantastic story of their very amateur efforts in subversion is told graphically by Blanco's biographer, Víctor Villanueva. As a first step, two banks in Lima were raided in order to obtain money for the purchase of arms. This action was justified by the F.I.R. on the Robin Hood theory that while some people might consider it bad to rob a bank, it was an even worse crime to be a banker. The first raid on a branch of the Banco Popular in Lima produced only the meagre return of 105,000 pesos, and most of this sum was in new notes of which the police had the serial numbers. The second attack, this time on the Banco del Credito in the exclusive suburb of Miraflores, raised the impressive sum of 2,950,000 pesos. But revolutionaries have their human failings, and a large part of this stolen money found its way into the pockets of individuals who seem suddenly to have realized the merits of the capitalist system. With what little money remained, a party of seven F.I.R. militants embarked upon a lorry bound for Cuzco. They spent three uncomfortable days and nights bumping over the rough mountain roads hidden under a tarpaulin. But somebody in their organization must have betrayed them, for the police were waiting for the lorry when it arrived at Cuzco at 2.30 in the morning, and both the money and the militants were seized. Bressano, who had kept well in the background while these stirring events were taking place, slipped quietly away in an aeroplane to the safety of his native Buenos Aires.

A more professional attempt at guerrilla action was organized by renegade *Apristas* who, disgusted with Haya de la Torre's *convivencia* with Prado, had broken away from the party and formed their own militant left-wing group, *Movimiento Izquierdista Revolucionario* (M.I.R.).[1] Its leader, Luis de la Puente Uceda, conferred with Hugo Blanco in Cuzco in October 1962. It does not seem, however, that any firm agreement for combined action was reached by the two men. Nevertheless, in the following year a detachment of Cuban-trained guerrillas of the M.I.R. entered Peru from Bolivia; near Puerto Maldonado, with the object of striking towards La Convención and joining forces with Hugo Blanco's peasant syndicates. But they were dispersed by the army before reaching their destination.

Undaunted, the M.I.R. in 1965 launched a series of guerrilla offensives designed to create a new and militant mass movement of the extreme left. At one time in that year there were no less than five small guerrilla groups operating in widely separated parts of the

[1] For a summary of guerrilla activities in Peru see Alain Joxe, 'The Sino-Soviet Dispute and Revolutionary Movements' (*Latin America and the Caribbean – a Handbook*, London, 1968), pp. 456–64.

Peruvian *sierra*. But although each group adopted romantic Inca names, such as Tupac Amarú, Pachacutec, and Atahualpa, they failed to attract the support of the peasants. Even so, this outbreak of guerrilla fighting was enough to shake Belaúnde's government to its foundations and to cause the army to mobilize a large part of its effective strength for the difficult task of hunting down an elusive enemy. Finally, outnumbered 100 to 1 by the army, the guerrilla bands were defeated one by one. Two of the principal leaders, De la Puente and Pablo Escobar, were killed in 1965. By the beginning of 1967 all the guerrilla bands had been eliminated.

It would be optimistic, however, to assume that because of this initial failure Peru has seen the end of guerrilla warfare – it was still going on in Bolivia in 1968. There is, however, perhaps a comforting moral to be drawn from these two initial experiments in left-wing subversion in the Peruvian Andes. The guerrilla movement in 1965 failed to obtain support because the Indian peasants, in their barely awakened state of political consciousness, were not interested in taking part in a Castro-style national revolution. This parochial attitude towards national politics may very well change with time and education, but for the moment the revolutionary potential of the Indians appears to be weak, except in relation to matters directly affecting their own local interests. Hugo Blanco has demonstrated that, under competent leadership, the peasants can be induced to take up arms and risk death in order to obtain land or conserve what little land they may already possess. But this seems to be the end of their revolutionary aspirations. Once he is in firm possession of his own plot of land the Indian peasant becomes as conservative in outlook as any other landowner.[1]

If this assessment of the Indian character is correct, it follows that the Peruvian government, or any future Peruvian government, has only to act energetically on the front of agrarian reform to reduce greatly the risk of serious trouble arising among the peasants. But if insufficient progress is made to satisfy the demands of the peasants for land, then it is more than likely that the Indians, whether egged on by extremist leaders or not, will once again be tempted to take the law into their own hands. Hugo Blanco has taught them how to do it, and they are not likely to forget the lesson.

[1] This was the sad conclusion reached by Villanueva, op. cit.

Chapter 19

Agrarian Reform – A Progress Report

THE AGRARIAN REFORM LAW OF 1964 is a compromise, not only between the views of *Acción Popular* and APRA, but between two different points of view, the one political and the other economic. Its motivation is political – social justice for the Indians and war against the evils of feudalism – but the practical problems are mainly economic. Thus, the law recognizes that there can be no real social progress by the Indian peasants until the rural economy has been not only thoroughly modernized, but also greatly expanded.

The need for expansion arises because, with all but a tiny fraction of the national territory occupied by deserts, mountains, and jungles, there is an overall insufficiency of cultivated land to provide most of the farming population with a tolerable standard of living. The 'man–land equation' is such that feudalism could be utterly destroyed and all the existing land redistributed without this doing much to improve the economic conditions of the peasants. About one million farmers own 25 million hectares[1] of land, of which 2 million are cultivated, 12 million are natural pasture, and 11 million – mostly very poor land – are unused. If the usable land were to be divided into equal parcels, the result would be $2\frac{1}{2}$ hectares for each family. It is estimated, however, that the minimum viable landholding to support a family in Peru is between 10 and 15 hectares. On this basis there is clearly not enough land to go round.

It follows then that the first objective of any agrarian reform programme in Peru must be to bring new land under cultivation. Estimates of the possibilities vary, but a reasonable long-term target might be to seek to double the present area of cultivated land, with perhaps another half-million hectares produced by irrigation on the Pacific coastal strip, and possibly as much as 25 million hectares of new land developed for agriculture in the *selva*.[2]

The next problem, which is partly social and partly economic, is the very uneven manner in which the available land is distributed, giving rise to the twin phenomena of *latifundia* (over-large estates)

---

[1] One hectare = 2·471 acres.
[2] These are not official estimates; but they represent what was the thinking in 1967 of officials in O.N.R.A. (National Office of Agrarian Reform).

and *minifundia* (parcels of land which are too small to support a family). On the Pacific coast only 10 per cent of the landowners hold 89 per cent of the land, leaving the remaining 90 per cent of the farmers in possession of the meagre 11 per cent of land which remains. In the *sierra* and the *selva* the position is even worse, with only 3 per cent of the landowners possessing 83 per cent and 93 per cent of the land respectively. And this is not the worst of the story. It is estimated that in Peru as a whole there are 417,357 mini-holdings of between only one and five hectares, or an average holding for each farmer of only 2·2 hectares, i.e. well below the limit of viability. Worse still, 290,900 families own less than one hectare. This is *minifundia* reduced to the point of absurdity. A peasant could not possibly live off such a small parcel of land and would have to find some additional source of income.

At the other extreme of *latifundia*, there are 1,091 landowners with properties larger than 2,500 hectares occupying some 60 per cent of the total land area available. Some large estates cover an area of more than 200,000 hectares, i.e. about the size of the prov-ince of Lima.[1] However, in assessing the social and economic evils of the *latifundia*, it is necessary to distinguish between the large, well-run, commercially operated *haciendas* on the coast and the few efficient cattle-ranches in the *sierra*, and the primitive estates of feudal landowners in the *sierra* which are inefficiently run, often with large areas of potentially useful land left uncultivated for want of capital.

In general, with the exceptions noted above, the standard of agriculture, as practised almost everywhere in Peru, is deplorably low. So relatively unproductive is the agricultural sector that, while 51 per cent of the working population of Peru are engaged in agri-culture, it contributes only 17·4 per cent to the gross national pro-duct. As against an annual increase in agricultural productivity of only 2·8 per cent, the population of Peru is increasing at the rate of 3·02 per cent, with the result that the country is having to import more and more of her essential foodstuffs, to the detriment of the balance of payments and the economy as a whole.[2]

In the face of these hard economic facts, the Agrarian Reform Law is very cautious – much too cautious to please the left wing in Peruvian politics – in its approach to the problem of land redistri-bution. It envisages that eventually the *colonos* in the *sierra* and the small tenant farmers on the coast should be given titles of outright ownership to the plots of land which they work. In the case of mini-

[1] Villanueva, op. cit., pp. 15–16.
[2] Figures quoted by President Belaúnde in his message to Congress on 28 July 1966.

holdings these plots will be reconcentrated and expanded so that each peasant will have a viable lot. But it is recognized that it would be folly merely to break up the great estates, the efficient with the inefficient, and hand out small parcels of land indiscriminately to thousands upon thousands of illiterate peasants, who in their present state of ignorance would simply cultivate them in their traditional way. Under the prevailing conditions of feudalism the tenant farmer or *colono* depends entirely upon the *hacienda* for credit, seed, tools, equipment, and the marketing of his product. Thus, before land-titles can be usefully granted to the small farmers, the umbilical cord which ties them to the *hacienda* has to be broken. In short, land redistribution must go hand in hand with education and a radical improvement in farming methods, backed by an adequate system of government credit for small farmers, technical assistance, and proper arrangements for the co-operative marketing of their produce.

Accordingly, the law does not call for the wholesale expropriation of the properties of the big landowners. It is left to the discretion of the government to 'designate' specific areas in the country where, on social and economic grounds, land redistribution is considered desirable. Moreover, within these designated areas, each individual case has to be examined by the authorities on its merits, with compensation paid in cash and bonds to the owner of any land that may be expropriated. The areas designated by the Belaúnde government for agrarian reform were all situated in the *sierra*, in the departments of Pasco, Junín, Puno, and the province of La Convención y Lares near Cuzco. These are parts of the country where the feudal system of *gamonalismo* is still to be found in its most extreme form, with grossly inefficient use made of the land and often cruel exploitation of the *colonos* who work it. They are also significantly the areas where the agitation of the peasants has been most intense, posing a political problem for the government.

No attempt has been made so far, under the laws, seriously to tamper with the large, well-run *haciendas* on the coast, producing export crops such as sugar or cotton, or the big commercially operated cattle ranches in the *sierra*. Indeed, the sugar estates have been specifically exempted by decree. With their refineries and private railways they are regarded as being essentially industrial enterprises. For example, the Empresa Agrícola Chicana, owned by the firm of Gildemeister and Company, embraces more than sixty formerly independent *haciendas*, cultivates 37,000 acres of cane and 12,000 acres of other food crops, and covers a total area of 220 square miles. This might seem to be *latifundia* in its most extreme form. But it is an example of efficient *latifundia*. The company's land

forms part of a self-contained industrial complex. Its villages are
well kept, with housing far superior in quality to that in the smaller
haciendas, let alone in the Indian villages. It not only pays good
wages (mainly in cash), but it provides its workers with schools,
cinemas, and other social amenities. In short, in the view of
Belaúnde's government, there would be no advantage on either
social or economic grounds in breaking up such an enterprise into
smallholdings.[1]

So much for the Agrarian Reform Law considered by itself. But
the measure was conceived by Belaúnde as being only one essential
part of a comprehensive national development plan which, insofar
as it related to the problems of rural Peru, included such additional
basic requirements as roads, irrigation, colonization, education,
housing, and health. In his mid-term message to the nation, on 28
July 1966, Belaúnde reported to Congress on the progress made
with the national plan during the first three years of his administration. He spoke for three hours non-stop and without notes – a
veritable *tour de force*. Those who witnessed this performance could
hardly fail to be impressed by the President's sincerity of purpose
and his tremendous grasp of detail in all branches of his government. But it was when he was dealing with development projects –
roads, irrigation schemes, and so on – that his eyes lighted up. He
was able to impart to his audience (only his *Aprista* critics remained
grimly silent) something of his tremendous faith in the future of his
country. It was only afterwards in the cold air of the street, and
even more after reading the massive documentation of the President's message, that the observer was left wondering how much had
really been achieved, and how much was a glorious pipe-dream. For
it must be admitted that a large part of the message – and this was
perhaps inevitable after only three years of office – related to un-
realized projects rather than concrete achievements. Belaúnde himself was well aware of the limitations imposed upon him by the
time-factor. He has been heard to complain to visitors that he had
so little time to do so much. In fact, he had less time than he had a
right to expect.

At the heart of Belaúnde's plan for Peru's future was his vision
of the rich tropical valleys of the *montaña* – the valleys on the
eastern side of the Andes leading down to the rain-forest of the
Amazon – being opened up by means of roads and settled and developed by landless Indians from the *sierra*. In this way, as he saw
it, the population pressure in the *sierra* would be relieved, the un-
welcome mass migration of Indians to the coastal cities diminished,
and a new potentially rich area of the country opened up to com-

[1] But see p. 237, footnote.

mercial exploitation. Towards the fulfilment of this dream a high priority was given by his government to an ambitious plan to complete by 1975 no less than 11,424 kilometres of new motor-roads at a cost of 17,850 million soles. In most of its aspects this plan was no more than a logical extension of the road-building programme initiated by Leguía in the 1920s, and to which other Presidents such as Benavides and Odría also made their contribution. The plan envisages that Peru should have three parallel longitudinal highways running from north to south: the first (which was already more or less completed before Belaúnde's time) along the Pacific coast between the frontier towns of Tumbes and Tacna; a central highway, of which some 500 kilometres still have to be built, along the backbone of the *sierra*, following more or less the path of the old imperial highway of the Inca from Lake Titicaca to the border with Ecuador; and the *carretera marginal* linking and opening up the valleys of the tropical *montaña* to the east of the Andes, and eventually providing links with the road systems of Ecuador, Colombia, Brazil, and Bolivia. Criss-crossing these longitudinal highways, lateral 'roads of penetration' – eighteen were reported to be under construction in 1966 – would link the Pacific ports with the interior. Finally, the isolation of the provincial centres in the hinterland was to be broken down by a network of rough and ready access roads, to be built by the inhabitants themselves under the scheme of *cooperación popular*. In one year, it was reported in 1966, 2,700 kilometres of such home-made roads had already been completed.

The distinctive and most controversial feature of Belaúnde's road plan is his much beloved *carretera marginal*. As fast as his budget allowed, and using both civilian and army teams, he vigorously pushed forward with his plan to construct some 800 kilometres of new roads in this virgin tropical region. The labour of clearing the jungles was tremendous. It was a heartening experience to witness, as the author did in 1966, the dedication of the army engineers, sometimes almost up to their necks in mud, working enthusiastically on this mammoth task under the hardest conditions imaginable.

Belaúnde's concept of the *carretera marginal* has been criticized on two grounds. First, it is asked whether there is any point in linking together a series of tropical valleys each producing very much the same kind of crops. Would not the roads of penetration, providing each principal area in the *selva* with an outlet on the Pacific coast, be sufficient? Secondly, it is questioned whether these roads through the jungles will ever pay their way by encouraging the creation of sufficiently important and viable areas of agricultural land to support large-scale settlement. To the untutored eye the jungle seems fertile enough. But the cost of bringing the land in this

tropical region to a productive state and its administration is very
heavy and requires a great deal of capital. Moreover, experience
has shown that much of the land in the *selva* is more suitable for
cattle than crops. But ranching employs little labour and would not
help very much to relieve the population pressure in the *sierra*.

A pessimist could point his finger at the failure of all attempts
made in the nineteenth century to colonize the *selva*. A German
colony, founded in 1849 in Loreto, was a fiasco, as were colonies of
Irish immigrants in 1851 and of Italians in 1867. In 1857 a colony
of Germans at Pozuzo just managed to survive, but only at subsistence level. The explanation of these failures usually given is that
this tropical country was altogether too tough for Europeans; and,
without communications, the colonies were too remote to attract
native labour.

An optimist, however, could retort by pointing to the comparative
success of the venture in Tingo María, where in 1938 an agricultural experimental station was established under the joint spon-
sorship of Peru and the U.S.A. He could further draw the moral
that it was the completion of the Lima–Pucallpa highway, linking
this part of the *montaña* with the outside world, which made it possible for this colonization scheme to succeed. The road was completed in 1945. By 1950 the population of Tingo María had already
grown to 6,000 and a considerable area of land in what had
formerly been bush now supported a thriving little farming community.

To a large extent, then, but not perhaps entirely, Belaúnde's
marginal highway in the *selva* must be regarded as an act of faith.
But so also for that matter was the building of the railways in the
sierra by President Balta in the nineteenth century. At the time
when they were constructed there was no revenue in sight to justify
them economically. But the investment then made by the Peruvian
government with the help of foreign loans has been amply rewarded
by the subsequent development of mining in central and southern
Peru which the railways made possible. And so it may prove to be
with Belaúnde's roads in the jungle. Meanwhile, there are several
pilot projects in the pipeline for colonization in the *selva* whose progress it will be interesting to watch. The most ambitious is a scheme
concerted with the United Nations, for developing an area of $3\frac{1}{2}$
million hectares of land alongside various stretches of the *carretera
marginal* in northern Peru.

The irrigation of new land in the coastal desert might seem to
present fewer problems, since it is a matter of common observation
that it only needs a few drops of water to turn a desert into a garden
– even a heavy dew will cause a multitude of little flowers to poke

their noses through the sand. But the economics of irrigation have their own stern discipline – it is in practice an immensely expensive and difficult business, usually involving major works of engineering in the high Andes, to control and utilize the waters of the turbulent and unpredictable rivers on the western slopes, some of which dry up at certain seasons of the year, while at other times they become raging torrents.

The Inca performed wonders in irrigating the coastal valleys with very limited engineering equipment, and some of their works are still in use. However, in modern times Leguía must be regarded as the pioneer, with a large-scale irrigation scheme in the Cañete valley which was completed in 1923. During the following twenty-five years successive Peruvian governments irrigated some 80,000 hectares of land in various parts of the coastal desert, while private schemes added a further 170,000 hectares. It is a fascinating experience to inspect one of these newly created irrigated estates on the coast. For example, at San Lorenzo in the vicinity of Piura in northern Peru, the visitor is rewarded by the sight of a lush green oasis stretching as far as the eye can see, with model farms, good housing, schools, clinics, pools of agricultural equipment, banking facilities, and every other kind of social amenity. It is a foretaste of what may be the conditions one day in the new Peru. But San Lorenzo is no more than an oasis, catering at great cost for the needs of a few thousand very fortunate farmers. Out in the surrounding wilderness there are still millions of peasants living in the old unregenerate way.

The national plan of Belaúnde's government called for the irrigation of 636,800 hectares of new land and improvements in the irrigation of 272,800 hectares which are already under cultivation. In his message of 1966, Belaúnde noted that, while in 1962 only 98 million soles were being invested in irrigation, by 1965 the figure had risen to 462 million soles. But major irrigation schemes require a lot of capital, which will usually have to be borrowed abroad, and extensive 'feasibility' studies have to be made by experts. These studies and negotiations, as Belaúnde found to his chagrin when dealing with organizations such as the World Bank, take a great deal of time. Thus most of Belaúnde's projects for irrigation – for example, an ambitious scheme at Olmos involving the driving of a tunnel for 20,000 metres through the solid rock of the high Andes in order to divert water to the Pacific desert which otherwise would have flowed uselessly back into the Amazon – were still not very far beyond the blue-print stage when he was dismissed from office. However, good progress was made during his term with a major irrigation scheme at Tinajones in Lambayeque, on which German engineers are working, and on a number of smaller projects. It seems likely that, thanks to Belaúnde's initiative, the 1970s will see a considerable increase in the area of irrigated land on the coast.

While his financial policy may be open to criticism – he probably tried to do too much too fast – nobody can reasonably accuse Belaúnde of neglecting the problem of rural development. He put his heart and soul into the task, spending what was probably an over-generous amount of his time closeted with experts and poring over blue-prints. (He might have spent it more profitably defending his political position.) Whenever he had a moment to spare he liked to take off in his private plane to inspect the progress of the work on the ground. Distinguished foreign visitors to the palace, who expected no more than a short formal interview, were likely to be taken personally by the President to the state banqueting hall and shown a collection of models and plans of housing estates, hospitals, roads, bridges, dams – in short, a panorama of the new Peru of Belaúnde's dreams. An architect by profession, it was no idle boast when he used to describe himself as the Architect of Peru.

He was criticized by the right wing for spending too much money and by the left wing for dragging his feet when it came to the social and political aspects of agrarian reform. It is not at all easy, however, to establish the facts. On 14 March 1967 the newspaper *La Tribuna* published a report under the headline 'the farce of agrarian reform in Puno', which accused Belaúnde of having deceived and defrauded the farmers in this region. The report claimed that, although the area now teemed with highly-paid officials who badgered the farmers with plans, maps, and censuses, and travelled through the entire department like tourists, they had not produced 'a single reform in the structure nor a single expropriation beneficial to the communities'. As against this, at a press conference reported in *La Prensa* on 21 November 1967, three of Belaúnde's former Ministers of Agriculture, Rafael Cubas Vinatea, Javier Silva Ruete, and Eduardo Villa Salcedo – three Christian Democrats, not members of Belaúnde's own party – claimed that 2,853,000 hectares of land had been 'processed' in four years of agrarian reform. During the same period 100,000 peasants had taken possession of land, with about 7,000 property titles handed to settlers in the *selva*. The Ministers stressed that this had been achieved in the face of tenacious opposition and with very meagre financial resources. For example, they said that only 500 million soles had been authorized by Congress for agrarian reform during the four years, although some time before a technical commission headed by President Prado's former Prime Minister, Pedro Beltrán, had concluded that at least 10 billion soles would be required.

Whatever the truth may be, it is not difficult to understand why Belaúnde was unable to push ahead with agrarian reform as quickly as his left-wing critics demanded. When it came to politics, the President was not master in his own house. He could go no faster and further with agrarian reform than he was allowed by the opposition majority in Congress, *Apristas* and *Odriístas*. The landowners, organized in the powerful *Sociedad Nacional Agraria*, were not without their friends in this Congress, and they had a vociferous mouthpiece in Pedro Beltrán's conservative newspaper *La Prensa*. This influential organ hammered away almost daily at the government, criticizing it for wasteful expenditure, bureaucracy, and the mishandling of agrarian reform. On 9 June 1966 *La Prensa*, alarmed by a statement of the then Minister of Agriculture, Silva Ruete, that agrarian reform would affect 3½ million hectares of land, lectured the Minister on the need to go slow until there was a sufficient number of trained experts to handle such a task. Or again, on 24 October 1967 the same newspaper was accusing the Office of Agrarian Reform of expropriating land in Puno, amounting to 2,508,000 square metres, contrary to the law, and then not putting it to any productive use.

Some of this criticism was no doubt justified. There are not enough trained technicians in Peru to carry out an ambitious programme of agrarian reform. Many of the officials engaged in this task are political appointees without proper qualifications for their job. It was for this reason, for instance, that Belaúnde's plan of *cooperación popular* was so unpopular with the *Apristas*. They feared, perhaps with some justification, that the officials who administered this scheme for government-assisted self-help in the villages, all hand-picked members of *Acción Popular*, were using the organization for political ends. Alleging graft in the bureaucratic organization of this department, the opposition in 1965 refused to provide funds for the programme.[1] Politics in Peru are a cut-throat business. It was not in the interests of the opposition that Belaúnde should succeed in his policies and gain in popularity.

In the face of so much conflicting evidence, how can one fairly sum up the progress made in recent years in tackling the daunting problems of the Peruvian countryside? A traveller in the Andes, observing the dull-looking, coca-chewing Indian peasants grimly pursuing their traditional tasks in the immensity of their formidable environment, might come back saying with some truth that nothing much has changed in Peru since the time of Pizarro. He would be as right as a lone mariner on a Kon-Tiki raft who concluded that the Pacific ocean consists mainly of water. But the Kon-Tiki did eventu-

[1] Pike, op. cit., p. 318.

ally make its landfall on an island. The signs – one might almost call them the symbols – of rural progress in Peru – the occasional model farm or experimental agricultural station, the isolated green irrigated patches in the desert, those rare and precious clearings in the jungle – are like the scattered islands in a Pacific archipelago. It needs a voyage of discovery to learn that there is, in fact, a good deal of a hopeful nature going on in Peru.

For the first time in her history – thanks to the military government of 1962–63 – Peru has a national development plan, drawn up with the help of foreign experts, and covering all aspects of her economy. Never before in Peru have there been so many experts, both Peruvian and foreign, at work on so many schemes designed to help the peasant: agricultural research projects of every kind; a growing number of strategically-placed pools of mechanical equipment to help the small farmer; government-sponsored schemes to help the small man with credit and co-operative marketing; roving teams of experts giving technical assistance and advice; clubs for young farmers. Even recently an optimistic Englishman could be found trying to persuade the scrawny hens of the Andes to lay more eggs at an altitude of 12,000 feet – and he may still be there. Over and above these attempts to grapple with the immediate problems of the peasant, Belaúnde, as we have seen, did his utmost to improve the economic and social infrastructure of rural Peru, with roads, irrigation, colonization, and, perhaps most important of all, by increasing the number of schools in the villages and improving the facilities for technical and higher education throughout the country. No doubt, as his critics assert, some of Belaúnde's programmes were misguided or misdirected. In his government's swollen bureaucracy there may well have been cases of nepotism, graft, and inefficiency. But these evils are endemic in Peru in her present state of development. In spite of these obvious limitations, it is difficult for any fair-minded person to escape the conclusion that things have begun to move in rural Peru, and that they are moving, generally speaking, in the right direction.

But are they moving fast enough to stave off the danger of renewed trouble among the peasants in the Andes? One can presume that this is a problem which will not escape the attention of Peru's latest military government. It was, after all, the military government of 1962–63 which took the first practical step towards agrarian reform when faced with the land invasions in the valley of La Convención. Soldiers who only a few years ago had to mount a large-scale military campaign against the guerrillas, and may at any moment find themselves faced again with the same problem, will be only too conscious of the importance of having the peasants on their side. There is no reason to expect, then, that because of the change in 1968 from civilian to military government, there will be any slackening in the momentum of rural development and agrarian reform. The reverse is more probable. Belaúnde had the vision, but lacked the political support, to turn much of his dream into reality. The army have the power to get on with the job.[1]

[1] These words were prophetic. The military government has since (see *B.O.L.S.A. Review*, No. 31, July 1969) announced a radical land reform law which in theory goes a long way beyond Belaúnde's law of 1964. The intention now, apparently, is to break up *all* large private landholdings (including the large sugar plantations which Belaúnde had exempted from expropriation), abolish the small inefficient family units (*minifundia*), and establish a system of peasant co-operatives. Payment for expropriated land is to be made according to region, size, and the state of upkeep, in cash and bonds. It remains to be seen in what manner and to what extent this measure will be implemented, and what will be the reactions of the landowning oligarchy and any foreign interests that may be affected. Meanwhile, it is significant that the military government's first Minister of Agriculture, General Benavides, who had close ties with the oligarchy, has resigned.

Chapter 20

The Problems of Urban Assimilation

HAVING BEEN CONDUCTED through the luxurious marble halls
of the new airport to his waiting car, the foreign journalist on some
hasty mission to Peru is likely to receive a shock as he drives along
the highway towards Lima and gets his first glimpse of the vast
sprawling shanty-towns, or *barriadas*, which almost completely surround the capital. He only needs to question the chauffeur to discover that these horrible-looking slums – for with their jumble of
straw-built shacks, untidy building lots, and unpaved streets, the
latter full of mongrel dogs and dirty little boys playing football in
the dust, they look like slums to anybody unaccustomed to Peruvian
conditions – provide the home for an estimated 500,000 of the city's
grossly over-swollen population of 2 million. Here, even before
reaching the hotel, is a lurid human-interest story which will make
the people sit up at home. The versions vary, of course, but their
common denominator is something like this. Poor, illiterate, landless peasants are depicted as flocking to the city in their thousands
and finding themselves destitute and without anywhere to live. And
so they squat in the desert on the outskirts of the city in miserable
little straw shacks under conditions of the utmost squalor – conditions which it is presumed are conducive to crime, juvenile delinquency, and prostitution, and provide a perfect opportunity for the
communist agitator.

Such a story is sufficiently close to the truth in some of its more
superficial aspects to obtain widespread credence abroad. But it
misses the point of what in social terms the *barriadas* are found to
represent in Peru when the phenomenon is studied in greater depth.
This, at least, is the opinion of two highly competent professional
observers – William Mangin, Professor of Anthropology at Syracuse
University and John Turner, a British-born Professor of City Planning at the Massachusetts Institute of Technology – who have spent
the best part of ten years studying the conditions in the *barriadas*
which surround Lima. They reject as 'grossly inaccurate' the popular view of the *barriadas* as cesspools of misery and vice, claiming
that in reality these 'communities-in-development' – and this is their

238

technical designation – are 'highly successful solutions to the problem of mass urbanization'.[1]

Mangin studied the case-history of a Peruvian family – the Pérez – which migrated from the highlands of southern Peru to Lima in the late 1930s and in the mid-1960s was comfortably settled, with its own substantial house, in the *barriada* of Benavides. This community, a fairly typical *barriada*, was formed in 1954 by about 100 families who squatted on a bare hillside on the edge of the desert, just outside Lima. Since then about 400 more families have joined the *barriada*, and the whole hill is now covered by their shacks and houses.

Bernardo and Dolores Pérez, together with their seven children and a nephew, were among the original invaders of Benavides. Like most recently arrived Indian immigrants they had, before the invasion, been paying high rent for a crowded, deteriorating three-room apartment situated in a narrow alley in down-town Lima – in what Mangin describes as a 'typical inner-city slum area'. There were constant rumours that the *callejón* (as these rented tenement buildings are called in Lima) would be torn down to make room for new construction. Moreover, the Pérez needed more room for the growing family. Many of their friends in the neighbourhood were in a similar predicament; and so the plan was formed by a group of these slum-dwellers to stake out a claim for themselves in the desert on the outskirts of Lima, on which each family could build its own house. Significantly the group formed for this purpose were all members of a regional association of peasant families which had migrated to Lima from the same district in the southern highlands – an interesting example of the communal traditions of the *ayllu* being transferred to urban life. Significantly, too, it was on the whole members of the second generation of immigrants, i.e. men and women who had already become more or less adjusted to city ways, who were the ringleaders in planning the invasion. In the case of the Pérez family it was the eldest son, Max, together with his mother, Dolores, who took the initiative. The old father, Bernardo, agreed to go along with the plan, but only with misgivings.

On the evening of D-Day, in 1954, the Pérez family loaded themselves and their belongings, which included the prefabricated straw walls of a shack, into a taxi. During that same night they erected a straw house on a previously chosen lot on the side of the bare hill. Their fellow conspirators were simultaneously engaged in the same task. By the time the police arrived – for the invaders were illegally squatting on government land – dozens of shacks had already been

[1] William Mangin and John C. Turner, article in the *Peruvian Times*, 12 July 1968.

erected. For fear of violence, the officer in charge of the police decided not to resist the invasion, but merely to contain it within certain defined boundaries. In this the invaders of Benavides were lucky. According to Mangin, in other instances of urban invasions the police had attacked the squatters, and there had sometimes been bloodshed and loss of life.

In this manner yet another hundred families of former peasants emerged from the squalor and misery of the slums of central Lima, in which some of them had lived for twenty years, to begin a new and more hopeful life in their own *barriada*. At first sight it might seem that they had merely jumped from the frying-pan into the fire, for such amenities as water, sewers, and lighting, which their slum-dwellings had provided, were totally lacking at first in the new site. Nor were their hastily erected straw shacks anything to boast about; a British or North American working man, however poor, would never dream of living under such conditions. But a straw shack is quite good enough, in the rainless conditions of the coastal desert, to give temporary shelter to a family of Peruvian peasant background. After all, the one-room windowless *adobe* hut which Bernardo and Dolores had left behind in their village in the southern *sierra* had been no palace; and what could be worse than their subsequent experience of living in overcrowded rooms overlooking the stinking alley of a city slum? The invaders could now at least breathe the fresh air of the desert. More important, there were now no rents, rates, or charges of any sort to pay, making it possible for each family to put something by each week towards the cost of the family house which would one day be built. For the straw shack was only the first step. As soon as possible each owner, working on the 'do-it-yourself' principle, would build himself a more substantial house, adding new rooms, or even a new storey, as the financial situation permitted, and in order to meet the growing demands of his family.

Peruvian working-class families are apt to be large. The household must have room not only for the parents and their probably numerous children, but in many cases for grandparents, uncles, aunts, and other dependants as well. That is why nobody ever, or hardly ever, starves in Peru, however poor he may be. There will almost always be some relative to give the destitute person shelter, and to share with him for as long as may be necessary the frugal fare of the household. Thus, as John Turner points out, what the sociologists call 'the extended family' is a positive asset in an under-developed society. It means that every member of the family who is capable of any kind of work can contribute something towards the family budget, and in the aggregate the income may be quite substantial if there is more than one generation of adults in the household.

Thus, there tends to be, in Turner's words, 'a classic sequence' in the housing needs of Peruvian urban immigrants as their circumstances change. The original peasant immigrant will probably come to the city because he has a friend or relative there already who is prepared to offer him shelter until he has found his feet. Once established in the city with his own family of young children the newly-arrived immigrant will most likely rent an overcrowded tenement room in one of the slums of central Lima. But when, as happened with the Pérez, the family comes to consist of two or three generations, with probably more than one of the adults in reasonably well-paid jobs, then by far the most practical solution of their housing problem, under Peruvian conditions, is to move out to a *barriada* and start building a house of their own.

The Pérez, having staked out their claim in Benavides with a straw shack, did not in fact move there immediately. The old father, Bernardo, who was not much use for anything else, was left in charge of the shack as a caretaker. The rest of the family moved to the middle-class suburb of Lince where Max, the principal breadwinner, had a job with a construction company. Here they built for themselves two more temporary straw shacks in the yard of the construction site in order to be near the job and to save transport and rent. In this way they were able to accumulate savings with which eventually to build a proper house for themselves in Benavides. Max was now an active member of a trade union and earning good money. At night he earned extra money as a watchman. His mother added to the family income by cooking for the construction workers, while Max's wife looked after the small children. In all, the family was now earning just about three times as much as the bare level of subsistence with which it had started when Bernardo and Dolores had first come to Lima, and the eldest daughter was in a good school in Lince. Meanwhile every week-end the whole family would go to Benavides to work on the construction of their new house.

We can now begin to see the true social significance of the *barriada* as a means of helping an immigrant family like the Pérez to find their feet in the city. None of this would have been possible, John Turner points out, had the family been living in a model low-cost workman's housing estate, of which there are now a number in Lima. The rents and mortgage payments would be prohibitive for the Pérez who were trying to pull themselves up in the world. Hence Turner's conclusion – and he is a town-planner by profession – that in Peru the squatter's straw shack 'is a positive aid for survival and

an opener of opportunity. It is a *good* environment, however poor
its material quality. Even the lowest-priced modern project dwelling
is a *bad* environment, since it will block progress and perpetuate
poverty'. Turner goes on:
    'If the family can settle permanently, if they are free of the obli-
gation to pay high rents (or mortgage payments) and are therefore free of the threat of eviction (or foreclosure), then they can
secure and consolidate their improved status. And, by investing
their growing savings margin in the construction of a modern
house they can boost their social status to higher levels without
increasing their incomes – the "property-mobility" phenomenon.
Those no longer on the edge of starvation and misery can easily
slide down or back into that condition as long as they live in a
highly competitive labour market without adequate sickness and
unemployment insurance – and, especially, if they are relative
new-comers to urban society. . . . The overriding priority for families in this situation – typical of the majority of the (largely immigrant) population of rapidly growing cities in the early stages
of industrialization – is . . . secure home tenure. A family owning
or at least in secure de facto possession of its own dwelling, even
if this is no more than a rude shack on an unserviced hillside plot,
has an anchor to hold it from sliding down the slippery slope into
abject poverty.'
    The Pérez family certainly never had any reason to regret their
decision in 1954 to take part in the Benavides invasion. Here is a
picture of the family when Mangin last visited it in 1966. Max had
now moved out with the rest of the family to Benavides, and added
a two-room wing to his already quite substantial house. Dolores
had invested in a food stand in a neighbouring market and did good
business with the factory hands on their way to and from work. The
children were all in good schools. Bernardo, with his old-fashioned
peasant's outlook, was treated by the neighbours with amused toler-
ance. But Max fitted well into the *barriada* mould – he had become
a typical suburbanite with all the usual city tastes – cinemas, football
matches, television, etc. As for the children, representing the third
generation, there was no reason why, with their good education,
some of them with luck might not break through into the white-
collar middle class. The Pérez family had travelled a long way in
thirty years from that now dimly remembered peasant hut in the
mountains.
    The *barriada* of Benavides had also changed out of all recogni-
tion as compared with the original squatter settlement of straw huts
on a bare hillside on the edge of the desert. Not that even now it
was a very beautiful sight. It could still quite easily be taken for a

slum by somebody, used to the amenities of well-to-do suburbs like Miraflores and San Isidro, speeding past in a car on the way to one of the beach resorts. With each of the squatters building his own house at his own pace and in accordance with his own taste – and with no regulations to hamper him – it is hardly surprising if a *barriada* is unsightly. The shacks and houses may be built of anything from straw to *adobe* and brick, and are of all sizes, shapes, and styles. The unpaved roads, paths, and stairways climb up the hillside at crazy angles and are full of sand and boulders. There is no foliage except for an occasional householder's carefully tended potted tree. The streets, especially in the summer, are hot and dusty. Within their private compounds the erstwhile peasants cannot resist keeping chickens and even sometimes sheep and goats (to say nothing of numerous barking dogs), so that a *barriada* tends to look and smell much more like a rural village than a suburb of a capital city. But it is very far from being a slum according to Peruvian standards.

Benavides was at first without services of any kind, but by 1966 it had acquired the most essential amenities. Missionaries had moved in and built a church. The government had contributed a school, but only after a resident had been killed falling from the roof of a school which was being built illegally by the inhabitants. Bars, stores, bus and taxi co-operatives, and other types of small businesses, owned and managed by *barriada* residents, had sprung up. Max had been involved in an abortive scheme to build a water-tower (to which it later transpired no water could be pumped) and a sewer-line (through which no sewage ever flowed). But the problem of water and drainage for Benavides had subsequently been solved by a lucky accident. It so happened that a private developer had built a lower-middle-class housing estate at the base of the hill. He found that he could not sell the lots or the houses because of the smell and the unsightliness of the rubbish and sewage from Benavides that had been dumped for ten years at the foot of the hill. So the developer used his political influence and was able to accomplish what the local residents had dismally failed to achieve in spite of frequent representations to the authorities. Benavides was linked up to the water supply and sewers of the housing estate at the base of the hill.

Thus, Mangin was able to conclude his report on Benavides on an optimistic note. Most of the original straw houses had been converted into brick and cement structures with an investment totalling millions of dollars in labour and materials – it had not cost the government a penny. Employment rates, wages, literacy, and educational levels were all higher than in the central city slums, from which most of the original squatters had escaped. The residents worked in the city, bought things in the city, belonged to clubs and associations, and enjoyed movies and soccer games. Their occupations covered an enormous range. Crime, juvenile delinquency, and prostitution were rare. The morale of the residents was high and their community spirit strongly developed. Although no official land-titles had been issued, the residents now felt fairly secure in their tenure, and some lots and houses had changed hands with home-made titles. The municipality of Rimac, the district of Lima where Benavides is located, had provided some police protection and garbage collection. The local congressman, no doubt with an eye to the next election, was now paying regular visits to the *barriada*. In short, Benavides, in many respects, had become just another suburb of Lima.

Nor is the experience of Benavides in any way unique. In 1963 John Turner, working in this instance in collaboration with the British Embassy in Lima, arranged for a party of young British volunteers to come out from England to work in the *barriada* of Comas, situated in another part of the outskirts of Lima. These eighteen-year-old boys, who had just finished their secondary schooling at home, undertook the practical task (which they had first to learn themselves) of helping the 'do-it-yourself' householders of Comas to install electric wiring in their homes. Just before the roof was due to go on a house, the British volunteers would map out the circuits with the owner, lay down tubing for them before the roof was concreted, and later put in the wiring. As a sideline they trained groups of local residents in electrical work so that in future the residents could do the job for themselves. This severely practical approach to the problem of aid for the *barriadas* paid handsome dividends in goodwill. These independent householders do not like to be the object of pity or charity. But they took to their hearts these nice, cheerful, and unassuming young English boys, who were prepared to come and rough it in the *barriada* under the same conditions as the residents and do something really useful.

This is what one of the boys, Maurice de Bunsen, had to say about conditions in Comas on returning to Britain.[1]

'Physical conditions ... were less advanced than in other barriadas. No street-lighting at all, and only a little privately generated domestic lighting, which worked erratically for a few hours night and morning. Stand-pipes for water had been installed just before we arrived (before that, everyone had relied on tanker lorries). Sanitation was limited, with only one W.C. in the whole

[1] Quoted George Pendle, *The Land and People of Peru* (London, 1966), pp. 72-3.

barriada.... Otherwise each house had an earth closet or merely a garbage pit...'

As regards the social conditions in Comas, he had this to say:

'All the people we worked for were employed, and reasonably well at that. At the top of the scale were a police N.C.O. and a dentist married to a hairdresser. Some were skilled or semi-skilled in factories, and even in white-collar jobs... of course these were not of the lowest barriada level....'

And finally this quite encouraging conclusion from a young Englishman used to the conditions in his own much wealthier country:

'In time, and given help to improve the barriadas before the inhabitants have been there so long that they lose hope, they will become perfectly reasonable working class districts, with proper roads and so on'.

Such being the evidence of responsible eyewitnesses, one may reasonably conclude that the *barriadas*, far from being slums, play an invaluable part in the process by which the peasant immigrants are assimilated into urban life. They should not be the objects of indignation, pity, or despair, but regarded as symbols of hope. This is now recognized by the Peruvian authorities. In 1961, realizing that the squatters could not, and should not, be resisted by force, Congress enacted legislation for the supplying of water and sanitary services to the *barriadas*, with provision made for the granting of legal title to the land (mostly government-owned patches of useless desert) that had been occupied. Since this time both the government and religious and charitable organizations have been paying increasing attention to the needs of the *barriadas*, building schools, clinics, and every other kind of amenity.

If one looks for it, there is, of course, still a great deal of poverty, with its inevitable accompaniment of vice, crime, and misery, in Lima, a huge overcrowded city. The Pérez family belong to the fortunate minority of immigrants who have found their place in urban society; there are no doubt many more such families who do little more than just manage to survive by means of marginal activities of one kind or another. For it must be faced that peasants are flocking to the cities on the coast at a rate much faster than they can possibly be absorbed into industry. Pike quotes the following statistics.[1] Between 1940 and 1961 the Peruvian population rose from 7 to nearly 11 million. But in 1963, the Peruvian economy was supplying only some 10,000 new job opportunities a year, while most economists agree that within ten years the annual number of new employment openings would have to rise to at least 100,000 if the country is to avoid staggering problems of unemployment and

[1] Pike, op. cit., pp. 303–5.

economic stagnation. It is, of course, a characteristic of Latin American cities, even in highly developed countries like Argentina, that a large proportion of the urban population (perhaps as much as 70 per cent) subsist by marginal activities – as house-servants, gardeners, porters, watchmen, pedlars, and as small craftsmen and tradesmen – while only a chosen few are recruited into the much higher-paid ranks of unionized labour in industry. Thus in Peru there is a sharp distinction to be drawn between the peasants and the only half-assimilated urban proletariat who are seeking to escape from being peasants, and those fortunate individuals, like Max, who have made good in their new urban environment, and either joined the ranks of unionized labour in industry or, as white-collar workers, put their feet on the lowest rung of the ladder leading towards the middle class.

What is lacking in the cities of Peru, however, is the hopeless poverty of the ghetto, such as is to be found in more highly developed countries where there is racial prejudice as well as economic and social stratification – to make it extremely difficult for a man to escape from the environment into which he is born. In Peru there is nothing in theory to prevent the Indian or *mestizo* from improving his position in society, once he has taken the plunge of leaving his village and coming to the city. That is why, no doubt, communism has made so little progress (except among students and intellectuals) with the urban proletariat of Peru. Most of the city-dwellers, however poor they may be, have escaped from something worse and consider themselves to be on the way up in the world. It is only necessary to build a straw shack on the edge of the desert to become a man of property. Such budding Forsytes are not of the stuff from which revolutions are made.

Chapter 21

Power, Politics, and the People

PERU IS IN THEORY a democratic republic. But, as in most Latin American countries, democracy of the kind practised in Britain or North America has seldom been much more than an ideal. It is necessary to delve beneath the surface of the written constitution to discover what are the motivating forces in politics and the real sources of power. Not that the written constitution can be ignored. It represents the legal framework, even if the law is not applied. Many Peruvians have fought passionately for democracy; probably the majority of educated Peruvians think of their country as democratic, even though they know that it falls far short of this ideal. In fact, in spite of all the obvious defects in the system, there is to be found in Peru a kind of grass-roots democracy at work through which, increasingly, the people are making their wishes felt.

One does not have to go any further than the presidential palace to become aware of the gulf which separates theory from practice in the government of Peru. According to the constitution, executive power is vested in a President of the Republic who (together with the First and Second Vice-Presidents) is supposed to be elected by direct suffrage for a term of six years.[1] But, as we saw in 1968, Velasco Alvarado seized power by means of a *coup d'état*. His authority as *de facto* President rests on the pragmatic argument that the democratic system failed to produce good government and allowed the country to sink into financial and administrative chaos. There are so many precedents of military interventions, designed to save the country from this or that disaster, that the *golpe* has become almost a respectable institution in Latin America, whatever else the rest of the world may think of it. Many Peruvians would consider that the generals were falling down on their jobs if they failed to protect the nation's interests in this way.

To return to the constitution, the President's powers are supposed to be limited by an elected legislature and subject to the rule of law as interpreted by an independent judiciary – a system of

[1] Having served his term of six years the President cannot be immediately re-elected.

247

checks and balances similar to that enshrined in the U.S. constitution. The Peruvian legislature consists of a bi-cameral Congress, with a Senate and Chamber of Deputies, numbering 45 and 140 members respectively. Senators and deputies are elected to represent districts by direct suffrage at the same time and for the same term of office as the President. The Judiciary comprises a Supreme Court in Lima, and lower Courts in the departments and provinces. Members of the Supreme Court are elected by Congress from among ten nominees of the executive, which also nominates magistrates to the lower Courts.[1]

Ever since Independence the division of powers between the Congress and the executive has been a bone of contention: the liberals wanting a strong Congress and a weak President; the conservatives, more realistically, insisting that there must be a strong executive in a country whose tradition is one of centralized, authoritarian government. This conflict of motives has been reflected in the widely varying constitutions (seven in all) which Peru has had since Independence. But thanks to Ramón Castilla's compromise constitution of 1860, it was the conservative philosophy (with some liberal trimmings) which prevailed in the end and is enshrined in the existing constitution of 1933. By this document the President is given ample powers. He is personally responsible for maintaining national security. He can convoke Congress, nominate and dismiss the President of the Council of Ministers, and all other Ministers of state, dictate decrees and resolutions, administer the national income, direct diplomatic negotiations, and appoint or dismiss members of the diplomatic service. In effect, he combines in his person not only all the symbolic and representational functions of a monarch or Head of State, but also the leadership of the government, with powers of decision considerably greater than those of, say, a British Prime Minister.

On another important issue which divided the politicians in the nineteenth century – federation versus centralism – the conservative preference for strong centralized government likewise prevailed. Administratively Peru is divided into twenty-three departments and the province of Callao. The departments are subdivided into provinces and districts. The chief administrator in a department is the prefect who is appointed by the President. Lesser provincial appointments – sub-prefects, governors, and lieutenant-governors – are appointed by the prefects. The only concession made in the constitution towards provincial autonomy is provision for the setting-up of departmental councils, the members of which are elected on a system of proportional representation for a term of four years. In

[1] R. J. Owens, op. cit., pp. 61–3.

practice, these councils seem to have achieved very little. It is the prefects and their minions who rule the roost in the provinces under the close control of the government in Lima.[1]

Thus throughout most of her republican history Peru has maintained the Incaic and colonial tradition of centralized, authoritarian, and bureaucratic government; Congress has normally played second fiddle to the executive; indeed, there have been long periods in the twentieth century when the legislature, if it was allowed to function at all, was little more than a rubber-stamp for dictatorial Presidents such as Leguía, Benavides, and Odría. A very different situation prevailed, however, during the two relatively short periods when Bustamante and Belaúnde occupied the presidency. Both of these constitutionally elected civilian Presidents believed sincerely in the democratic system and tried to make it work. They were both, however, hampered by a hostile *Aprista* opposition, which, with its allies, could command a majority of the votes in Congress, and thus possessed the means to impose a much greater measure of congressional control over the executive than had ever been attempted in the past. Now a hybrid system of presidential and parliamentary government, such as the *Apristas* sought to establish,[2] might have worked satisfactorily in a situation where the President, like a British Prime Minister, could count upon the support of a majority of his followers in Congress. But both Bustamante and Belaúnde lacked this essential requirement. The opposition parties in Congress adopted harassing tactics, censuring and dismissing Ministers, blocking measures, and refusing to approve tax proposals and budgets, which made it virtually impossible for the two Presidents to govern. In the case of Bustamante the result was near-anarchy; in that of Belaúnde financial chaos culminating in a crisis of confidence. In both cases parliamentary democracy conspicuously failed to work, providing the pretext for its replacement by military government.

What, one might ask, was the reaction of the Peruvian people to the arbitrary dismissal of two democratically elected Presidents whom the majority of the electorate had chosen only a few years before for the highest office in the land? The author was in Lima when Bustamante was removed from office in 1948. He heard the news on the radio and, like everybody else, was taken completely by surprise. There was virtually no opposition shown by the people towards General Odría's action in seizing the presidency. The next day everybody went to work as usual and minded his own business. In the case of Belaúnde, who during his first three years of office

[1] Ibid., p. 62.
[2] In 1945 the *Aprista* majority in Congress amended the constitution of 1933 in order to give Congress greater powers.

had been a very popular President, the reaction of the people seems
to have been equally luke-warm. According to newspaper reports,
the students protested and there was a clash with the police, but
the trouble was all over in twenty-four hours. All the main political
parties (with the notable exception of Seoane's left-wing faction of
Acción Popular) uttered protests, and most of the newspapers carried
editorials condemning the takeover. But there was no follow-up to
this press campaign; no sign at all of anything like spontaneous or
widespread public indignation. While it is impossible to quantify
any such assertion, there seem to have been a good many Peruvians
who welcomed the military takeover. 'Belaúnde was a well-meaning
chap, but his head was in the clouds – the change had to be made'.
This comment was made to the author in London by a leading
Peruvian businessman, and no doubt reflects what was being said
at the time in the *Club Nacional* and in oligarchical cocktail parties
in Lima. At the more popular level there were some patriotic folk
who tossed their hats into the air and shouted 'Viva Velasco' when,
six days after the *coup d'état*, the hated I.P.C. was expropriated.
There is nothing like the heady air of nationalism to rouse the
people to enthusiasm for a new government.

But, unless something like this happens to arouse them, the Peruvian people are inclined to be apathetic towards politics. Possibly
this is because the electorate is so small. Under the constitution
voting is compulsory for literate adults (men and women) between
twenty-one and sixty years. But the literacy test is a very selective
filter. In 1963 only some 2 million adults out of a total population
of 12 million were qualified to vote. Thus the voters belong to a
privileged minority. At the lower level they are likely to be relatively
well-paid unionized workers in industry and on the coastal farms,
together with artisans, small shopkeepers, clerks, and the like – i.e.
people who have already come up quite a long way in the world
and hope to go farther. At the next level the voters will be professional men – doctors, dentists, lawyers, civil servants, schoolteachers,
university professors, etc. – in short, the educated élite of the middle
class. Finally, driving to the polls in their limousines, will come the
members of the oligarchy – men and women of property and wealth,
whose influence in society is a great deal more weighty than the
flimsy pieces of paper which from time to time they may drop into
a ballot-box. Apart from a minority of eccentrics and intellectuals,
this is not the kind of electorate which is likely to set the country
on fire.

Outside in the cold, without any say whatsoever about the choice
of their President or the senators and deputies who are supposed to
represent them in Congress, are the mass of the peasants (some 40

per cent of the population), together with a large floating population of recently arrived urban immigrants, who are still at the stage
of scraping a living in the cities by marginal activities. Now these,
of course, are precisely the two classes of the population who most
urgently need the help of the politicians and the goodwill of the
government. But only insofar as the rival political candidates, and
those who are in power, may be prepared for their own good
reasons to espouse the cause of the disfranchised majority can this
part of the population be said to have any political representation.
For members of the proletariat it makes no difference, therefore,
whether their benefactor has been elected to office in the democratic
manner laid down by the constitution or is a soldier who has seized
power by force. When it comes to hand-outs, military dictators, like
Benavides or Odría, have just as good a record of munificence as
any of the constitutionally elected Presidents of Peru.

For the majority of the Peruvian people, therefore, politics is not
so much a question of votes and elections, as one of finding effective
ways and means of securing the assistance and goodwill of the government of the day. The bureaucratic machine in Peru, much of it
unchanged since colonial times, is cumbersome and slow, and in
some cases it may also be corrupt.[1] For the ordinary citizen, who
has neither money nor pull, it can be an agonizing experience trying
to get action on quite simple things. Ill-paid junior civil servants are
mostly nothing more than unwilling and inefficient wielders of
rubber-stamps – to obtain a decision on anything of the slightest
importance it is necessary to see a Minister; indeed, all really important decisions in Peru are taken by the President himself. With
queues of petitioners lined up in their anterooms every day seeking
favours, it is extremely difficult for the President and his Ministers
either to give good service to the public or find time to deal with
fundamental questions of policy; there is no competent body of
permanent officials to whose broad shoulders the burden of either
of these two tasks can be transferred. But it is the public which of
necessity suffers the most from this defective system of government.
Unless he is a personal friend of a Minister, the individual petitioner
is not likely to get very far in his dealings with government departments. But experience has shown that union means strength. Both
Ministers and civil servants very quickly sit up and take notice
of their problems when ordinary citizens combine together in
political parties, trade unions, peasant syndicates, *barriada* councils,
trade associations, and similar groups. If it is true to claim that

[1] A contributory cause of Belaúnde's downfall in 1968 was a scandal concerning graft in the Peruvian customs, in which high officials were alleged
to be involved.

democracy of a kind exists in Peru, it is very largely through the agency of such pressure groups (rather than through the formal machinery provided by the constitution) that it expresses itself.

Take, for example, the trade unions. They were created originally in order to increase the bargaining power of labour in its relations with management. But in Peru, as in Latin America generally, the trade union movement very soon acquired a political orientation. Rather than bargain from weakness in a market saturated by cheap labour, the unions found that a more effective way of protecting their interests and getting what they wanted was to bring pressure to bear upon the government. Unstable Latin American governments, living in constant fear of a military takeover, are very sensitive to the threat of strikes, street demonstrations, and violence, and will go to great lengths to avoid such troubles. Certainly in Peru even the toughest dictators, like Benavides and Odría, always had an attentive ear open to the demands of labour (even at times when most of the *Aprista* labour leaders were in jail), and social benefits were heaped into the laps of this feared and favoured class of the population. As a consequence an enormous gulf now separates the relatively affluent unionized workers in factories, mines, oilfields, and railways (including some of the farm-hands in the large coastal *haciendas*) from the mass of the peasantry and the unskilled urban proletariat. The latter live at the margin of subsistence. The former enjoy good wages, together with such amenities as medical services, good houses, radio sets (sometimes even television), social centres, sports grounds, and cinemas. In short, the unionized workers of Peru have become a privileged aristocracy within the working class.

In the early part of the twentieth century the Peruvian labour movement tended to be Marxist in its ideology. But with increasing affluence its revolutionary fervour has very largely disappeared. It no longer dreams of overthrowing the established order in which it has found quite a comfortable place. The vast majority of the unions are affiliated to the *Aprista* dominated *Confederación de Trabajadores del Perú* (C.T.P.), founded in 1944, and with a membership now of over 500,000 workers. But there is intense competition between the political parties, including the various extremist groups — Moscow- and China-orientated communists, Trotskyists, anarchists, the dissident *Aprista* M.I.R., etc. — to gain a foothold in the labour movement. The Christian Democrats have had some success through C.L.A.S.C. (Latin American Confederation of Christian Trade Unions), but Belaúnde's *Acción Popular* was always very weak in its penetration of the unions, and had to rely very largely upon the support of the extremist labour leaders.

As we saw in Chapter 18, this competition between the political parties has now been extended to the organization of peasant syndicates in the *sierra*, the way having been successfully pioneered by the Trotskyist F.I.R. in the La Convención valley. More recently the Christian Democrats, with the encouragement of Roman Catholic missionaries, have made good progress in this field in an attempt to beat the 'extremists' at their own game. So it rather looks as though, through the instrumentality of peasant syndicates, politics in Peru are entering upon a new dimension – nothing less than the political emancipation of the peasants. This is, of course, something which is bound to come quite soon in any case, as the new generation of schoolchildren (the vast majority of children in Peru now go at least to a primary school) come of age and qualify as voters.

For the moment, however, it is a combination of unionized industrial labour and the new and expanding middle class (what has been called the 'middle sectors')[1] that dominates the electorate and holds the balance of power in politics, even though the ultimate power – economic and military – remains in the hands of the oligarchy and the army. The emergence of the middle class as a major force in politics is reflected in the decline of purely oligarchical parties (like the old *Civilista* Party of the early twentieth century) and their replacement by more broadly-based 'popular' parties such as APRA and *Acción Popular*. The tragedy for Peruvian democracy is that these popular parties are split asunder by personal rivalries, and have never been able to combine, as in logic they ought to do, in support of a single leader or programme.

Not that the middle class in Peru represents anything like a homogeneous political group. It is split between a majority who on the whole are conformist in outlook and emotionally identified with the institutional *status quo*, and a minority – mostly among the students and intellectuals – who are 'hell-bent for reform'.[2] This 'extremist' element, in its turn, is split between a multitude of warring factions, whose only common denominator is an undying hatred of the oligarchy and a burning dissatisfaction with the present state of Peruvian society. But opinions are divided between those who seek to overthrow the capitalist society by force, as Castro managed to do in Cuba, and those (for example, the Moscow-line communists) who, for tactical reasons, advocate a more moderate course.

In 1963 it was estimated that the extremist groups in Peru represented some 100,000 votes (which mainly were given to Belaúnde) or, say, about 5 per cent of the electorate. However, their pulling power in politics is a good deal greater than is suggested by this

[1] Pike, op. cit., p. 303.
[2] Peter Nehemkis, 'The Middle Class' (*Latin America and the Caribbean – a Handbook*).

figure. It only needs one or two determined 'extremist' leaders to take over the management of a trade union with a membership running into thousands. For example, in 1961, it was estimated that at least six important workers' organizations, with a membership of 21,000 (construction workers, taxi drivers, and bank clerks, together with important nuclei of workers in Cuzco and Huancayo), were under extremist control of one sort or another.[1] The student bodies in the universities likewise offer a tempting target for the professional extremist agitator. Here are young men of the middle class still with tender social consciences; many of them disgusted with the caution and ineffectiveness of the older generation of politicians. It is in any case traditional for Latin American students to regard themselves as the shock-troops of revolution. By these various means the 'extremists' can bring pressure to bear upon political parties and governments out of all proportion to their numbers. If the Peruvian government is today paying attention to agrarian reform, this is largely the result of fear of extremist agitation among the peasants. Even a military government has to keep its ear closely to the ground in order to try to discover what plots are being hatched in the extremist network. Like the political parties, the soldiers, too, must adopt a 'popular' policy in regard to social reform, if only to take the wind out of extremist sails.

The vast majority of the Peruvian middle class, however, although naturally keen to get all the material benefits they can out of the politicians, are very far from being revolutionary in their political outlook – and this seems to go equally for the humble *barriada* dweller[2] who is engaged in converting his straw shack into a proper house, and the already well-established professional man who probably has at least one car in his garage. In both groups there may be jealousy of the oligarchy, but this feeling is normally accompanied by the desire not to destroy, but to be admitted into, the charmed circle. As the Chilean writer Claudio Véliz has pointed out,[3] the industrialization and consequent rise of the middle class in Latin America have not brought about the substantial social, political, and cultural changes associated with the similar phenomenon in nineteenth-century Europe. There the industrial bourgeoisie presented a challenge to tradition which attained its fulfilment in the heyday of Victorian England. To quote Véliz: 'A great social and cultural distance was covered between the times of the Prince Regent and the Prince Consort. . . .'

But things turned out very differently in Latin America.

---

[1] Payne, op. cit., p. 101.   [2] See Mangin and Turner, op. cit.
[3] Claudio Véliz, 'An Historical Introduction' (*Latin America and the Caribbean – a Handbook*).

'Far from adopting an anti-traditionalist or anti-aristocratic stand, the Latin American groups who have acquired wealth from industry have tended to join the established groups, reinforcing their social standing and lending their own vitality and resourcefulness to the perpetuation of the existing social structure. The result of three decades of intensive industrialization has not been a frontal attack on tradition but rather the institutionalism of social climbing.'

This is certainly true of Peru, where it is almost impossible to draw any clear-cut line between the upper levels of the middle class and the oligarchy.

The kernel of the modern Peruvian oligarchy[1] is the owners of the large coastal plantations, producing sugar and cotton for export. These modern estates are totally unlike the old-style feudal *haciendas* in the *sierra*. They are essentially capitalistic enterprises, quite often organized as limited liability corporations and managed by competent engineers and administrators. They employ wage-earning, sometimes unionized, labour, require a good deal of capital, plant, and equipment, and have to compete in fluctuating international commodity markets. Thus, the typical oligarch is a businessman of modern and indeed international outlook. He has very little in common with the ancestral type of feudal landowner – the backbone of the nineteenth-century oligarchy – who lorded it over immense territories, exploited the work of enslaved Indians, and usually had all the local officials in his pocket. This unregenerate type of landowner (*gamonal*) still survives in Peru and may still have some local influence in politics, but he is no longer important nationally. In other words, oligarchy in Peru, originally based very largely on the regional power of feudal 'barons', has now been replaced by plutocracy.

Bourricaud's investigations into the composition of boards of directors reveal that the same small circle of business tycoons, who own the coastal plantations, have a finger in every other kind of pie, and indeed effectively control the economy of Peru. They run the banks – all the big sugar and cotton fortunes were found to be represented at the highest level in these organizations which control the distribution of credit. They dominate in the field of exports and imports. They speculate in mines, land, and real estate. Rather cautiously – they prefer to leave others to take the initial risks – they are moving into industry. Many oligarchs keep part of their fortunes abroad to be out of harm's way.

[1] The analysis which follows is based very largely upon François Bourricaud. *Structure and Function of the Peruvian Oligarchy* (Social Science Institute, Washington University, 1966).

A characteristic feature of the Peruvian oligarchy is the importance of the family – as Bourricaud puts it: 'it is in essence a network of families controlling wealth'. Nor, he points out, are they necessarily old families; in fact only a very small group among them would have serious claims to reaching back to the colonial period. Many oligarchical families are of fairly recent foreign origin – Italian, German, French, British, Arab, and Jewish.[1] The oligarchy is exclusive in a snobbish sense, and it has its different layers of social prestige – nothing can beat a Pardo or a Prado – but there is likewise nothing to prevent the newcomer from crashing his way in, provided that he is rich. Poor relations are tolerated. Each family has its head, who may be the elder son of the elder branch or simply somebody who is generally recognized as being the most active, most competent, and best placed of all the brothers, cousins, brothers-in-law, sons-in-law, and nephews of which the family is composed. The responsibilities of the head of the family extend not only to his own children, but to all the members of the clan, rich and poor alike, who will come to him, as a matter of course, for help and advice, to seek jobs or positions on the board of one of the family concerns, and for protection or assistance in dealing with the government or the law.

In its economic organization an oligarchical 'empire' is likely to consist of a loose federation of family-controlled interests – agricultural, banking, financial, and possibly mining and industrial – with members of the family and their friends serving on interlocking boards, or in professional capacities as managers, administrators, lawyers, architects, engineers, and so on. These Peruvian 'conglomerates' are not, however, designed primarily to maximize profits like their North American equivalents – they may quite often be weak in productivity and poor in organization. Their more fundamental purpose is to secure the family's position in society, preserving not only its wealth, but also its political influence and social prestige.

In politics the oligarchy does not normally seek to govern directly, but prefers to exert its influence from behind the scenes. As we saw, during most of her history as a republic (with occasional interludes of civilian rule), Peru has been ruled by a series of military *caudillos* – men for the most part of modest birth and mixed blood, who had no family ties with the oligarchy. The basis of co-operation was an implicit recognition on both sides that the government must be allowed to get on with the job of governing (preferably with the

---

[1] For example, names such as Gildemeister, Schreiber, Schroder, Dibos, Montagne, Carnevaro, Ricketts spring to mind. Fernando Belaúnde's mother's name was Terry.

help of oligarchical Ministers and advisers), but it should not meddle
more than absolutely necessary in affairs which the oligarchy considers to be its own preserve. In particular, oligarchy should not be
taxed beyond a certain point, monetary stability should be maintained, and the economy run 'soundly' on the traditional *laissez-
faire* lines.

Thus the influence of the oligarchy in politics is essentially negative. Its aim is not so much to make things happen, as to prevent
decisions being taken without its advice or against its interests. In
relation to government, the oligarchical 'clan' is essentially a pressure group like a trade union, and it has to steer its way very carefully in politics. With rival military *caudillos* and political parties
competing for power, it is prudent for an oligarchical family to have
a foot in several camps; but this cannot always be accomplished.
Thus, every government tends to bestow its favours on a given
oligarchical sector, while those oligarchs who are left out in the cold
will lend their support to an opposition group. If a government
succeeds in maintaining itself in power for a relatively long time, as
Leguía did between 1919 and 1930, it may be able considerably to
alter the basis of oligarchical power by rewarding the 'good' – that
is to say friends – and punishing the 'bad'. To quote Bourricaud,
'The endless struggles and inexpiable hatreds which place the clans
of the Peruvian oligarchy against each other can basically be ex-
plained by the competition for favours'.

Some of these family feuds have gone on for generations. For
example, the Miró Quesadas, the owners of the newspaper *El
Comercio*, have never forgiven Haya de la Torre for his alleged
responsibility for the murder, in 1935, of Antonio and his wife.[1]
Ever since this crime was committed the editorial policy of the
newspaper has been coloured by a relentless hatred for APRA. All
the other oligarchically owned newspapers, such as Pedro Beltrán's
La Prensa, are likewise highly polemical, with violent 'loves' and
'hates' for this political leader or the other. Far from being, then, a
monolithic force in politics, the oligarchy lends its support to party
faction in Peru, and to this extent can be said, perhaps, to serve the
purposes of democracy.

Oligarchy's greatest peril would consist in a coalition of the
'underprivileged' Indian peasants, the urban proletariat, and the
more radical sector of the middle class. Such a combination of
political forces very nearly came into being during the hunger and
misery of the Depression years (1930–33), when the revolutionary
fervour of APRA was at its height. In the years which followed,
however, the oligarchy was able to take shelter behind a series of

[1] See above, p. 164.

military 'strong-men' (Sánchez Cerro, Benavides, and Odría), until, with the increasing affluence of the middle class, the danger receded; but it has not disappeared. As the spread of education results in an enlarged electorate, the peasantry becomes politically emancipated, the urban proletariat grows in size and political strength, and the competition between 'popular' and 'extremist' political parties becomes more intense, so inevitably the bastions of oligarchical power will become more difficult to defend.

If oligarchy represents the economic prop of the Establishment, the Roman Catholic Church provides its moral foundations. It exerts its influence, not perhaps so much upon the rising middle class, as at those two poles of society – the oligarchy and the peasants. Traditionally the political outlook of the Church (it is a major landowner in Peru) has been conservative. But today there is a 'new look' in the Church's attitude towards social problems in Latin America, based on recent papal encyclicals. In January 1969 the Roman Catholic bishops of Peru, stimulated no doubt by the Pope's visit to Latin America in August 1968, announced the new policy in the most uncompromising terms. They put the blame for the ills of the country firmly upon the shoulders of 'a privileged minority of rich Peruvians acting in complicity with an imperialistic economic system'. The present reality of social, economic, cultural, and political inequalities was denounced as a 'state of sin'. One of the bishops, Mgr Luciano Metzinger, is reported to have declared that half the population of Peru was suffering injustices and that 6 million Peruvian Indians were 'totally abandoned' by the national community.[1] These are sentiments that Haya de la Torre might have uttered in his heyday as a revolutionary leader; they come strangely from the mouth of a prelate of the Church in Peru.

To what extent these brave words will be matched by deeds remains to be seen. Truly progressive bishops are in a minority in the Peruvian hierarchy. The priests are very thin on the ground – only one for every 7,257 inhabitants; and in the country parishes they are often of low calibre. There are, however, some encouraging signs of progress by the Church in the direction indicated by the new policy.[2] As long ago as 1956 it was reported by the archdiocese of Cuzco that the Church had divested itself of some of its land, selling it at half its market value to rural labourers on easy terms of credit. In many parts of the *sierra* Roman Catholic foreign missionaries (as well, incidentally, as various sects of Protestant missionaries) are doing excellent work running schools and clinics, and even

[1] Report from Buenos Aires to *The Times* by Richard Wigg, 28 January 1969.
[2] See Pike, op. cit., pp. 312–15.

helping the Indians in such practical matters as the establishment of credit and consumer co-operatives and the organization of peasant syndicates. Since 1963 the Maryknoll fathers, in Puno on the shores of Lake Titicaca, have been running a radio school. It broadcasts in Quechua, Aymara, and Spanish and provides lessons in reading and writing as well as on such practical matters as hygiene, sanitation, and modern farming methods. The *barriadas* surrounding the great cities are likewise a target for missionary activities, both clerical and lay; indeed, there is scarcely a lady in the oligarchy who does not engage in some sort of charitable work, often under conditions of considerable discomfort. Nor is the political field – with the danger of the spread of communism in mind – being neglected by Roman Catholics of progressive outlook, working through such organizations as the Christian Democratic Party and its various ramifications in the field of organized labour.

To complete this balance-sheet of the forces making for, or inhibiting, social progress in Peru, it only remains to consider the position of the army, the third and ultimate prop of the Peruvian Establishment. Here, too, there is to be found a 'new look' concerning social problems. True, the army leaders (like the Roman Catholic Church) are rigorously opposed to 'communism' (a term employed very loosely to describe any form of extremism). They are also highly allergic to anarchy – public order must be maintained at all costs. It would be wrong, however, to conclude from this that the army is 'reactionary' – nothing more than a tool of the oligarchy. In politics the new generation of army officers act rather as an autonomous estate and intervene to defend their own group interests or what they conceive to be the national interest, not those of civilians they may well despise. The soldiers regard themselves as being more efficient – and more patriotic – than civilians. They pride themselves on forming part of the technical intelligentsia in an age when 'planning' and 'technology' have become something of a cult. Nor is this by any means entirely an empty claim. The standard of education received in Peru's C.A.E.M. (*Colegio de Altos Estudios Militares*) compares favourably with that to be found in any of the secular institutions of learning or technology.[1]

In social background most officers in the Peruvian army come from the *mestizo* middle class and the troops they command are mostly Indian. Moreover, the army gets about the country, chasing guerrillas in the mountains, guarding the frontiers, and building roads. In the *selva* the Peruvian armed forces – the navy in this case – use their British-built gunboats to patrol the upper reaches of the

[1] See Alistair Hennessy, 'The Military in Politics' (*Latin America and the Caribbean – a Handbook*).

Amazon and its tributaries, providing medical and social services and police protection to the scattered hamlets of this wild jungle region. The claim of the armed forces to be in closer touch with the people than the city-bred and city-bound civilian politicians (Belaúnde was an outstanding exception) is not therefore without some foundation.

Whether it is right to describe the modern generation of army officers in Peru as 'Nasserite' is a matter of terminology. Probably the only real example to date of 'Nasserism' in Latin America was the Argentine phenomenon of Perónism, with its initial support by radical army officers, its populist base, and neo-socialist policies. It is apparent that the Peruvian army has not yet gone as far as this along the road of social revolution; but one does not know, of course, what plans are being made by unknown colonels lower down in the military hierarchy. All that can be said for the moment is that both the military government of 1962–63 and the one inaugurated by Velasco Alvarado in October 1968 differ in an important way from any previous military régimes. In both cases the decision to intervene was taken not as in the past by an ambitious *caudillo* greedy for power, but by the Joint Command of the Armed Forces acting in unison. In 1962, ironically enough, the object of the military intervention was to stop Haya de la Torre and Odría and pave the way to the presidency for Fernando Belaúnde, whose social policies were fully supported by the army leaders of that time. Six years later, in 1968, a new Joint Command of the Armed Forces found themselves in the unpleasant situation of having to dismiss a President whom the army had supported, not because his policies were too radical for the military taste, but because, in the view of the soldiers, the country had been allowed to sink into chaos.

It is significant that the new military government has made no promises at all concerning the holding of presidential elections and an eventual return to civilian government. The plan seems to be to stay in power until, in their own good time, the soldiers themselves decide that the mess has been cleared up and the country is ready for a new bout of democracy.

We conclude, therefore, on an unsatisfactory note of uncertainty. It might almost seem that Peruvian politics are doomed to go round in an endless circle of alternate civilian and military governments, without getting anywhere. But if one examines the record over a long enough period of time, say from the turn of the century, it will be seen that the movement has been not a flat circle, but an upward spiral, with a good deal of progress made on each turn.

The political future of Peru is obscure – benevolent despotism or democracy? Evolution or revolution? Or are we to expect some kind of a Nasserite solution, with the soldiers acting as the agents of revolutionary change? Only time can tell. What is, however, virtually certain is that the interconnected processes of 'mestization', industrialization, and urbanization will continue upon their relentless course, gradually changing the face of the country, creating a new racial and cultural balance in the population, putting new strains upon the economy, and giving rise inevitably to an ever-increasing pressure from the grass-roots for social reform.

Chapter 22

Peru in the Modern World

PERU HAS A GREAT DEAL to offer as a field of study, if only because of the glamour of her Incaic and colonial past. But there are, of course, a number of Latin American countries which outrank her in importance by any modern yardstick. She occupies only the fourth place in size and the fifth in population, her 12 million inhabitants comparing with a total population for Latin America estimated at 261 million. In terms of wealth (as measured by her income *per capita*) she comes very far down in the list, with a figure of $268·5, compared with 799 for Argentina, 644·5 for Venezuela, and 415·4 for Mexico. Indeed, there are only six mostly very small republics in Latin America poorer than Peru, the poorest being her neighbour, Bolivia.[1] If industrialization is the yardstick, Lima, in spite of its 2 million inhabitants, is exceeded in factory output by seven Latin American cities – Buenos Aires, São Paulo, Mexico City, Rio de Janeiro, Santiago, Havana, and Caracas.[2] Socially, large areas of Peru are still very backward even by Latin American standards.

For the student of Latin American affairs some knowledge of Peru is essential, however, to understand the peculiar problems of the Andean area – problems of racial and cultural integration and economic underdevelopment, which have no parallel in countries such as Argentina and Uruguay. Three of the republics of the area – Peru, Bolivia, and Ecuador – formed part of the Inca empire and the domain of the original viceroys of Peru. The wider area includes Colombia and Venezuela – two countries of somewhat different character from Peru – which were intended to have been part of Bolívar's Confederation of the Andes. Although the five republics have all gone their own separate ways since Independence they have retained a certain family resemblance. In particular, there are close affinities between the highland 'Indian' regions of Peru, Ecuador, and Bolivia. It is indeed tempting to make comparisons. Why, for

[1] Carmen A. Miró, 'Population of Latin America' (*Latin America and the Caribbean – a Handbook*). The figures relate to 1961.
[2] Peter R. Odell, 'The Geography of Latin America's Economic Development' (*Latin America and the Caribbean – a Handbook*).

example, did Bolivia, a much more backward country than Peru in most ways, have a social revolution in 1952 which has destroyed the feudal system in the *haciendas*, while Peru is only just beginning to grapple with the problem? Part of the explanation, no doubt, is that Bolivia has no 'coast'. The capital, La Paz, is in the heart of the Indian country. In Peru, by contrast, most of the wealth of the country is concentrated upon the coast, and the Indian highlands have always been a neglected hinterland. If the Peruvian capital had been established in Cuzco the problems of the Indians would probably have been very much more to the fore.

One can profitably ask the same question about Mexico and Peru. Here are two countries with a remarkably similar historical background. Both were the cradles of the most highly developed Indian civilizations of the New World, culminating with the Aztecs in Mexico and the Inca in Peru. Mexico City and Lima were the two great viceregal centres of Spanish power in America. Since Independence both republics have been faced with precisely the same basic problem – the integration of the Indian and Spanish races and cultures within the framework of a modern industrial society. To compare Peru with Mexico is rather like looking at one of those 'before' and 'after' advertisements. During the last fifty years Mexico has consolidated the gains of a major social revolution – started in 1910 – of which Professor Humphreys wrote in 1946: 'what is remarkable is not that it has achieved so little but that it has achieved so much'.[1] Not all Mexico's problems have been solved, of course. But oligarchy, which still flourishes in Peru, has long since disappeared in Mexico and been replaced by a large and prosperous *mestizo* middle class. There are still peasants living at a bare level of subsistence in what Cline calls 'Remote Mexico', but today they account for only 30 per cent of the population; the corresponding figure for Peru would be more like 50 per cent. Why the great difference? Here again geography has probably been a major factor in determining the rate of social change. Mexico City was built by the Spaniards on the site of Aztec Tenochtitlan, in the heart of the former Indian empire, whereas Lima was built on the coast. 'Mestization' has proceeded much more rapidly in Mexico than in Peru, where the Andes have been a barrier to integration. Moreover, Mexican proximity to the U.S.A. has served the dual purpose of hardening the Mexican character, in resistance to U.S. cultural infiltration, without preventing the absorption of Anglo-Saxon ideas on such matters as business efficiency and go-getting, and the need for social change. Peru, in contrast, being remote from the great

[1] Quoted Howard F. Cline, *Mexico – Revolution To Evolution 1940–1960* (Oxford, 1962), p. 24.

centres of industrial power in the world, has been relatively immune from such 'foreign' influences.

In her relations with the outside world Peru does not perhaps cut very much ice on her own, although together the twenty republics of Latin America represent a formidable concentration of power. Economically, Latin America is rich in raw materials, and some of the more advanced republics are already well forward along the road to industrialization – in terms of economic development the area is a half-way house between 'poor' Asia and Africa, and 'rich' North America and Europe. Its population, 261 million, is growing more rapidly than in any other part of the world – a mixed blessing, no doubt, but providing the potential for almost unlimited economic growth. Politically, Latin America is also of considerable international importance, not only in relation to the security of the U.S.A., and hence of the western world as a whole, but as a bloc of countries holding the balance between 'East and West' (or if one prefers it 'North and South') in the United Nations.

In the Organization of American States, in which all the Latin American republics, with the temporary exception of Cuba, are represented, the essential political problem has always been to harmonize the interests and obtain a working partnership between the U.S.A. – the Colossus of the North – and a large number of much weaker countries, proud of their Latin American heritage and jealous of their independence, but all to a greater or lesser extent dependent upon the U.S.A. for their security and economic well-being. After a century of uninhibited U.S. imperialism in the Caribbean, President Franklin Roosevelt, in 1933, inaugurated the 'Good Neighbour Policy' and there was a marked improvement in hemispheric relations. The last marines left Haiti in the following year. In 1961 another important step towards hemispheric solidarity was taken with the creation of the 'Alliance for Progress', described by President John F. Kennedy as 'a vast new effort unparalleled in magnitude and nobility of purpose, to satisfy the basic needs of the American people for homes, work and land, health and schools'.[1] Kennedy's initiative followed shortly on Fidel Castro's announcement of his revolutionary plans for remaking the hemisphere. 'The Andes must become the Sierra Maestra of Latin America', Guevara told a shocked and hostile ministerial meeting of Latin American states at Punta del Este, Uruguay, in August 1961. To quote a present-day writer:[2] '1961 was a year of gloriously competing visions – Castro's and Kennedy's – of the future of Latin America. The

---

[1] The speech was made in the White House in March 1961.

[2] William D. Rogers, 'The United States And Latin America' (*Latin America and the Caribbean – a Handbook*).

years since have disappointed the dreams of both. Castro has become a bad joke. But Kennedy's hope for a rapid "revolution in freedom" has surrendered to the grim truth that political, social and economic development is, at best, the work of decades in Latin America.'

With her Indian backyard wide open to the danger of infiltration by Cuban-trained guerrillas (a danger which materialized in 1963) Peru took the lead in calling for a conference of Pan-American Foreign Ministers, which met in San José, Costa Rica, in August 1960, to consider the Cuban danger. The difficulties with which the delegates to this conference, presided over by Dr Julio César Turbay Araya of Colombia, were faced have been described.[1]

'The Latin American view, never wholly unanimous, generally opposes communism, but is sceptical that the Cuban movement is much more than a radical, but nationally supported, social upheaval to put an end to political and economic abuses that have plagued Cuba since its relatively late achievement of independence at the end of the nineteenth century. Governments such as those of Mexico and Venezuela, where undercurrents of sympathy for the Castro régime are especially strong among the politically potent Left, and whose main policies also point towards social and economic reforms demanded by their own successful revolutions, must tread with special care a path that is full of political booby-traps.'

In the event, the U.S. Secretary of State, Christian Herter, was able to avoid the booby-traps and obtain the unanimous approval of the delegates to a 'Declaration of San José', which energetically condemned intervention, or 'the menace of intervention', by extra-continental powers in the affairs of the hemisphere, while reiterating that no American republic has the right to interfere with the affairs of another, imposing its own ideology or social, economic, and political principles. There is, of course, a contradiction of aim here, which is reflected in the fact that, while Peru wholeheartedly supported the U.S.A. in the Cuban crisis of 1959–60, she was highly critical of U.S. intervention in the Dominican crisis of April 1965.

Peru was a founding member of the United Nations, which came into being at the San Francisco Conference in 1945. Of the fifty participating nations, no less than two-fifths, or twenty, were the republics of Latin America, giving them at the beginning a tremendous, and indeed inflated, influence in the affairs of the world organization. While remaining free to take their own individual line when voting in the various committees, the Latin American republics, conscious of their united strength, work fairly closely together as a bloc and hold regular informal meetings to discuss matters of

[1] Cline, op. cit., p. 316.

importance. With varying degrees of emphasis, they mostly support the U.S.A. and the Western Powers on 'Cold War' issues, although they can sometimes be a thorn in the flesh of a country like Britain on 'colonial' questions. Indeed, with the United Nations increasingly swamped by new ex-colonial countries, there is a tendency for the Latin American delegations to seek to purchase support for economic development measures, in which they have a special interest, with reciprocal support for anti-colonial measures.[1] The Peruvian delegation to the United Nations, under the leadership of Víctor Andrés Belaúnde (President Belaúnde's uncle) from 1949 until 1967, was usually very helpful in its attitude towards the Western Powers, although falling short of support for Britain on such awkward topics as the Falkland Islands, British Honduras, Gibraltar, etc. Víctor Andrés Belaúnde became something of an institution in the United Nations and was president of the fourteenth session of the assembly in 1959. Peru had a seat on the Security Council in 1955–56.

In her capacity as a member of the various specialized agencies of the United Nations and of the O.A.S., and in her bilateral relations with the U.S.A. and other developed countries, Peru, like all the Latin American republics, is vitally interested in such economic problems as development finance and aid, Latin American integration, and the terms of international trade between Latin America and the rest of the world. In 1942 the first U.S. Technical Cooperation Mission was invited to Peru to advise the government on such matters as agriculture, health, education (rural and teacher-training), manpower, transport, and public administration. In 1954, under the guidance of its able Secretary-General, Raúl Prebisch, the U.N.'s Economic Commission for Latin America (ECLA) put forward some far-reaching proposals for a Latin American policy of economic growth. It was envisaged that there should be a massive increase in long-term financing for the development of Latin American industry, agriculture, and mining, to be contributed by all the developed countries of the free world, while the Latin American republics for their part should each individually draw up a long-term economic plan on the basis of a close analysis of all the empirical data available. With ECLA's assistance, Peru was already working in 1959 on her first national plan.

Under the dampening influence of Secretary of State John Foster Dulles, who with his preoccupation about East-West relations never had much time for Latin America, the U.S. government showed very little enthusiasm for the ideas put forward by ECLA; nor was it at all keen about a plan for economic co-operation propounded

[1] John A. Houston, *Latin America in the United Nations* (New York, 1956).

in 1958 by President Kubitschek of Brazil, known as *Operacāo Panamericana*. The Latin Americans for their part resented this lack of U.S. interest in their affairs, a feeling to which they gave vent when Vice-President Nixon visited South America in 1958. In Lima he was the victim of a hostile demonstration of students. But, as we saw, in 1960 the attitude of the U.S.A. towards Latin America was transformed when in his election campaign President Kennedy outlined his visionary plan of the Alliance for Progress. In August 1961 at Punta del Esté the Latin American republics committed themselves to a revolutionary programme of social and economic reform – comprehensive agrarian reform, fair wages and satisfactory working conditions, illiteracy to be wiped out, tax laws reformed, tax evasion severely punished, the national income re-distributed more fairly, the integration of Latin America accelerated – all this to be achieved under conditions of monetary stability (i.e. without inflation) and 'through the institutions of representative democracy'. The U.S.A. agreed to make available a major part of the minimum of $20 billion needed to make the programme possible. In effect, Kennedy was offering to underwrite a social revolution in Latin America on 'new frontier' lines.[1]

As the 1960s draw to their close it is clear that, in regard to its social aspects at any rate, the Alliance for Progress has not worked out according to plan. The social ills of Latin America, as we have already seen in our survey of Peruvian problems, are deep-seated, and it will probably take several generations before they can be cured, if indeed they can ever be entirely eradicated. On the other hand, the U.S.A. has kept its promise about 'aid', and a great deal of capital has been pumped into the area in the last few years. In 1964 Latin America received $1,018 million, mainly from the U.S.A., but with contributions from most of the other developed countries of the free world and through multilateral agencies.[2] In 1968 Peru received $15 million in loans and grants from the U.S.A. alone. The U.S. commercial investment in Peru was estimated to be $460 million.

As regards progress towards Latin American integration, Peru, in June 1961, became a founding member of the Latin American Free Trade Association (LAFTA), to which all the South American countries, plus Mexico, belong. The Central American republics have their own separate organization, CACM. In April 1967, the Heads

[1] Peter Nehemkis, 'The Alliance for Progress' (*Latin America and the Caribbean – a Handbook*).
[2] This figure relates only to aid provided by member countries of the D.A.C. (Development Assistance Committee of O.E.C.D.), i.e. all major countries except communist countries, Australia, New Zealand, and Israel.

of State of the member countries of O.A.S. who met in Punta del
Esté, Uruguay, pledged their support for the eventual merger of
LAFTA and CACM in a common market for the entire region by
1985. Enthusiasts for economic integration in Latin America believe
that none of the republics can fully develop its potential in isolation.
There must be a joint harnessing of natural resources, a pooling
of productive capacity and markets, and the formation of an economic bloc for the conduct of Latin America's foreign trade. But as
has been pointed out,[1] there are a great many practical snags. In
its initial stages, which involved the liberalization of existing trade
between the member countries, progress was rapid, since 'existing
trade' then consisted mainly of the primary commodities normally
exchanged between tropical and temperate regions. The difficulties
arose when this stage was completed and consideration had to be
given to competitive manufactured products. It is easy, Huelin re-
marks, for Ecuador or Paraguay to make tariff concessions to
Argentine and Brazilian manufacturers, as no real element of industrial competition is involved. But it is much more difficult for
Peru, Colombia, Chile, or Uruguay to make such concessions because manufacturing costs in the smaller markets are higher than
in the large countries, and liberalization would put many of the
industries out of business. The beneficiaries of integration would be
the advanced industrial countries – Argentina, Brazil, and Mexico –
which are beginning to replace the U.S.A. and Europe as sources
of industrial products.

Dissatisfaction with the rate and direction of LAFTA's progress,
coupled with uneasiness about the predominance of Argentina,
Brazil, and Mexico, were the basic reasons for the emergence in
1967 of a sub-regional group within the LAFTA framework – the
so-called Andean group – consisting of Bolivia, Colombia, Chile,
Ecuador, Peru, and Venezuela. There have been several meetings
of this group and initial progress was rapid and enthusiastic. For
example, on 7 February 1968 an agreement was signed setting up
the *Corporación Andina de Fomento* to promote and finance regional industrial and infrastructure projects that would normally be
beyond the means of private enterprise acting alone. But the liberation of trade between the Andean countries seems to be causing the
same dissensions that have divided LAFTA. Both Venezuela and
Peru, where costs are high and industry of recent origin, are doubtful about the ability of their manufacturers to compete successfully
even in a limited sub-regional free market of some 60 million people.
Consequently, while Chile and Colombia have been pressing for the

[1] David Huelin, 'Latin America: A Summary of Economic Problems'
(*Latin America and the Caribbean – a Handbook*).

elimination of tariffs among member countries over a six-year period and the establishment of a common external tariff within twelve years, Peru and Venezuela have preferred to emphasize the other aspects of integration, such as the co-ordination of economic policies, the harmonization of development plans, and the sponsoring of large international projects.[1]

Of very special interest to Peru, as a major exporter of food and raw materials, is the question of her terms of trade with the rest of the world. While working in ECLA on his economic plans for Latin America, Raúl Prebisch propounded the doctrine that the mechanism of free markets and international trade combines to favour the industrial countries at the expense of the exporters of primary commodities. The latter suffer the full loss occasioned when prices of raw materials fall, but benefit from only a part of the rises resulting from cyclical expansion. For when prices of raw materials rise on world markets the industrialized countries find ways of economizing in their use, either by improved technical processes or by the development of substitutes. To put it in layman's language, under the 'Prebisch Effect', the rich countries become richer, while the poor countries, even though they may not become poorer in absolute terms, are retarded in their development.[2] In Peru export earnings are the most important source of capital formation and they also determine how much the country can import. Moreover, foreign trade in both directions is a major source of government revenue. It is no exaggeration to say, therefore, that the economic expansion and social progress of Peru depend more upon the ability to obtain favourable terms for her trade than on aid and foreign capital, important though the latter may be.

There is no easy solution of this problem in a free-enterprise market economy. To some extent export prices can be stabilized by means of commodity agreements, quotas, etc., and trade barriers can be removed by the reduction of tariffs. But more drastic action is probably needed. Accordingly, the rich countries are coming under increasing pressure in the United Nations to consider ways and means of improving the terms of trade for the developing countries, and a special agency, UNCTAD (U.N. Conference on Trade and Development), of which Raúl Prebisch was the first secretary, has been exploring the possibilities of action. Its deliberations are of the greatest interest to Peru.

Peruvian relations with the U.S.A., traditionally very friendly, are under a temporary cloud, but there is no reason yet (i.e. in early 1969) to expect that the quarrel will be lasting or that it de-

[1] *B.O.L.S.A. Review*, Vol. 2, No. 23, pp. 624–7.
[2] Huelin, op. cit.

notes any fundamental change in the direction of either Peruvian or U.S. foreign policy. The chancelleries of the two countries are both confined to the straightjacket of domestic politics. The new military government of Peru is bound by political necessity to take a tough line over the expropriation of the I.P.C. If it refuses to pay compensation on the grounds that the company owes the Peruvian government $690·5 million in back-taxes, this is because such a claim, whatever may be its legal validity, has become a part of the nationalistic folklore of Peru. One can be sure that the officials in the U.S. State Department are perfectly well aware of this psychological background to the dispute; but their hands are equally tied by their own recalcitrant Congress, which has become tired of foreign ingratitude and has ruled, under the Hickenlooper Amendment, that aid should be suspended from countries which expropriate American properties without paying due compensation. One can only hope, for the sake of both countries, that some way out of the impasse will soon be found. It is perhaps a hopeful sign that the U.S. business community seems to have taken at their face value Peruvian statements that the I.P.C. is a 'special case', and that the Peruvian government will continue to guarantee the safety of all U.S. and other foreign investments in Peru. For example, the Southern Peru Copper Corporation are reported to be going ahead with their plans to invest $335 million in the Cuajone copper deposits. More significantly, in view of the experience of I.P.C., two U.S. oil companies, the Texas Petroleum Co. and Occidental Petroleum, have been granted concessions to explore for oil in eastern Peru and off the coast between Lambayeque and Chimbote.[1]

Whether there will prove to be any political significance in the Peruvian government's decision, on 1 February 1969, to establish diplomatic relations with the U.S.S.R. remains to be seen. Any immediate shift of Peruvian policy towards 'neutralism' seems unlikely so long as there is hope that Peru's fences with the U.S.A. can be mended. On the face of it, diplomatic relations with the U.S.S.R. are no more than a logical extension of a policy which was initiated by Belaúnde's government in 1967, when Peru rescinded a 1953 ban on imports of manufactured goods from communist bloc countries. In June 1968 an official Peruvian delegation started a tour of the iron-curtain countries in order to explore the possibilities of trade. Since then, in 1968 and the first months of 1969, Peru has signed commercial agreements with Hungary and Romania and established diplomatic relations with Czechoslovakia, Romania, and the U.S.S.R. A trade agreement was signed with the U.S.S.R. on 17 February 1969. Commercially, Eastern Europe offers a useful additional

[1] *B.O.L.S.A. Review*, Vol. 3, No. 26, p. 117.

market for Peruvian fish-meal, and in return Peru will presumably be able to count on a certain amount of economic aid. Already a Hungarian commercial mission is reported to have expressed interest in the possibilities of establishing an industrial estate in the northern Peruvian city of Trujillo.[1] Politically, any offers of aid and trade from iron-curtain countries may be useful to Peru as a bargaining counter with which to extract more aid on better terms from the U.S.A.

Not that one can exclude the danger that Peru, like any other of the Latin American republics, might be swung, if events moved in a particular way, into the 'neutralist', if not right into the communist, camp. Cuba has already gone that way. Brazil might have gone there in 1964. It was touch and go whether Frei would be able to beat the communists in the Chilean election of 1964. As for Peru, the danger of a communist takeover does not seem to be imminent, but the potential for revolution is obviously there so long as her social ills remain without a cure. It is always well to remember how in 1930–31, during the Great Depression, the bottom fell out of the Peruvian economy, and for a time the country lapsed into a state very close to anarchy. President Kennedy saw the danger clearly when he launched the Alliance for Progress. Where he went wrong was in pinning his hopes for social change in Latin America on the leaders of non-communist parties of the democratic left, such as Muñoz Marin of Puerto Rico, Betancourt of Venezuela, Figueres of Costa Rica, Frei of Chile, and Belaúnde of Peru. In early 1969 all these 'democratic' politicians, except Frei, were out of power, and five of the Latin American republics had military régimes. It is obviously asking too much that there should emerge in one Latin American country after another a smooth model of parliamentary democracy. But communism is not the necessary alternative, provided that Latin America is able to produce governments which are sincerely dedicated to the task of removing social injustice, and are 'democratic' at least to the extent that public opinion has the means of making its influence felt. According to these two criteria, Peru passes the test.

With Western Europe it has always been an object of Peruvian foreign policy to maintain the closest possible links. Peruvians are very conscious of their European cultural heritage; there is still, in spite of everything, a great love for the mother country, Spain, and French culture also is held in the highest esteem. Here again, of course, the fundamental motive, both political and economic, is to reduce her dependence upon the U.S.A. and preserve the integrity of the Latin culture, not out of any feeling of hostility towards the

[1] *B.O.L.S.A. Review*, Vol. 3, No. 26, p. 116.

North American republic, but as a matter of common prudence – it is bad to have too many eggs in one basket. Thus, the new Peruvian government can be counted upon to continue President Belaúnde's efforts to build up good relations with the developed countries of Europe – Germany, France, Italy, and Britain in particular – as well as with such non-European countries as Japan and Israel, who have shown a desire to participate in Peru's development plans.[1]

Peru's relations with the United Kingdom could not be more friendly, although they are tinged with a certain sadness because of Britain's reduced status as a world power. The days have long gone by when the principal activity of the British Embassy (or the British Legation as it was in the nineteenth century) was the presentation of claims against the Peruvian government for alleged wrongs suffered by British citizens and traders. Today the Embassy's main task – and this goes for the Ambassador as well as his commercial staff – is to assist British exporters to get a foothold in the Peruvian market, and British contractors and engineering firms to get their fair share of the many lush contracts for ports, dams, roads, irrigation works, etc., which from time to time the Peruvian government put out to tender. The international competition for this kind of business is fierce. Britain's commercial position in Peru is not, of course, anything like what it was in the nineteenth century – the opening of the Panama Canal and two World Wars have seen to that. At the turn of the century Britain supplied 45 per cent of Peru's imports and took 50 per cent of its exports. By 1965 these figures had been reduced to a pathetic 5·2 per cent and 5·8 per cent respectively, with the U.S.A. now in the predominant position and supplying 39·8 per cent of Peru's imports. But beggars cannot be choosers, and Britain cannot afford to neglect an export market in Peru, in which in 1967 she sold more than £12 million-worth of goods, as compared with £167 million for Latin America as a whole.

Britain's policy towards Peru, and towards Latin America generally, has the double objective of promoting trade with the area, while at the same time doing everything possible, within her limited means, to assist in economic, social, and political development. For, as a leading democratic country and a member of the Western Alliance, Britain shares with the U.S.A., albeit as a junior partner, a political and economic interest in the success of the Alliance for Progress.

[1] It remains to be seen, however, how foreign business opinion will react to the new Agrarian Reform Law of 1969 (which might, for example, affect the sugar plantations of the W. R. Grace Co.), or the proposal to nationalize foreign-owned telephone companies.

Britain's reawakening interest in Latin America is shown by such encouraging developments as the establishment since 1962 of no less than five centres of Latin American studies in British universities; the appearance in 1967 of two British periodicals devoted exclusively to the area – the Latin American edition of *The Economist* and *Latin America*; an increase in educational and cultural exchanges under the auspices of the British Council; and a modest programme of economic aid and technical assistance. Most of Britain's contribution in economic aid is channelled to Latin America through her participation in international lending agencies such as the World Bank, the International Monetary Fund, and the Inter-American Development Bank. But she occasionally makes direct grants to individual Latin American republics – for example, in 1966 the sum of £500,000 was loaned to Peru for the purchase of bridging equipment.

In the financial year 1965–66 Britain spent £614,000 on technical assistance to Latin America, of which the largest share (£166,000) went to Peru. This may not seem to be a very large sum (Britain cannot afford to be lavish in her overseas expenditure), but if properly chosen the value of technical assistance to the recipient country can be out of all proportion to the amount of money spent – expert advice is often more valuable than mere cash. In Peru British technical assistance projects have included a team of five geologists who are assisting the Peruvian government in the vitally important task of geological mapping; the gift of equipment worth £156,000 and the loan of three British instructors for the National Apprenticeship Training Centre, where young Peruvian artisans are being taught their crafts; a gift of scientific equipment to the National Engineering University; and the loan of British experts, at Peruvian request, on such miscellaneous subjects as housing, nature conservation, the feasibility study for a garbage disposal plant, a professor of law for one university, and a lecturer in fluid mechanics for another. If the still British-managed railways of Peru remind one of her influence in the past, these gifts and loans are a tangible proof of Britain's continuing goodwill. In a modest way, the British people can feel that they are helping the Peruvians in their gigantic task of 'conquering Peru'.

The Revolutionary Government 1968

EXCERPTS FROM ITS MANIFESTO (3 OCTOBER 1968)

'The action of the Revolutionary Government will be inspired in the need of transforming the structure of the State in a way that will permit a more efficient Government activity; transforming the social and economic and cultural structures; maintaining a defined nationalistic attitude, a clear independent position and the firm defense of national sovereignty, and dignity; fully re-establishing authority, respect and observance of law and the prevalence of justice and morality in all fields of national activity.

'The Revolutionary Government declares its observance of the international treaties of which Peru is a part, its resolution to remain faithful to the principles of the Christian and Western tradition and its determination to encourage all foreign investments which are willing to abide by the laws and interests of Peru.'

ARTICLE 2 OF DECREE LAW NO. 17063

Goals of the Revolutionary Government

The Revolutionary Government of the Armed Forces has chosen as its principal endeavour the attainment of the following goals:

(*a*) to transform the structure of the State making it more dynamic and efficient as required for a proper Government action;

(*b*) to promote the less favoured segments of the population to higher standards of living compatible with the dignity of the human being. This is to be achieved through the transformation of the economic, social and cultural structures of the Nation;

(*c*) to impress upon all acts of the Government a spirit of nationalism and independence, based on the firm defense of national sovereignty and dignity;

(*d*) to raise the moral standard of the Country in all fields of activity and to fully re-establish the principle of authority, respect for the Law and the prevalence of Justice;

(*e*) to promote the unity, harmony and the integration of all Peruvians; strengthening the national conscience.

EXCERPTS FROM MESSAGE TO NATION OF PRESIDENT VELASCO ALVARADO (5 DECEMBER 1968)

Strategy of Socio-Economic Development

It is necessary that the citizenry be aware that Government action must conform to a permanent planning process which visualizes future or Long Range Goals; mediate or Medium Range Goals; and immediate or Short Term Goals.

National planning must be related to the Government Program and it is for this reason that the Revolutionary Government in defining its political goals, has coordinated them with the Economic and Social Development Program formulated by the National Planning Institute. The Long Range Goals will lead towards a total change of structures and will assure the continuity required to achieve the goals of development that the Nation demands. Thus, the Long Range Goals will be conveniently adapted to the Revolution, in order to set the Country in the course it requires, and to effect the proposed transformation of structures and development.

Finally, the Short Term Goals will be reached by means of annual programs and adequate priorities.

The citizenry knows the Fiscal and Financial reality of the Country. Any Government Program requires economic resources for its implementation. Herein lies a limitation being faced by the present Administration. Nothing would be gained by showing a fully comprehensive Government Program, if results thereof might be detained or delayed by this limitation which the Revolutionary Government is firmly set in overcoming.

Long Range Goals

The great purpose of national development must be shared by all Peruvians and their responsibility refers to the following:

1. To achieve an intense growth which might facilitate the integration of all the population, reducing the margins which separate social groups and affording real possibilities of well-being to the majority of Peruvians.

2. To assure a wide domestic market which might be conducive to an increasing participation of the population in the process of development.

3. To achieve a better distribution of the population within the economic scope of the Nation by means of the formation of compensatory poles of development in strategic areas.

4. To reach an internal change in the structures that might insure

a larger measure of participation of the population in the economic, social, political and cultural processes.

5. To modernize and technically qualify the State for its role of true promoter of national development.

6. To gain for the Country a position in accordance with its importance within the Latin American community.

7. To attain the capacity to mobilize surpluses for investment purposes and thus make it possible to build the infrastructure required for the development of agriculture, mining, and industry in the Nation.

8. To develop the cultural potential by creating forms of living in accordance with the national scale of values and a strong national conscience.

In brief, these efforts define the three great goals to be reached in the next twenty years:

(a) To integrate the national population in order to bring about a full utilization of the human resources as well as the basic possibilities of the Country.

(b) To substantially improve the distribution of a per capita income to no less than twice its present level.

(c) To activate the contribution of the External Sector to national development policy, reducing the present conditions of dependence and vulnerability which are present in the economy.

Medium Range Development Goals

Considering the above mentioned limitations, the Revolutionary Government proposes to reach the following medium range goals:

1. To accelerate the process of agrarian reform throughout the Sierra (Andean area);

2. To begin the process leading to a better distribution of the population within the economic scope of the Country, reducing the concentration in the metropolitan area of Lima-Callao, which however will continue to be the most dynamic pole of the national economy;

3. To effect important changes in the national structure of production which are to be related to a scheme of regional development, designed to increase the participation in the Gross National Product of the strategic sectors of agriculture and cattle raising, mining and industry, and the building industry;

4. To increase the employment field especially in the areas of agriculture, cattle raising and the building industry, as well as in all activities related to the poles of development:

5. To render more dynamic the contribution of the External Sector, by promoting exports, obtaining a larger share of the

profits generated by foreign investment, attracting new capital from abroad and preparing the productive sectors of the economy for participation in the process of Latin American integration and the Andean Group;

6. To strengthen the role of the Public Sector as promoter of national development, using central planning as the principal instrument of the Revolutionary Government, stimulating a higher production of the strategic sectors and orienting the activity of the private sector toward objectives of national interest;

7. To make the instrument of credit accessible even to small and medium businessmen both in the city and in rural areas. The State supervision (control) of the sources of credit will be assured;

8. To reform the business enterprise, guiding it towards a policy of workers sharing in the profits and in management and the protection of the cooperative enterprises organized by the workers:

9. To establish the basis of a national policy with regard to technology, such as will assert the autonomy of national development and will permit a better use of the productive resources of the Country.

Source: Central Bureau of Information, Lima.

Bibliography

Agüero, José de la Riva, *Por la verdad, la tradición y la patria* (Lima, 1937–38), 2 vols.

Alegría, Ciro, *Novelas completas* (Madrid, 1959).

Arciniegas, Germán, *Latin America: A Cultural History* (New York, 1967).

Basadre, Jorge, *Historia de la república del Perú* (Lima, 1964), 10 vols.

Baudin, Louis, *A Socialist Empire – The Incas of Peru* (New York, 1961).

Belaúnde Terry, Fernando, *La conquista del Perú por los peruanos* (Lima, 1959).

—— *Pueblo por pueblo* (Lima, 1960).

Bennett, Wendell C., 'The Andean Highlands: An Introduction' and 'The Archaeology of the Central Andes' in *Handbook of South American Indians* (Washington, 1946), Vol. 2, pp. 183–330.

Bourricard, François, *Pouvoir et société dans le Pérou contemporain* (Paris, 1967).

—— *Structure and Function of the Peruvian Oligarchy* (Washington, 1966).

Bushnell, G. H. S., *Peru* (London, 1956; New York, 1957).

Bustamante y Rivero, José Luis, *Tres años de lucha por la democracia en el Perú* (Buenos Aires, 1949).

Chávez, Hector Cornejo, *Nuevos principios para un nuevo Perú* (Lima, 1960).

—— *Que se propone la democracia cristiana* (Lima, 1962).

Clissold, Stephen, *Latin America: A Cultural Outline* (London, 1965; New York, 1966).

Cossio del Pomar, Felipe, *Haya de la Torre el indoamericano* (Lima, 1946).

Descola, Jean, *La vida cotidiana en el Perú en tiempos de los Españoles* (Buenos Aires, 1962).

Deustua, Alejandro O., *La cultura nacional* (Lima, 1937).

Ford, Thomas R., *Man and Land in Peru* (Gainseville, Fla., 1962).

Garcilaso de la Vega, *The First Part of the Royal Commentaries of the Yncas* translated and edited by Clements R. Markham (Hakluyt Soc. Publications, Nos. 41 and 45, 1869–71), 2 vols.

278

Haring, C. H., *The Spanish Empire in America* (New York, 1947).
Haya de la Torre, Víctor Raúl, *Construyendo el aprismo* (Buenos Aires, 1933).
—— *A donde va Indoamerica?* (Santiago, 1935).
Hoyle, Rafael Larco, *Peru* (Geneva, 1946).
Humphreys, R. A., *The Evolution of Modern Latin America* (Oxford, 1946).
Kantor, Harry, *The Ideology and Program of the Peruvian Aprista Movement* (Berkeley, Calif., 1953).
Latin America and the Caribbean – A Handbook, edited by Claudio Véliz (London and New York, 1968).
Madariaga, Salvador de, *The Rise and Fall of the Spanish American Empire* (London and New York, 1947), 2 vols.
Mariátegui, José Carlos, *Siete ensayos de interpretración de la realidad peruana* (Lima, 1928).
Markham, Clements R., *Travels in Peru and India* (London, 1862).
Mason, J. Alden, *The Ancient Civilisations of Peru* (London, 1957).
Means, Philip Ainsworth, *Ancient Civilizations of the Andes* (New York, 1931).
Memorias de los vireyes que han gobernado el Perú (Lima, 1859), 6 vols.
Métraux, Alfred, *The Incas* (London, 1965; New York, 1966).
Miró Quesada, Aurelio, *Costa, sierra, y montaña* (Lima, 1947).
Mishkin, Bernard, 'The Contemporary Quechua' in *Handbook of the South American Indians* (Washington, 1946), Vol. 2.
Osborne, Harold, *Indians of the Andes* (London and Cambridge, Mass., 1952).
Owens, R. J., *Peru* (London and New York, 1963).
Palma, Ricardo, *Tradiciones peruanas* (Lima, 1899).
Parry, J. H., *The Spanish Seaborne Empire* (London and New York, 1966).
Payne, James L., *Labour and Politics in Peru* (New Haven, 1965).
Pendle, George, *The Land and People of Peru* (London, 1966).
Pensamiento politico de Haya de la Torre (Lima, 1961), 5 vols. (A compilation of Haya de la Torre's political philosophy.)
Pike, Fredrick B., *The Modern History of Peru* (London and New York, 1967).
—— 'The Old and the New Apra in Peru; Myth and Reality' (*Inter-American Economic Affairs*, Vol. 18, Washington, 1964).
Platt, D. C. M., *Finance, Trade and Politics in British Foreign Policy* (Oxford, 1968). (Chapter 6 deals with British commercial relations with Latin America.)
Prescott, William H., *The History of the Conquest of Peru* (New York, 1847).

Robinson, David A., *Peru in Four Dimensions* (Lima, 1964).

Romero, Emilio, *Historia económica del Perú* (Lima, 1949).

Rowe, John Howland, 'Inca culture at the Time of the Spanish Conquest' in *Handbook of the South American Indians* (Washington, 1946), Vol. 2, pp. 183–330.

Taylor, Milton C., 'Taxation and Economic Development – A Case Study of Peru' (*Inter-American Economic Affairs*, Vol. 21, No. 3, Washington, 1967).

Urquidi, Víctor L., *The Challenge of Development in Latin America* (New York, 1964).

Valcárcel, Daniel, *La rebelión de Tupac Amarú* (Mexico, 1947).

Valcárcel, Luis E., *Tempestad en los Andes* (Lima, 1927).

Villanueva, Víctor, *Hugo Blanco y la rebelión campesina* (Lima, 1967).

Visión del Perú en el siglo XX (Lima, 1962). (A useful collection of articles on twentieth-century Peru.)

Von Hagen, Victor Wolfgang, *Highway of the Sun* (New York and London, 1955).

Wagner de Reyna, Alberto, *Historia diplomatica del Perú* (Lima, 1964), 2 vols.

Ybarra, T. R., *Lands of the Andes: Peru and Bolivia* (New York, 1947).

Index

Guerrilla warfare, 116, 122, 225, 226
Guevara, Che, 264
Guild of Lima Merchants, 62, 67, 68
Guise, George Martin, 87
Gutiérrez, Tómas, 103–4; brothers, 104

Haciendas, 55, 58, 149, 187, 211, 212, 217, 220, 221, 223, 229
Haiti, 128
Haya de la Torre, Agustín, 164
Haya de la Torre, Víctor Raúl, 150, 152, 156, 157, 158, 159, 160, 167, 170, 171, 178, 182, 184, 185, 186, 188, 189, 194, 220, 257, 275; deported, 151; prisoner, 175; released from prison, 164; 'shadow-President', 171; 'space–time' theory, 153
Hercelles, Osvaldo, 194
Hernández de Pinzón, Luis, 112, 113
Herrera, Bartolomé, 96
Hidalgo y Castillo, Miguel, 74
Honduras, 186
Hoover, Herbert, 145
Huaca del Sol, 37
Huallaga, River, 94
Huancavelica, 138
Huancayo, 26, 97, 213
Huánuco, 26, 94
Huaraz, 35
Huáscar, 115
Huascar, 51
Huascarán, 24
Huaylas, Callejón de, 26, 35
Huayna Cápac, 39, 51
Humboldt current, 29–30, 31, 94, 199
Hurtado, Federico, 174, 175

Ica, 97
Iglesias, Miguel, 117, 121
Illiteracy, 125, 126, 212
Imports, 62, 193
Inca dynasty, 38–9; as gods, 41, 45
Inca peoples, 22, 23, 27, 36, 38–9, 40–49, 70, 262
Inca society, 40–49; economic organization, 45–9, 149; nobility, 44, 50; officials, 43; organization, 40–41; religion, 45; viceroys, 43; women, position of, 45
Income, average, 199; *per capita*, 262
Independence movement, 67–80, 84
Indians, Peruvian, 22, 27, 28, 32–9, 48, 50, 53, 54, 55–8, 68–9, 72, 83, 84, 90, 93, 125, 127, 141–2,

148, 149, 150, 154, 158, 177, 179–80, 208–16; agriculture, 34, 35, 36, 56, 207, 210; architecture, 35; arts and crafts, 213–14; characteristics, 32, 215; communities, 24, 34, 41–3, 56, 84, 204, 217–19; diet, 211; education of, 155; grievances, 141–2, 216; herding of animals, 210–11; houses, 211; illiteracy, 125, 212; kingdoms, 30; landless (*yanacuna*), 44, 58, 182, 216–26, 234; migration to cities, 125, 128, 230, 245; miners' revolt, 146; origins, 32–3; percentage of population, 83, 125, 209; pottery, 34, 35, 57; religious cults, 34, 37, 214; revolts, 69, 71, 223–4; rituals, 210; schools, 212–213; strikes, 222; textiles, 37, 57
Industry, 124, 150, 179, 202–3
Inflation, 123, 133, 169, 172, 181, 191–2, 205
International Development Bank, 192
International Monetary Fund, 206
International Petroleum Company, 124, 140, 172, 194, 195–6, 250; expropriated, 196, 202, 270
Iquique, 95
Iquitos, 23, 137, 139, 161
Irigoyen, Hipolito, 133
Iron ore, 199, 202
Irrigation, 22, 36, 138, 166, 201, 232–3
Iturbide, Agustín de, 75

Jaen, 82, 169
Jáuregui, Agustín, 70
Jiménez, Gustavo, 159
Jones, J. Wesley, 191
Juárez, Benito, 111, 112
Juliaca, 102, 174
Junín, 138, 229
Junín, Battle of, 78
Junta Electoral Nacional, 123, 165, 186
Junta Nacional de la Vivienda, 188

Kaiser Group, 202
Kennedy, John F., 186, 264, 265, 267, 271

Labour code, 130
La Convención, 187, 223, 224, 229
La Fuente, Antonio Gutiérrez de, 78, 87, 89, 90
Laguna, 94
Laissez-faire policy, 85, 100, 176, 200
Lambayeque, 138, 233, 270
Land, 217–26; area cultivated, 21;